T0319706

Institutions, Economic Performance and the Visible Hand

Institutions, Economic Performance and the Visible Hand

Theory and Evidence

Ashok Chakravarti

Senior Visiting Lecturer, Department of Economics, University of Zimbabwe, Africa

Edward Elgar
Cheltenham, UK • Northampton, MA, USA

Published by
Edward Elgar Publishing Limited
The Lypiatts
15 Lansdown Road
Cheltenham
Glos GL50 2JA
UK

Edward Elgar Publishing, Inc.
William Pratt House
9 Dewey Court
Northampton
Massachusetts 01060
USA

A catalogue record for this book
is available from the British Library

Library of Congress Control Number: 2012930610

MIX
Paper from
responsible sources
FSC
www.fsc.org   FSC® C018575

ISBN 978 1 78100 137 0 (cased)

Typeset by Cambrian Typesetters, Camberley, Surrey
Printed and bound by MPG Books Group, UK

Contents

List of figures and tables   vi
About the author   vii
Preface   viii

1   Introduction   1
2   The neoclassical model and its critique   11
3   The old and new institutional economics   35
4   Development strategies and performance: an overview   54
5   Institutions and governance: the new empirical evidence   74
6   Institutions in economic history   97
7   Discontinuous institutional change   122
8   Southern Sudan: a case study in discontinuous institutional
    change   147
9   Markets and institutions   170
10 Mechanisms of institutional transition   197

Appendix   210
Bibliography   214
Index   231

Figures and tables

Figures

9.1   Institutions and market performance   183
9.2   Institutions and opportunism/predation   193
10.1 Institutions and economic rationality   200

Tables

4.1   Per capita GDP growth rates 1950–2001   54
4.2   All developing country regions: per capita GDP growth
      rates 1975–2005   55
4.3   Savings and investment rates 1995–2005   66
4.4   Economic and political governance indicators   68
4.5   Sub-Saharan Africa: aid dependency ratios   72
4.6   Aid/gross capital formation 2006   72
5.1   Contribution of total factor productivity to growth of output   76
5.2   Decomposition of growth of output   77
5.3   Contributions of capital, human capital and productivity   78
5.4   Impact of economic and institutional variables on economic
      growth   82
5.5   Impact of democracy on economic growth   90
6.1   Per capita GDP levels and growth rates – major regions   97
6.2   Per capita GDP levels   98
7.1   Per capita GDP – annual compound growth rates   126
7.2   India – per capita GDP levels   131
7.3   India – per capita GDP growth rates since 1950   137
7.4   Number and assets of private firms 1988–2005   137

About the author

Ashok Chakravarti has been involved with the field of development for the past 30 years. During this period he has worked in an advisory role for the World Bank, USAID, DFID, UNDP, UNCTAD and other international agencies. In his last advisory position he was Chief of Party of a USAID-funded programme in South Sudan (2004–2007) that was focused on building institutions of democratic governance. Between 2002 and 2009, he was a Visiting Fellow at Oxford University on several occasions. Since 2009 he has been attached to the Department of Economics, University of Zimbabwe, where he teaches an institutions-oriented curriculum to students of Development Economics and Macroeconomics.

Preface

My research agenda over the past ten years has focused on institutions and how the structure of economic and political governance affects economic performance and developmental outcomes. This interest was a direct consequence of my experiences as a development practitioner, mainly in Africa, where I have been managing institutional development programmes on behalf of various aid agencies since 1980. I found that these experiences strongly contradicted the standard economic models and development theories that emerged from these models. Consequently, my initial programme of research focused on the impact of aid on development and culminated in the publication of my first book entitled *Aid, Institutions and Development* (Edward Elgar 2005). In this study I concluded that the evidence indicated that aid in general has had a very limited impact on development. However, in countries with good economic and political institutions, where good governance and favourable macroeconomic policies are being followed, aid can have a much more significant impact.

Standard economic theory postulates that growth and development are a function of technology, and the level of resources – primarily physical and human capital – invested in a society. What I observed in the many countries I worked in was that the institutional framework of a society (i.e. the economic and political rules that govern its functioning) was far more important in determining economic outcomes. That conclusion was reinforced by the events surrounding the recent sub-prime related financial crisis and subsequent world recession. This crisis has shown that even highly developed markets in the advanced economies do not have self-regulating and self-equilibrating characteristics and cannot function efficiently without proper institutional and governance-related frameworks. My experiences, and recent economic events, led me to consider other more fundamental questions, such as: What is the real content of human economic behaviour? What are the institutions of good economic and political governance? Why do they encourage individuals and governments to act in a productive manner? And how do these institutions come into being? These in turn have resulted in this book.

In undertaking this study, I was privileged to have been given the opportunity to play a role in South Sudan's incipient institutional development. This gave me a first-hand insight into what institution building and institutional change are all about. South Sudan became an independent country in July 2011, after a brutal civil war that commenced in 1956 and lasted over 50 years. During this period social order was primarily maintained through tribal structures and informal traditional institutions. At a formal level, the few governance structures introduced by the central government in Khartoum never achieved any level of credibility. Consequently, they never became established as functional institutions. In spite of the long period between 1956 and 2011, however, South Sudan did not see any evolutionary or endogenous development of its political or economic institutions. Rather, society became frozen in some sort of low-level homeostatic equilibrium. The fact of conflict does not change this assessment. Historically, after all, war and conflict have played a major catalytic role in many countries in bringing about the emergence of new institutions. But no such process was observed in South Sudan.

Thus when I went there in 2004 on behalf of a major international development agency, and found that the ruling group that had emerged through the civil war had progressive political and economic ideas and was interested in building a democratic capitalist society, following on from my research hypotheses, it seemed to me that what was required was an activist institutional engineering programme. My analysis of the historical experience of other developing countries that had achieved favourable institutional transitions indicated that in most cases successful institutional change was a result of the conscious efforts of small domestic ruling groups, or sometimes even external forces, inspired by progressive ideas and ideologies. Institutional change, particularly in the developing world, was therefore not a consequence of grand endogenous forces, but the result of good ideas, good leadership, and the conscious and forceful intervention of human agency. Subsequent consultations between the Sudan People's Liberation Movement and my agency resulted in the design and implementation of a major programme of institutional development that was led by the domestic elite and supported by external forces. This commenced in 2004 and is still ongoing. Chapter 8 discusses the successes and failures of this programme.

I am grateful to Piet Hein van Eeghen, Johann du Pisanie, John Toye, Geoffrey Hodgson, Takawira Mumvuma, Tony Hawkins and three anonymous referees for their comments on earlier drafts of the study. I am particularly indebted to Piet Hein van Eeghen and Johann du Pisanie for reviewing each individual chapter over a period of two years and providing me with suggestions and detailed comments. I dedicate this book, however, to the leaders and the brave people of South Sudan who fought repression and tyranny for over five decades – a fight that resulted in the death of over two million people – to win the right to create a society of their own choice. It is also dedicated to my colleagues, and to the many other external actors in South Sudan's institutional development programme since 2004, who lived in tents and *tukuls* (huts) in

40°C for extended periods of time; suffered from repeated bouts of malaria, bilharzia, and other tropical diseases; and, accepted AK47s going off, mines being found in close proximity, and ammunition dumps blowing up, all in order to engage the domestic leadership in an active dialogue to bring about institutional change that would prove favourable to economic and social progress.

Ashok Chakravarti
Harare, Zimbabwe
November 2011

1. Introduction

This study is about economic performance – both the long-run performance of developing countries, as well as short-run fluctuations in the advanced market economies. The neoclassical view, which continues to dominate mainstream economic theory, postulates that the problems of growth and development can be solved without reference to the institutional dimension of markets. Reflecting on this issue, Furubotn and Richter (2005: 1) state that 'as the technical development of neoclassical theory has progressed and economic models have become increasingly abstract, institutional phenomena have received less and less attention'. The standard free market paradigm of this theory holds that unfettered markets are efficient and self-adjusting. Further, it is argued that given the natural ability of the market mechanism, under certain conditions which enable competitive markets to be established and optimality conditions to be achieved, interfering with its functioning will reduce the impact of existing resources on incomes and welfare. It is of course accepted that there are caveats to this paradigm. The existence of public goods or externalities can cause free markets to be sub-optimal. Unfettered markets can also be characterised by persistent unemployment. But as Stiglitz (2010: 17) indicates, although a considerable body of economic theory now exists which shows that unfettered markets do not yield efficient solutions even when small and realistic changes are made to the model – e.g. when there are information imperfections or asymmetries (Greenwald and Stiglitz 1986, Grossman and Stiglitz 1980) – this view continues to be the 'ruling' or 'standard' paradigm in economics. Thus, until very recently, such efficiently functioning and self-regulating free markets were seen as the basis for economic stability and growth in the advanced economies. However, the recent world recession, which commenced in 2007 with problems in the US sub-prime mortgage and financial markets, has seriously undermined the credibility of this model and necessitated a rethink on what constitutes a basis for good economic performance.

In the context of the economic development of poor countries, based on the same neoclassical vision, the adequacy of resources to create both human and physical capital is seen as being key to sustained economic growth. In recent years there has been increased discussions on the importance of a favourable institutional environment, and the need for good economic and political governance, for achieving improved and sustainable levels of growth and poverty reduction. In spite of this, however, the fundamental strategies of development followed by the developing countries themselves, supported by World Bank and IMF programmes based on the Poverty Reduction Strategy and other similar approaches, have focused on the resource-based vision of development. Consequently, the weak growth observed in most developing country regions over the past 60 years has been ascribed to a lack of resources, or to inappropriate government policies and interference in markets, which it is argued will cause economic distortions and a misallocation of resources. In this model therefore, the problem of economic development is not one of the absence of an institutional framework or mechanisms to bring about the best use of available resources, but one that focuses on a paucity of the resources themselves. A significant consequence of this thinking has been that economic theory, policy and practice over the past 60 years have tended to underplay the role of institutions in influencing economic performance.

NATURE OF INSTITUTIONS

Of course, writers in the neoclassical tradition accept that various types of economic, social and political institutions exist in a society and have an impact on social interaction. However, it is generally argued that such institutions are not very relevant when it comes to theorizing about economic behaviour and economic outcomes (Marshall [1920]1956: Appendix C). Even those in the neoclassical school who give greater significance to the role of institutions tend to assume that any institution that may be required to sustain free contracting amongst agents will emerge spontaneously and support the efficient functioning of the system (Hayek 1945, Hayek 1973, Menger [1883]1963). In a formal sense, therefore, the neoclassical model is based on an 'institution-free' view of the functioning of the economic system. The existence of a market and a 'ghostly' auctioneer is presumed (Toye 1995). However, such a market has no independent characteristics and no independent existence apart from the actors who trade within it. The market is, therefore, just a place where trading occurs and prices are formed, and the role of the auctioneer is to communicate the price information so that re-contracting can occur such that the market clears. In view of this, it is useful to start off by defining what we mean by institutions. An encompassing definition of institutions can be found in North (1989, 1990) who holds that institutions are the rules of the game of a society, or more formally the humanly devised constraints together with their enforcement characteristics that structure human behaviour. Institutions can be formal rules such as constitutions and laws, or informal constraints such as habits, customs or tradition. Generalizing this concept, Hodgson (2006) argues that social rules are the essence of an institution. Institutions are thus systems of established and prevalent overt or implicit social rules that structure social interaction.

The debate on the nature and relevance of institutions is extensive. As the definitions above indicate institutions can be formal or informal, explicit or tacit, and they can include a wide range of entities such as codified laws, rules, conventions and norms. Contributing to this discussion, Aoki (2007) states that there are two views of institutions. In the first, institutions are seen as rules in a hierarchical order. These rules are pre-determined exogenously, outside the domain of economic transactions, and economic institutions, such as markets, operate within these constraints. The second is the endogenous view, in which the institutions or rules are seen to emerge spontaneously or be endogenously shaped from within the economic order. This debate suggests that to facilitate the discussion here, a more fundamental ontology of institutional reality needs to be elaborated upon. Such an ontology should help us to understand why institutions should be considered as central to the functioning of an economic system. In Searle (2005) we can find such an analysis. Searle states that there are facts or features of the world that exist independent of human thought and belief. These include physical and chemical phenomena and the relations that exist between them. On the other hand, there are those facts or features which exist as entities only relative to human feelings and attitudes, such as government, money, marriage, etc. The difference between these two groups is that the first set of features is observer independent, whereas the second set is observer dependent. On this basis Searle argues that an institution is any collectively accepted system of rules, procedures, practices, that enables us to create institutional facts, and that the nature of institutions is that they are deliberate human devices which have the capability of constraining or enabling human behaviour.

This ontology of institutional reality enables us to more accurately understand the fundamental nature of institutions and why they play a central role in influencing economic performance. Nabli and Nugent (1989) emphasize three characteristics of institutions which are of relevance. The first is their nature as rules and constraints on human behaviour. The second is their ability to govern the relations amongst individuals and groups. The third is their predictability, and through this characteristic, their ability to play an enabling role by providing a structure for repeated human interaction. As a consequence of these characteristics institutions not only limit the choice set of economic and political actors, but they also define the matrix of incentives that will influence and determine the manner in which human beings will behave. Following on from this view, Williamson (2000) argues that the problems of resource allocation and maximization, which are the central concerns of neoclassical economics, are in fact embedded in three higher levels of economic and social structure. All these levels influence human behaviour.

The deepest underlying level is that of social embeddedness, where informal institutions, customs, traditions and religion are located. These factors have a pervasive influence and change very slowly. The second level is that of the formal institutional environment. This includes constitutions, laws, the formal nature of the political system, property and contractual rights, etc. While much of the formal framework in the world today is a product of evolutionary processes, rare windows of historical opportunity to effect radical reforms in these institutions also occur as a consequence of social disorders, wars, occupations, or other breakdowns. The third level relates to governance structures. These are structures that have been crafted by human beings in order to take advantage of the incentives created by the other two levels of institutions and facilitate transactions between individuals and groups. They include the legal system where contracts are enforced; business enterprises of various types; political and civil associations; and other organizational structures.

Within this framework, the interaction between individuals and institutions can be seen as a two-way relationship. On the one hand individuals through collective action, which may be spontaneous or involving direct action, can bring about the creation of institutions that will reflect their ideas and beliefs. This has been termed as a process of upward causation. Hodgson (2006) indicates that the process of upward causation, whereby lower level changes fundamentally alter higher level structures, is widely accepted. However, as we have noted above, the reverse process by which institutions affect individual behaviour is equally significant. This is a process of downward causation originally hypothesized by the psychobiologist Roger Sperry (1964, 1969). Hodgson (2003, 2006) argues that this can take two forms. First, if there are systemic properties and tendencies, all processes at the lower level of an ontological hierarchy can be restrained by and act in conformity with the laws of the higher levels. In this case all individual aspirations, dispositions or constraints are influenced by system-wide processes. Second, there can be reconstitutive downward causation. In this case individuals and populations are not only restrained but also changed by the causal powers associated with higher levels of the hierarchy. Thus new institutions can lead to changes in behaviour and concordant habits based upon congruent purposes and beliefs amongst significant sections of the population, who initially may not have necessarily shared these beliefs and values. Downward causation is therefore an important mechanism through which institutions can influence and change human behaviour, and consequently impact on the performance of an economic system.

Based on the discussion above, we can state the three fundamental questions that this book seeks to answer:

- Is the exclusion of institutions from orthodox theory defensible from a theoretical point of view?

- What does the historical and empirical evidence tell us about the relative importance of institution-related factors in explaining modern economic growth and the more recent performance of developing countries? And can such factors be used to develop a useful model to explain the recent fluctuations in advanced market economies?
- How do the necessary institutions which underlie successful economic performance emerge? Do they come into being spontaneously based on endogenous forces, or are exogenous interventions – either in the form of shocks or direct interventions, important factors that bring about their emergence?

These questions are not new, and there is a substantial literature, some of which goes back to the 19th century, that has attempted to address them. This book's contribution is to review and consolidate the major themes and issues that have emerged from this literature, and in doing so to try to arrive at a set of more coherent hypotheses and consistent conclusions that may prove useful in explaining economic performance. Consequently the study neither intends nor claims to have taken into account the views of all authors who have written on this subject or the vast literature that is available covering all the relevant topics. Rather, only the major works in each area of concern have been considered and used in arriving at certain conclusions.

METHODOLOGY

In terms of its analytical approach the study follows the inductive methodology embedded in the mainstream institutional economics literature (Greif 1998, 2006; North 1981, 1990; Olson 1965, 2000). In this literature it is accepted that whether in the natural sciences or the social sciences, any understanding of a phenomenon must start with good observation. Based on observation and fact, valid generalizations can then be drawn. Such generalizations may in turn be used to formulate working hypothesis or deductive theories. Therefore, the starting point for any serious theory that attempts to explain reality must be inductively derived generalizations.

In the case of economics, economic history provides the most reliable and varied set of observations about how economic processes function. For an economist, therefore, economic history is his laboratory. Economic history is not just narrative: the recent applications of statistical and econometric methods to large amounts of historical and cross-country data have generated a substantial quantum of empirical evidence. This evidence reveals which patterns or associations are recurrently found amongst the key variables that are considered important to the functioning of an economic system. In this book, therefore, we shall use historical evidence, case studies and cross-country empirics to develop and buttress the arguments. However, as Greif indicates, such evidence is atheoretical. He states (2006: 309) that the purely inductive method which involves classifying and generalizing – whether through narrative or statistical method – is insufficient, because it does not inform us about what the lines of causation are. This is particularly so as many important variables that may play a key role in the functioning of the economic system are unobservable. As a result, a more useful approach here is to adopt a theoretically informed inductive method within which theoretical predictions are combined with historical narrative. In this way, theoretical insights drawn from a single or alternative hypothesis can be stated and tested against valid generalizations which have been arrived at on the basis of historical and empirical fact. If a correspondence is found between the hypothesis and the generalizations, then a realistic theory can be built in the confidence that reasonable and empirically grounded assumptions are being used to build this particular theory. The predictions of such a theory can then be used to test its validity and confirm the lines of causation between the variables which form part of the theoretical system.

Neoclassical economics does not take this approach. Hausman (1989) provides us with a historical overview of this subject. He indicates that the deductive method of neoclassical economics finds its origins in the classical thought of J.S. Mill ([1843]1949, [1836]1967). Mill's view was that basic psychological or technical laws were established through introspection or experimentation. Based on these premises, the economic implications can then be deduced and empirical verification conducted as to whether the deductively derived conclusions are valid or not. However, confidence in the theory is based on a direct confirmation of the assumptions rather than any serious tests of the implications. The neoclassicals agreed with Mill. Thus Robbins (1935) indicates that the basic premises of economics are well justified and empirical failures do not cast any doubt on their validity. Referring to the core rationality assumptions of neoclassical economics he states that they 'are so much the stuff of our everyday experience that they have only to be stated to be recognized as obvious' (Robbins 1935: 79).

This view was challenged by the positivists such as Hutchison (1938) and Popper (1959) who argued that economics should measure up to the standards of a responsible empirical science and accept only those theories that were well confirmed by the empirical data. According to the standards set by the positivists, the emergence of empirical studies which showed that individuals or firms do not behave in the manner postulated by microeconomic theory undermined the claim of neoclassical economics to be a scientific discipline. Friedman (1953) proposed a way out of these empirical difficulties. His interpretation of positivism was that a good theory was one that sought significant and usable predictions, not an understanding or explanation of the phenomena. Thus he stated that a theory would be more fruitful the 'more precise the predictions, and the wider the area within which the theory yields predictions' (Friedman 1953: 10). In this approach, termed as instrumentalism, the validity of the underlying assumptions or principles is not very relevant, and assumptions that bear no relationship to reality are quite justified so long as they can generate a coherent theory which can then be tested against the facts. As Lucas (1986) put it, a theory does not have to have impeccable foundations. The axioms are abstractions and necessarily 'false'. However, the propositions need to have empirical validity to establish the range within which the abstractions will be adequate. Although many neoclassical scholars may prefer a more balanced approach wherein an effort is made to derive simplifying assumptions that capture the essence of reality, this instrumentalist methodology is deeply ingrained in neoclassical thinking.

My study rejects this positivist/deductive approach that underlies most of modern day neoclassical economics. As Hausman (1989) argues, Friedman's positivism (i.e. that the goals of science are exclusively predictive) is a contentious claim for which no justification has been offered. In fact, it stands to reason that unrealistic assumptions will result in false predictions, and when a prediction fails there is no way to employ a new theory without judging the validity of the original assumptions. Otherwise, the whole approach can degenerate into arbitrary guesswork. Discussing this issue, Clower (1994) indicates that in disciplines rooted in plausible inferences, such as physics and economics, the truth is of paramount importance. The aim is not to state and prove theorems but to proffer empirical conjectures that will persuade others of their plausibility in explaining phenomena. Such empirical conjectures based on plausible reasoning are the content of fact-oriented or inductive sciences. Clower also argues that opposed to this there can be hypothetico-demonstrative disciplines such as mathematics, in which the concept of truth is contained in formal ideas, and deductive methods are used to explore or discover what other propositions these ideas or axioms imply. Since economics claims to be an empirical discipline, the fact-based inductive approach is most appropriate. Clower (1995: 311) states that 'no empirical science has ever been generated by axiomatic thinking. One has only to mention Copernicus, Galileo, Newton and Einstein to see the absurdity of a contrary view'. We will argue in later chapters that the positivist/deductive approach in economics is misguided and harmful. One of its more recent consequences has been that it generated a model of the functioning of an economy, which in many ways can be considered as one of the causes of the present financial crisis and world recession.

The empirical analysis in this study focuses on economic growth, with growth performance being taken as a proxy for economic development. Of course, the two concepts are not synonymous, and economic development is a broader concept which goes beyond GDP growth rates to encompass structural changes in the economy, distributional issues, and improvements in poverty rates, literacy, life expectancy, and other social indicators. Also, in the short run, growth may not always be associated with improvements in the indicators of development or a reduction in poverty. However, growth matters, particularly sustained growth over long periods of time, because it results in rising incomes that will enable the poor to improve their standard of living, health, nutrition and educational status. As Sen (1993) indicates, while the enhancement of living conditions must clearly be an essential – if not *the* essential – object of the entire economic exercise, and such an enhancement is an integral part of the concept of development, an expansion of GNP, given other things, should enhance people's living conditions and typically bring about an improvement in social indicators such as life expectancy, etc.

Emphasizing the strong relationship between growth and development, Maddison (2006) states that while increases in life expectation are an important manifestation of improvements in human welfare, and our standard measures of GDP do not capture such changes, the historical data show that there has been a significant congruence over time, and between regions, in the patterns of improvement in per capita incomes and life expectation. In fact, there is a substantial body of empirical evidence which confirms this relationship. Thus Barro (1996a), using panel data for 100 countries over the period 1960–1995, finds that there is a strong association between growth rates and improvements in life expectancy and lower fertility. Dollar and Kray (2000), using data from 137 countries over four decades, find that there is a strong link between growth and poverty reduction, with this relationship holding across regions of the world, time periods and income levels. They also find that the incomes of the poor have a tendency to rise significantly at times of high economic growth. Similar conclusions are reached in the *World Development Report 2000/2001* (World Bank 2001). Given the close correlation between economic growth and the indicators of economic development, and the fact that the historical analysis in our study considers very long periods of time, the factors underlying sustained economic growth are also taken to be the main determinants of good development performance.

OUTLINE OF THE STUDY

Since the neoclassical model finds its origins in the works of the classical economists, in order to put the discussion in a historical perspective, in Chapter 2 we shall start with a consideration of the views of some of the main thinkers in this tradition. The chapter then continues with an outline of the basic neoclassical model and a critique of the fundamental behavioural assumptions underlying it based on the current thinking in cognitive psychology, genetics, and the findings of modern experimental and behavioural economics. Chapter 3 reviews the alternative model of the economic system as presented in the old and new institutional economics literature. In this literature informal and formal institutions, such as customs, habits, laws and other formal governance structures, are seen as being the fundamental guides to human behaviour and the economic system, rather than some immutable concept of self-interest, as assumed by neoclassical theory. In line with our theoretically informed inductive method, the chapter will extract the key insights that emerge from this body of thought and state these as working hypotheses in order that they may be assessed against the generalizations that will emerge from the later chapters which consider the historical and empirical data.

In Chapter 4 we shall outline the key elements of mainstream development theory as these have emerged out of neoclassical economics. The policies and strategies that have been followed in the developing world since the end of the Second World War, and the economic performance achieved by these countries as a consequence of the application of these policies and strategies, will also be considered. As part of this review, the successes and failures of the World Bank/IMF-inspired structural adjustment programmes undertaken since the early 1980s will be considered. The alternative approach taken by the East Asian tiger economies will also be discussed. In this group of countries a development strategy was followed based on the view that free markets do not provide an adequate mechanism to bring about the structural transformation of an economy and the achievement of high rates of growth. Rather, government intervention is necessary to alter market incentives and signals in order to achieve these objectives.

Chapter 5 undertakes a review of the considerable body of empirical evidence that has developed over the past 20 years or so, one that considers the role of institutional and governance-related factors in influencing economic growth and developmental outcomes. The evidence primarily consists of a large number of cross-country studies which find that while physical and human capital may be the proximate causes of growth, it nevertheless still needs to be explained why some countries accumulate, innovate and grow faster than others. In Chapter 6 we shall consider the fundamental question of how the institutional frameworks, which the empirical evidence suggests are necessary for an economy to function efficiently, can come into being. Institutions may matter both theoretically and empirically, but it needs to be understood how they come into being. The historical experience of Western Europe, and the relevance and applicability of this model of evolutionary institutional change to developing countries, will be analysed.

Chapter 7 consists of various case studies. The purpose is to evaluate how institutional transitions in the non-Western world have occurred and identify any common factors, if any, that have contributed to the successful absorption of more efficient institutions. For this purpose three countries from Asia and Africa have been chosen where successful institutional transitions seem to have occurred: these are Japan, India and Botswana. Chapter 8 is an analytical description of a programme of institutional change, which follows the central ideas of the book and has been under implementation since 2004 in Southern Sudan – a region which had been subjected to a devastating civil war for a period of almost 50 years. The chapter is entirely based on primary field work and active participation in South Sudan's institutional development process between 2004 and 2009. The successes and failures of this programme, which is being led by a progressive domestic elite and supported by an exogenously inspired and internationally supported institutional development programme, are discussed. Finally, Chapters 9 and 10 synthesize the findings of the earlier chapters and propose a new model for the functioning of markets and institutional change based on an assessment of the working hypotheses stated in Chapter 3, and a review of the empirical and historical generalizations that emerge out of Chapters 4, 5, 6, and 7.

2. The neoclassical model and its critique

INSTITUTIONS IN CLASSICAL ECONOMIC THOUGHT

The historical origins of the neoclassical model are to be found in the works of the classical economists. To establish what the classical thinkers said about the role of institutions in the functioning of an economy and how economic change occurs, we shall consider here the works of a number of key scholars in this tradition. These will include those who emphasized the natural liberty of an individual as being central to the functioning of an economic system, such as Adam Smith and John Stuart Mill, but also the ideas of those who were at the other end of the classical spectrum, such as Karl Marx and Frederick Engels. The latter group of thinkers – though they subscribed to many of the key concepts and theories of the classical liberal economists – emphasized the importance of social and historical forces in bringing about economic change. Finally, we shall consider the works of some of the flag bearers of the marginalist revolution, such as Jevons and Marshall, in order to understand the extent to which their ideas conformed to or differed from those of the classical thinkers.

Adam Smith argued that based on the principle of self-interest and the operation of the invisible hand 'the natural effort of every individual to better his own condition when suffered to exert itself with freedom and security, is so powerful a principle, that it alone and without any assistance … is capable of carrying on the society to wealth and prosperity' (Smith [1776]1904: 508). Underlying this view was his belief that natural processes operated to produce the happiness and perfection of the species. Smith originally developed this doctrine of a beneficent order in nature in his *Theory of Moral Sentiments* (1759). Harmony and beneficence were perceived to be inherent parts of the matter-of-fact processes of nature. Further, there were no serious flaws in the harmonious operation of natural forces even in the economic order, where self-interest was the main impulse for human action (Viner 1927). Thus, discussing the division of labour in the *Wealth of Nations*, Smith argued that beneficent economic institutions would arise naturally from human nature rather than the 'effect of any human wisdom' ([1776]1904: 13), namely conscious action.

However, Smith was also well aware of the role that the institutional framework played in determining the economic performance of nations. He argued that for natural liberty to succeed there needed to be a sovereign who, amongst other things, would undertake the 'duty of protecting, as far as possible, every member of society from the injustice or oppression of every other member of it, or the duty of establishing an exact administration of justice' ([1776]1904: 651). An impartial state that protected the rights of all individuals equally was therefore essential. Smith further argued that for this to be achieved the state needed to be based on the principle of a separation of powers between the executive and the judiciary: 'In order to make every individual feel himself perfectly secure in the possession of every right which belongs to him, it is not only necessary that the judicial should be separated from executive power, but that it should be rendered as much as possible independent of that power' ([1776]1904: 681).

As an historical example of how the nature of laws and institutions affects economic performance, Smith discussed the example of China. He stated that 'China seems to have been long stationary, and had probably long ago acquired that full complement of riches which is consistent with the nature of its law and institutions. But this complement may be much inferior to what, with other laws and institutions, the nature of its soil, climate and situation might admit of' ([1776]1904: 95). Stressing the importance of legal enforcement he further observed that, 'When the law does not enforce the performance of contracts, it puts all borrowers nearly on the same footing with bankrupts or people of doubtful credit in better regulated countries' ([1776]1904: 95). From these quotes it is evident that while Smith believed that natural liberty would automatically generate beneficent economic institutions, for such liberty to exist, the presence of certain types of laws and institutions was required, and these were not necessarily present in a particular country.

Apart from this emphasis on the importance of formal institutions, he was also conscious of the role played by informal norms. Thus, in the case of the invisible hand, he was explicit that for this mechanism to succeed people needed to share certain well-defined underlying behavioural characteristics. In his famous passage comparing market competition to a race, Smith indicated that for the race to be successfully run there must be no violation of fair play (quoted from his *Theory of Moral Sentiments* in Wilson 1976: 83). Further, for the economic system he was describing to function smoothly it was necessary that there would be people of common understanding, with this understanding consisting of acting in a manner based upon 'common prudence, frugality and industriousness' (Smith [1776]1904: 333). This discussion indicates that, in Smith's model, for competition to result in the social good it was assumed that there was not only an underlying harmony of interests, but also that economic actors would behave according to certain informal rules of the game. His system was, therefore, by no means institution free as compared with the later neoclassical model.

Subsequent to Adam Smith, a number of classical liberal thinkers elaborated on the view that economic progress was based on individual liberty and the development of free markets. Thus John Stuart Mill ([1848]1923), starting from the proposition that the accumulation of capital was central to the creation of wealth, outlined his reasons for what he termed as being the 'weak principle of accumulation' in many countries. According to him the means to increase accumulation were, first, 'a better government: more complete security of property; moderate taxes, and freedom from arbitrary exaction under the name of taxes', and second, 'improvement in the public intelligence: a decay of usages or superstitions which interfere with the effective employment of industry; and the growth of mental activity, making people alive to new objects of desire' ([1848]1923: 189). Expanding on this theme, Mill went well beyond what his predecessors such as Adam Smith advocated as being the most appropriate role for government. He argued that for the principle of individual liberty to function, and *laissez faire* to succeed, the institutional environment needed to include a democratic constitution, and a government that not only afforded protection of persons and property, but also guaranteed the enforcement of contracts and the regulation of natural resources for the common enjoyment ([1848]1923: 796–800). Further, he also believed that the presence of certain generalized modes of thinking – i.e. a public imbued with non-superstitious or rationalistic thinking – was necessary for the proper functioning of the economic system.

In opposition to the views of the classical liberal thinkers we have the 'historical determinism' of Marx and Engels, as well as the theories of the German historical school. The latter group included a number of social scientists such as Schmoller, Roscher and Knies. Although there were differences between these two groups, with Marx and Engels being closer to the classical liberal school in terms of concepts and methodologies, both groups nevertheless gave greater primacy to the role of historical and inertial forces in explaining social phenomena and the functioning of an economy, over that played by human action and individual behaviour. Human action was seen as being determined by natural, ethical/customary, and historical conditions. Therefore, in contrast to the classical liberal thinkers, the workings of social institutions could not be explained in terms of individual phenomena (Weber 1975: 85). The apogee of this thinking is to be found in the works of Marx and Engels ([1859]1958). Marx and Engels agreed with the individual liberty school that capital accumulation was the key to economic progress. In their model, at any given historical moment, men entered into certain relations with each other which they termed the relations of production. However, they also argued that within the framework of a capitalistic market economy based on *laissez faire*, over time the material productive forces in a society would come into conflict with these relations of production, and this would bring the accumulation of capital to a halt. This crisis of capitalism would bring about economic and social change with new relations of production being established; these would then enable capital accumulation and economic progress to commence afresh.

In Marx and Engels's view, the institutional framework of a society, though fundamental to its functioning at any given moment in time, did not play a key role in the process of change. To them the relations between the productive forces automatically generated the laws, institutions, property rights, etc., and determined the character of the state. Thus Marx stated that, 'The sum total of these relations of production constitutes the economic structure of society, the real foundation on which rises a legal and political superstructure and to which correspond definite forms of social consciousness' (Marx [1859]1958: 363). Institutions for Marx and Engels formed the 'superstructure' of a society and had no independent role other than to protect the existing relations of production. The state in this model was part of the superstructure of a society: it was not beneficent and it represented the interests of the ruling classes (Engels 1962: 396). Based on their materialistic conception of history, Marx and Engels argued that in the process of social change this superstructure would come into conflict with the productive forces in society and be swept away. In spite of the secondary role given to institutions, however, this model nevertheless emphasized that at any given time the social consciousness or thought patterns prevalent in a particular society would be largely determined by the existing institutional matrix. Thus in the *Grundrisse*, Marx stated that 'the human being is in the most literal sense a political animal, not merely a gregarious animal, but an animal which can individuate itself only in the midst of society' (1981: 84).

From the discussion above it is evident that both the classical economists, and their protagonists from opposing schools of thought, recognized that institutions played an important role in the functioning of an economic system. The institution-free model of the economy was therefore not of their making, but instead the product of much later thinking, and primarily the creation of Jevons ([1871]1970), Walras ([1877]1954) and Marshall ([1920]1956). Jevons and Walras – the neoclassical protagonists of the marginalist revolution – were inspired by Newtonian mechanics. They saw the economic system in a deterministic manner which conformed to the model of the physical world found in Newtonian physics. Although Adam Smith himself had drawn inspiration from the Newtonian system, particularly its vision of spontaneous natural harmony, he did not push the mechanistic analogy so far as to reduce human beings to being robotic optimizers whose behaviour paralleled that of natural objects. In the marginalist system, however, epitomized by the Walrasian model (Walras [1877]1954), all societies consisted of a mass of maximizing individuals who wished to trade goods and services for personal betterment. Left to themselves, they had the right motivational and behavioural characteristics to participate in an iterative process in a predictable manner, through which market prices were determined which cleared both production and consumption markets. Although the Walrasian model required that a market needed to exist, the market in this system was essentially a disembodied institution, which had no existence apart from the iterative price-making and clearing process that its participants went through. Such markets were assumed to emerge spontaneously, be ubiquitous, and potentially give the right signals for allocative efficiency to be achieved. Thus Jevons abandoned the term 'political economy' in favour of 'economics', and saw the new subject as a 'mechanics of utility and self-interest' (Jevons [1871]1970: 23).

Elaborating on this vision, and the subsidiary role played by both formal and informal institutions, Marshall distinguished between 'those outward forms and accidents of economic organization which depend on temporary or local aptitudes, customs and relations of classes on the influence of individuals; or on the changing appliances and needs of production' and 'that more fundamental substance of economic organization, which depends mainly on such wants and activities, such preferences and aversions as are found in man everywhere' (Marshall [1920]1956: 641). In other words, rational self-interest and utility maximization were considered to be universal principles on which the economic science should be based, whereas institutions, habits and customs were 'outward forms' or 'accidents of economic organization' that did not merit any fundamental consideration. While admitting that in backward countries there were still many habits and customs that influenced action, Marshall reaffirmed that in business matters in the modern world such habits would die away quickly. Thus the economic science should not concern itself with motives for action or conditions of life that were not reducible to any definite standard, as this would take the discipline way from its central stronghold ([1920]1956: 643).

In sum, therefore, we can see that although both the main opposing schools of classical thought – as represented by Smith, Mill, Marx, Engels, and other early economic thinkers – emphasized other factors as being central to explaining the functioning and performance of an economic system, they nevertheless recognized that institutions played an important role and formed an integral part of any such explanation. While the natural liberty school minimized this role by making certain assumptions about human nature, the historical determinists and the historical school gave primacy to what they called inertial or productive forces over institutions. The neoclassical school, however, moved the agenda of economic science away from this dualistic view of the economic system, and as its thinking developed, the role of institutions was completely pared away from the model. Subsequent elaborations that formalized a set of assumptions about human nature and the functioning of markets (Arrow and Debreu 1954, Debreu 1959) removed the necessity for any reference to be made to the institutional framework of a society. Human beings were now assumed to be utility maximizers, with this utility being defined in terms of general purchasing power or the command over material wealth. In the words of Marshall, 'this is so, not because money or material wealth is regarded as the main aim of human effort ... but because in this world of ours it is one convenient means of measuring human motive on a large scale' ([1920]1956: 18). Based on this assumption a large literature has developed showing that so long as economic agents are allowed to operate freely in markets where competitive forces predominate, an economy can achieve efficiency in its resource allocation between different uses and maximize incomes and welfare. This neoclassical model of the economy now forms the basis for most of the textbook teaching of economics.

CRITIQUE OF THE NEOCLASSICAL MODEL

Rational choice theory, with its maximization principle, is at the behavioural core of neoclassical economics (Caldwell 1993, Knudsen 1993, Vanberg 1993). According to this theory, all agents are self-interested optimizers whose behaviour is determined by economic rationality. The content of this economic rationality is that agents will undertake the constrained maximization of utility in the allocation of scarce resources among alternatives uses, and in doing so, will make choices that are transitive and independent of the utility of others. The assumption of rational maximization is the basis on which neoclassical theory – and its subsequent derivations that are part of the new classical school – has developed some of its core models to explain economic phenomena. This includes the consumption behaviour of individuals, the investment behaviour of firms, and the efficient functioning of markets. Thus we have the permanent income hypothesis of Friedman (1957), according to which a utility-maximizing consumer will base his consumption on the discounted value of current and future income (i.e. his wealth or permanent income). In the area of investment decision-making we have two major models. Modigliani and Miller (1958) argue that a profit-maximizing manager, in order to maximize shareholder value, will only make those investments where the risk-adjusted return exceeds the market rate of return on capital. Likewise, the q-theory of Tobin (1969) argues that a profit-maximizing firm will invest in capital up to the point where the cost of an extra unit of capital stock is equal to the present discounted value of the stream of earnings from a unit of capital. Finally, we have the efficient markets hypothesis (Fama 1970). Since within a rational maximization framework financial market prices or valuations should reflect the present value of expected cash flows, according to this hypothesis, in an efficient market – such as the financial markets that exist in advanced market economies – the information sub-set available to investors will be fully utilized by the market in forming the equilibrium expected returns and consequently current prices or valuations.

A critique of this view can be made at three levels. First, at the microeconomic level it could be argued that self-interested maximization is not an accurate or generalizable characterization of human behaviour. Thus from the field of psychology we have the findings of cognitive science, which indicate that the human mind, and our emotions, do not function in the manner proposed by neoclassical economics. Within economics itself, a wealth of evidence has now accumulated from behavioural and experimental studies to show that human behaviour does not conform to the characterizations of this theory. Even at a relatively less rigorous level, the central behavioural postulate of economics since Adam Smith that human beings behave in a self-interested manner is not as straightforward as it seems. A more precise elaboration of the various aspects of this concept indicates that it has not been adequately defined by neoclassical economics, and once the benign aspects of this required behaviour are made explicit, it becomes evident that such behaviour is not generalizable to the system as a whole. As discussed in greater detail below, self-interestedness can be defined in different ways, each of which has a certain type of behavioural pattern associated with it. And these behavioural patterns, if they occur in a significant enough manner, are likely to result in different types of market situations occurring, rather than there being a unique and efficient solution as proposed by neoclassical economics. Apart from its other implications, such an alternative view of market actors automatically renders unviable the neoclassical assumption of a representative agent who has unique behavioural characteristics. These arguments form the main content of this chapter.

Second, at a more macro level, it can be argued that constitutional and legal frameworks, habits, customs and cultural variables – that the classical economists did refer to, but gave relatively less importance to in their model in favour other factors – have a major influence on human behaviour, as well as being the key determinants of how an economic system functions. In this view, economic reality is necessarily embedded within a broader set of social relations, culture and institutions, and as argued in the basic sociological model, these social rules and norms must be viewed as the foundations for any cooperative social order. Thus, for instance, even the Walras-Arrow-Debreu framework on which much of neoclassical economics is based implicitly assumes that property rights are respected and contracts are adhered to, and this clearly requires constraining and enabling structures such as laws, courts, social norms, etc. Consequently, an entity such as the market cannot be represented simply as an arena in which individual maximizing agents collide. Rather, it is itself a social institution based on certain social rules, and reflective of a particular kind of social culture. A modern theory of pricing, therefore, cannot disregard corporate institutions through which a significant proportion of the prices in a developed economy are determined. An elaboration of this view would lead us in the direction of the old and new institutional economics literature that propounds an alternative view of the functioning of an economic system. We shall consider this literature, and the model of the economy that it proposes, in greater detail, in the next chapter.

Third, even if we grant rational maximizing behaviour, the core neoclassical model requires a number of stringent assumptions which are not consistent either with the actual conditions that prevail in markets, or with the nature of the all the goods and services produced and consumed in an economy. The presence of these distortions has already been widely discussed in the literature on welfare economics: it is accepted, even by neoclassical theorists, that their existence results in market failure and that such a failure prevents free markets from achieving efficiency and optimality conditions (Nath 1969). Therefore, we shall not discuss this issue further in any great detail. Distortions which result in market failure include the presence of uncertainty and the absence of perfect knowledge; the existence of indivisibilities in factors of production and increasing returns to scale; and the presence of non-market interdependencies between consumers or between production units. Uncertainty, for instance, is the inevitable characteristic of an economy where rapid technical change is occurring or the structure of production is changing. In these circumstances the prices of products will not be a given, and consequently none of the required marginal conditions will be met. Production interdependencies or external economies in the production of goods will result in the profits of firms being inter-related. Where such externalities exist, the market when left to itself will result in the sub-optimal production of such goods, or will even give rise to a situation where the production of these goods does not occur at all. The impact of consumption externalities, in particular the case of public goods, is well known. Here, the market will find it impossible to produce such a good, because its consumption has the characteristics of non-excludability and non-rivalrousness.

The factors underlying market failure discussed above indicate that from a theoretical point of view markets left to themselves will not necessarily bring about efficient allocative solutions. Therefore, even if we do not take into account concerns relating to the distribution of income and equity, for a market-based economy to function smoothly it is evident that there need to be laws, regulations, supportive policies and government intervention. At a minimum, the extent of this regulation or intervention will depend on the extent of market failure. Based on this view, a substantial body of literature now exists which argues that this is in fact the situation in developing countries, where achieving high rates of growth involves changing the structure of the economy, rapid technological change, and establishing industries which may be characterized by increasing returns. Thus, Stiglitz (1989) emphasizes that market failure is particularly common in developing countries. Such failures occur because the markets for knowledge and information are very imperfect and coordination problems are present that will prevent a scale of production being established – such as can be found in the advanced economies, whereby technological indivisibilities can be internalized. On these theoretical considerations, Chang (2011) argues that free markets may in fact be less good at generating growth than markets which are protected, regulated, or more generally subject to government intervention. Using the examples of Britain and the United States during the early stages of their industrialization, he provides historical evidence to support this contention (Chang 2002). These arguments are considered in Chapter 4.

HUMAN BEHAVIOUR

At the level of human motivation, the neoclassical model holds that self-interest is the primary motive underlying economic action. More specifically, it states that rationality consists of human beings attempting to maximize something called 'utility', the content of which is defined in terms of wealth or payoffs, and that this rational self-interest leads to a self-equilibrating economic system. Detractors of this view argue that human nature is far more complex than that assumed by neoclassical economics, with ideas, ideologies, altruism and standards of conduct derived from beliefs and culture being equally important determinants of economic behaviour. Therefore, any theory which requires generalizable assumptions about human motivation should take into account all these aspects of behaviour and arrive at its assumptions based upon a well-founded knowledge of actual behaviour in its historical, cultural and institutional context, rather than based on some *a priori* general principles (Hodgson and Screpanti 1991). In terms of the concept of rationality itself, as clarified by the Arrow-Debreu theorem, the model assumes an extreme form of rationality. This requires decision-makers to be omniscient and foresee all contingencies, so that maximizing behaviour leads to efficient inter-temporal market solutions. Such rationality has been termed 'instrumental' or perfect rationality. As North (1992: 1) has indicated, in such a 'world of instrumental rationality, institutions are unnecessary … efficient markets – both economic and political – characterize economies'.

In actual fact, however, our cognitive capabilities are limited, and we do not have the capability to perform the mathematical operations necessary to maximize utility based on a complete evaluation of the set of availabilities and contingent availabilities. Simon (1957, 1965, 1979) has used the term 'bounded rationality' to signify the fact that both the knowledge and computational abilities of the decision-maker are limited, and that an individual goes about making decisions in a procedurally reasonable manner based on a subjective assessment of the options available. Referring to the rationality of *homo oeconomicus* Simon states, 'He does not stand on a mountain top and, viewing the whole world at his feet, make a global, omniscient rational choice. He is rational within the bounds set by his social role of economic man' (1982: 6a). Simon's conception refers to the neuro-physiological limits of a human being, on one hand, and the limits of language on the other. As a consequence of these limits, it is impossible to identify all future contingencies, and given substantial uncertainty, it is more rational for economic agents to use experience-based 'selective heuristics ... to explore a small number of promising alternatives' (Simon 1979: 73) as a basis for decision-making. In simple markets, the limits of an economic agent's bounded rationality may not be reached. However, this is not likely to be the case in complex markets, where uncertainty and limited knowledge are ubiquitous. Self-interested behaviour under these circumstances will not yield the efficient solutions that neoclassical economics predicts. On the contrary, signalling equilibria may not fall within reasonable bounds, dramatic disquilibria may occur from time to time, and multiple equilibria may be common. Arrow (1986) confirms this view. He states that the implications of perfect rationality are derived from all the structural assumptions of perfect competition and the completeness of markets. Where there is incomplete information and uncertainty, even with perfect rationality, there will be multiple equilibria.

Leading cognitive psychologists Cosmides and Tooby (1994) go further here to indicate that the neoclassical assumption that rational behaviour is the state of nature which requires no explanation is decidedly odd from a scientific perspective. In fact, rational behaviour is definitely not the state of nature, and all behaviour – rational or otherwise – requires causal explanations that will necessarily invoke theories about the architecture of the human mind. In this context, evolutionary psychology, based on Darwin's theory of natural selection, can provide well-specified theories and general principles about how our cognitive mechanisms generate behaviour, including economic behaviour. In this view, human cognitive architecture resembles a large network of functionally specialized computational devices which have evolved in the past 100,000 years or so to solve the ancestral problems of our hunter-gatherer past. Since our ancestors had to solve natural adaptive problems, natural selection promoted the evolution of specialized problem-solving mental devices. These include domain-specific reasoning instincts, and learning and preference circuits which are applied without formal instruction or an awareness of their underlying logic. These circuits are hard-wired into the more primitive parts of the brain such as the limbic system and amygdala and control various elements of human motivation. The mind, therefore, cannot be seen as a *tabula rasa* guided by certain specific rules of functioning, and human mental content cannot be seen as being dominated by rational decision-making tools such as logic, mathematics and probability, because such general purpose rational methods are computationally incapable of solving natural adaptive problems. This view is supported by neurophysiological experiments. For instance, Moll and Grafman (2006) have found that both monetary rewards and charitable donations activate the mesolimbic reward pathway – a primitive part of the brain – showing that altruism is not a superior moral faculty which suppresses basic selfish urges, but is instead an activity which is pleasurable to the brain.

Modern genetic theory also holds the same views. Human behaviour is postulated to have a biological basis (Maynard Smith 1995, Wilson 2000). Altruism, for instance, is shown as having genetic roots (Hamilton 1964, 1996). Explaining this theory in popular terms, Dawkins (2006) indicates that evolution is based on the good of the gene, not the good of the species. Genes are the survival replicators and human beings are their survival machines. Natural selection favours those genes that control their survival machines in such a way that they make the best use of their environment and leave more surviving offspring. Since genes cannot manipulate the world directly, the human brain has evolved such that it is programmed in advance with rules, strategies and advice to cope with as many eventualities as possible in the struggle for existence. In other words, the mind is not a machine designed to conduct a rational calculus, but is a device functionally designed for the purposes of survival and reproduction. To achieve this end genes induce self-ish individual behaviour. However, since this selfishness is geared towards the survival and reproduction of one's genes, it includes altruistic behaviour towards ones kin, with whom of course we share our genes, and reciprocal altruism towards 'others', whose lives impinge on us directly and may of course play an important role in contributing to our survival. In these circumstances there is no reason at all for an individual to define self-interest in terms of wealth maximization.

As Plott (1986) states, from the point of view of evolutionary biology, the definition of individual self-interestedness could be seen as one of maximizing the survival potential of an actor and his or her genes in future generations. In such a socio-biological model, rational self-interest would imply altruism, reciprocal altruism, or even nepotism aimed at protecting the interests of one's relatives and other descendants. This would result in a totally different pattern of individual behaviour than that predicted by standard economic theory. Thus once the narrow assumption of individual maximization in terms of material payoffs is dropped, and a wider range of assumptions based on cognitive psychology or genetics is accepted to explain human behaviour, there is no longer any guarantee that the outcome of interactions between actors will result in the economic system functioning in the manner predicted by neoclassical economics.

Apart from the biological and psychological findings discussed above, within the economics discipline itself, over the years, a number of researchers have undertaken empirical studies to establish whether market actors do in fact behave in a manner predicted by the rational choice and individual maximization hypothesis. This body of literature has now developed into the field of behavioural economics in which psychology and economics have been connected. The issues considered in these studies include the extent to which motives other than pure self-interest are significant in influencing market behaviour; whether individual decision-making involves maximization based on stable, well-ordered, and externally determined preferences; and whether an individual's preferences are independent of the preferences of other individuals. By focusing on cognitive illusions and anomalies, the conclusion reached by this literature, as discussed in greater detail below, is that human behaviour deviates in significant ways from that assumed in the neoclassical model and consequently this model is a descriptive failure. The behavioural economics literature is vast. In the brief review below we shall therefore focus on some of the key areas where experimental studies undertaken in market settings have revealed the inadequacies of the rational choice model that is central to neoclassical thinking.

The first area we shall consider is where experiments have shown that the standard assumptions underlying the concave expected utility function of an individual do not hold. A central assumption of the expected utility model is that a person's utility will depend on the final state of that person's endowments or wealth. Kahneman and Tversky (1979), however, have shown that initial states are a relevant factor in estimating an individual's utility function. Their research shows that human behaviour is reference dependent (i.e. how the current situation differs from some habitual or other reference level, rather than the absolute characteristics of the situation). In the context of wealth, people are found to be much more averse to losses than to gains of the same size. This intense loss aversion, where people dislike even a small-scale risk, implies that an individual's utility function abruptly changes its slope at the reference level. Such a reference-based kink is not consistent with the standard concave utility function. Kahneman and Tversky also found that a pervasive pattern of human perception is that the perceived effects on well-being are greater for changes closer to one's reference level than for changes further out. This indicates that a person's utility function over wealth levels becomes flatter as the wealth level gets further and further away from this reference level. A combination of loss aversion and this diminishing sensitivity means that the utility function is more likely to be S-shaped, with a kink at the reference point, rather than concave as assumed by neoclassical economics. Additional support for the concept of reference levels, which are influenced by initial allocations, comes from the evidence on the 'endowment effect'. Experiments by Thaler (1980), and Kahneman, Knetsch and Thaler (2008), showed that once a person comes to possess a good, they will immediately value it higher than before they possessed it. Possession changes the reference point of the individual and the selling price of the possessed good, implying that preferences are influenced by initial allocations or endowments.

The second area in which a wealth of evidence has accumulated to show that human behaviour systematically departs from the assumptions of the neoclassical rationality model is that of judgement biases and inconsistencies in decision-making. Rabin (1998), referring to this literature, summarizes some of the major findings of these studies:

- *The law of small numbers* – people will exaggerate how closely a small sample will resemble the parent population and will consequently over-infer from a short sequence of events.
- *Belief perseverance* – once a strong hypothesis has been formed, people will become inattentive to new information contradicting the hypothesis. While such a confirmatory bias has not been observed in the case of visual perception, it seems to occur whenever the evidence is ambiguous and requires some degree of abstraction and interpretation. In particular, people will have a tendency to interpret ambiguous or disconfirming evidence in a manner which is less damaging to the adopted hypothesis.
- *Overconfidence* – mass psychological research shows that people are prone to overconfidence in their judgements, and while repeated experience or learning moderates this somewhat, it does not eliminate such biases.
- *Framing effects* – logically equivalent statements of a problem lead decision-makers to choose differing options depending on how the statements have been framed (Tversky and Kahneman 1986). Thus the manner in which a problem is framed influences preferences. One of the best examples of framing effects is money illusion, where people have been found to be attentive to nominal rather than real changes in wages and prices. Money illusion has, in fact, been noted to be widespread in spite of assumptions to the contrary being postulated by neoclassical and new classical economists (Kahneman et al. 1986, Shafir et al. 1997).
- *Preference reversals* – experiments showing that choices are not well ordered or stable have a long history (Grether and Plott 1979, Tversky and Thaler 1990, Tversky et al. 1990). Referring to this phenomenon, Tversky and Thaler (1990: 208) state 'the findings indicate that the preference reversal phenomenon is an example of a general pattern, rather than a peculiar characteristic of choice between bets'.

The third body of material relates to the assumption of rational choice theory that individual decisions are time consistent (i.e. inter-temporal choices do not depend on the decision date or when the decision is made). Contrary to this Pesendorf (2006), considering the experimental evidence on this subject, indicates that there is an 'immediacy effect' such that people will have a tendency to choose an earlier smaller reward over a later larger reward, but will reverse this preference when both rewards are delayed. More generally Rabin (1998), surveying this body of evidence, states that people will tend to make current choices according to which choice directly yields the highest utility without taking into account the choice's effect on the utilities from future choices. This short-term tendency to pursue immediate gratification is commonly inconsistent with our long-term preferences, and it indicates that our preferences are time variant rather than being unified or stable over time. Because of such time inconsistent propensities for immediate gratification, self-control and self-commitment devices become important, because through such devices future choices can be restricted and future behaviour controlled. Human beings will commonly use self-control and self-commitment mechanisms in order to make future options consistent with current preferences, in the knowledge that otherwise they are likely to behave in a manner in the future that they will not like given today's preferences. Such time variance in preferences is not consistent with the expected utility theory. However, models based on these insights do explain a wide range of savings (Laibson 1997) and choice reversal (Kirby and Hernstein 1995) behaviour, including the widely observed human effort to put in place self-control and self-commitment devices.

Finally, behavioural economics has considered the importance of motives other than self-interest in influencing market behaviour and outcomes. Rabin (1998: 16) states that there are hundreds of studies which show that economic behaviour is induced by equity, fairness, status-seeking and other departures from simple self-interest in non-trivial ways. These departures affect market outcomes in observable ways:

- *Altruism* – people will put a positive value on the well-being of others and consequently their utility function will include, to some degree, the well-being of others (e.g. family members). This violates the independence axiom of neoclassical utility maximization theory.
- *Reciprocal altruism* – many studies, such as that of Shafir and Tversky (1992), have found that others' intentions and behaviour are relevant to our own preferences and behaviour. Croson (1995), for instance, finds that there is a positive correlation between a person's contribution to a public good and their beliefs about how much other people are contributing. In a public goods situation the existence of such prefer-

ences will result in a high contribution efficient equilibrium or a low contribution inefficient one. Reciprocal altruism can also explain the widely observed higher than market clearing 'efficiency wages' that many firms pay their employees. The 'efficiency wage' is paid to induce workers to reciprocate by putting in more effort (Akerlof and Yellen 1990).

- *Fairness* – the importance of fairness as a motive underlying economic behaviour finds its origins in Adam Smith's *Theory of Moral Sentiments* (1759). In this work he argued that people have a natural sentiment towards fairness and justice and that these sentiments underlie the fabric of human society. According to Smith, human behaviour is an outcome of the internal struggle between our passions such as self-interest and the need for immediate gratification, and the 'impartial spectator' who was guided by such sentiments as fairness and justice (Ashraf et al. 2005). More recently, Kahneman, Knetsch and Thaler (1986) have shown the importance of fairness in economic decision-making through experimental studies. Fehr, Kirchler and Weichbold (1994), in their study of experimental labour markets, also found that because of notions of fairness and equity, people's behaviour need never converge with the outcomes predicted by self-interest.

Behavioural economics therefore shows that individual maximization based on rational choice is an unsafe hypothesis. However, Plott (1986) argues that the rejection of a theory of markets on such a basis is not a challenging objective. The issue is whether the magnitude of error in the predictions of market phenomena by this theory is acceptable, or if not, whether any alternative theory exists that better fits the facts. Elaborating on this view, Plott refers to three types of experiments that have been undertaken by experimental economists to test the individual optimization hypothesis. First, he describes the case where middlemen were used to intermediate between buyers and sellers in different rooms. If the middlemen were optimizers then the prices in both these markets should approach equality. In the experiment, with time and replication the prices were in fact found to converge to the market-clearing price. Second, Plott states that experiments with auctions have shown that the average actual prices achieved were close to the mean price predicted by the optimization model. Third, referring to a set of experiments conducted in 12 markets to capture the nature of the equilibrating process, he indicates that it was found that in two of the markets the results did correspond closely to the behaviour predicted by the rationality model.

Based on these experiments, Plott concludes that the optimization hypothesis does a pretty good job of capturing the essence of a very complicated phenomenon. Commenting on this literature, however, Coleman (1986) is not so sanguine in his conclusions. He states that the experimental literature shows that an English auction gives one set of outcomes; a central clearinghouse of bids and offers another; sealed bid auctions give another; a market with prices set by sellers and modified to produce market clearing gives another; and a market in which the participants must themselves develop trading structures gives yet another. Therefore, although all the actors within these markets were trying to optimize in terms of neoclassical behavioural assumptions, different equilibrium prices emerged because of the various institutional settings they were operating in. Therefore optimizing behaviour by itself does not generate a unique set of outcomes.

Summarizing these behavioural findings, Vernon Smith (1989) – one of the pioneers of testing in experimental markets – indicates that experimental testing has shown that:

- the institutional setting does matter because agents' incentives are affected by the institutional rules that convert messages into outcomes;
- there is overwhelming evidence that economic agents do not solve decision-making problems in the manner proposed by neoclassical economics;
- in spite of the behavioural anomalies, market outcomes are often consistent with the predictions of optimization theory.

Vernon Smith concludes that these findings show that mainstream economic theory has lagged behind the empirical evidence and economics has become an *a priori* science rather than an observational science in which there is interplay between theory and observation. To illustrate this point, he provides a parable comparing the reaction of neoclassical economists to evidence that individual choice behaviour is inconsistent with expected utility theory and the fundamental behavioural hypothesis in the theory of demand that there should only be a small difference between the willingness to pay and the willingness to accept. Referring to this as the flat world hypothesis, he states that evidence that some travellers have not returned is interpreted by neoclassical economists as showing that they fell off the edge, whereas evidence that some returned is interpreted as them not having gone far enough to fall off the edge. Based on such an interpretation of the empirical evidence, the neoclassical null hypothesis is never rejected.

RATIONALITY, OPPORTUNISM AND PREDATION

The discussion above suggests that the self-interest-based utility and profit maximization model is not well suited to explaining observed human behaviour. People do not seem to have a well-ordered objective function or to process information in a probabilistic manner. More generally, the evidence indicates that people misperceive their long-run well-being and do not attempt to maximize utility in the manner proposed by the rational choice paradigm. In spite of these findings, while an uncompromising and relentless drive towards utility or profit maximization may not be realistic, nevertheless *homo oeconomicus,* with his tendency to exploit most opportunities for personal benefit, is still held by many as a reasonable and realistic approximation of reality, especially when we confine ourselves to market behaviour. As Vernon Smith (1989) highlights, maximization in terms of payoffs is a good working hypothesis for predicting economic behaviour in general, particularly in the context of market activity. However, given the behavioural findings outlined above, the question still remains as to what exactly we mean by self-interested behaviour, since the concept of self-interest is itself open to a varied interpretation.

Rabin (1998) argues that given loss aversion, endowment effects, diminishing utility, judgement biases, and the tendency towards immediate gratification, human rationality – and therefore the content of self-interest – is quite different from that assumed by neoclassical economics. These behavioural characteristics, rather than being anomalies, should in fact be viewed as the real content of our rationality. For instance, if losses relative to the status quo are viewed as being something very unpleasant, then loss averse behaviour should be considered as being fully rational rather than an anomaly. To reconcile this view of what self-interested behaviour consists of and the fact that the constrained maximization model often does work in market settings, Vernon Smith (1989) suggests that the psychologists' reference frame is good for explaining a subject's short-run or initial behaviour which reflects all kinds of beliefs and expectations. But if these choices are found not to be sustainable, then subjects will adapt their expectations in a manner such that the standard economics maximizing paradigm seems to perform quite well in predicting the equilibrium reached over time. Even if we accept this interpretation, as a host of experimental studies have found (Plott and Vernon Smith 2008), given the behavioural attributes discussed above, as well as the existence of bounded rationality, opportunity costs and sunk costs, any inter-temporal adjustment process is likely to be sluggish, erratic and non-optimal. This implies that there is no guarantee that self-interested behaviour, even within a constrained maximization framework, will automatically result in the operation and continuance of a self-equilibrating system, particularly as markets depart from their Walrasian simplicity and become more and more complex.

We have already noted the views of Adam Smith on the parameters within which self-interest needs to operate for the competitive market-based system to function in a self-regulating manner. These include notions of fair play, common prudence, and common understanding. The latter implies some degree of harmony of interests. The same theme is to be found in Arrow (1974). Discussing the importance of market actors having a fair degree of reliance on each other and other people's word for the proper functioning of the market-based system, Arrow focuses on the role of trust. He says that, 'Trust is an important lubricant of a social system ... Trust and similar values, loyalty or truth-telling ... are commodities that have real, practical, economic value; they increase the efficiency of the system ... But they are not commodities for which trade on the open market is technically feasible' (1974: 23). Thus for the efficient functioning of a market, even a mainstream economist such as Arrow admits that self-interest needs to operate in the context of a universally accepted value system and code of behaviour. This indicates that the utility or profit maximizing behaviour of *homo oeconomicus* has in some sense to be benign because it is bound by informal rules that will include fair play and some degree of trust.

Elaborating on this issue Williamson (1985: 47) states that for the neoclassical system to work, when neoclassical man confronts self-interested others across markets, the bargain must be struck in a rule-bound manner on the basis of fully and candidly disclosed initial positions. There can be no problematic behaviour attributable to rule deviance amongst human actors. In fact, quoting the ample literature, Williamson (1985: 49) argues that human behaviour does not involve what he calls such 'simple self-seeking'. On the contrary, an observation of what actually happens in the economic sphere shows beyond doubt that in all societies a typical individual uses various stratagems to continually pursue an increase in that which they can legitimately claim as being theirs. Thus Williamson distinguishes between simple self-interest seeking and opportunism. Neoclassical economics assumes that there is simple self-interest seeking behaviour and excludes the possibility of opportunistic self-seeking behaviour on a scale large enough to affect market outcomes.

Opportunism, therefore, is the second type of self-interest seeking behaviour. Williamson (1985) defines such behaviour as 'self-interest seeking with guile'. When transactions are conducted on the basis of uncertainty and incomplete information, self-interest seeking opens the way to opportunism. If individuals were fully open and honest in their efforts to realize individual advantage, or if obedience to the rules could be presumed, then uncertainty in economic transactions would vanish and there would be no opportunism. However, as we have already noted this is not the case and the maximizing behaviour of the typical individual tends to be a continuous pursuit of an increase in that which they can claim to be theirs, using an incomplete or even distorted disclosure of information. Williamson (1985: 47) thus argues that opportunistic behaviour goes well beyond subtle forms of deceit, such as attempts to mislead, disguise, distort or confuse, to include more blatant efforts such as lying, cheating, embezzling or stealing. Furthermore, such opportunism can either be *exante* or *expost* (i.e. it can occur before or after a transaction has been completed). Williamson and Ouchi (1981) further point out that for opportunism to have a major impact on market performance, it is not even necessary for such behaviour to occur on a large scale. All that is needed is that some agents will behave in this manner and that it be costly to sort out those who are opportunistic from those who are not. Thus market-affecting behaviour need not even be the dominant or most common type of behaviour. And it follows on from this that if opportunism is an accurate representation of certain types of economic behaviour, then contracts will not be concluded in the market in the way assumed by neoclassical economics, and in particular, markets will not have the characteristic of being self-regulating or self-equilibrating.

Yet another type of self-interested behaviour emerges when we drop the neoclassical assumption that actors will limit their choices to a basket of opportunities that lie within their own budget and capabilities, and that they do not try to acquire goods, services or wealth by means which lie outside these parameters. The implications of this assumption are best brought out in Mill's definition of private property. He ([1848]1923: 218) stated that 'The institution of private property, when limited to its essential elements consists of the recognition in each person, of a right to the exclusive disposal of what he or she have produced by their own exertions, or received either by gift or by fair agreement, without force or fraud, from those who produce it'. This understanding presumes that some sort of institutional framework exists, such as an effective legal system with enforcement mechanisms, that will ensure all the actors limit themselves to their own budgets and capabilities rather than trying to take away the endowments of other individuals by choosing to rob, steal, plunder, or act in some other predatory manner (Bardhan 2001).

Self-interestedness in the neoclassical sense, therefore, precludes behaviour by individual agents or the state which could be construed as being predatory. However, this is not a realistic presumption because the scope for predation by private parties on each other is created by the inherent inequality between individuals in terms of physical strength, wealth, or other means that will give one person greater power than another. Veblen ([1899]1949) had hypothesized such behaviour as being characteristic of the leisure class, and suggested that predatory habits were an essential part of an individual's struggle for existence. However, it is evident that such behaviour can be generalized as being a potential characteristic of all economic agents. In addition to predatory behaviour by individuals, there is of course scope for predation by the state, or elites who control a state. This scope is created by the inherently coercive power of the state. Predation and government have, in fact, an integral relationship, because both are based on the use coercive force in one form or another. In both cases (i.e. potential predatory behaviour by individuals or the state), unless there are checks and balances in society that will ensure the rule of law is supreme and able to control or circumscribe the power of individuals and the state, predatory activities are likely to occur.

As it happens, the history of the development of capitalism and the emergence of modern economic growth in Western Europe is essentially one of how the arbitrary rule and predatory exactions of kings, lords and the nobility, were brought under control, and the security of property rights and the rule of law was established (Kohn 2005). Our narrative in Chapter 6 will show that in England and the Dutch Republic – the first countries where in the 17th century such conditions were established – sustained economic progress commenced. However, where predatory rulers and elites – such as the Hapsburgs of Spain or the Bourbon kings of France – continued to rule and extract as much revenue as possible from their subjects, the economic backwardness of these countries continued for many centuries (Olson 2000). Predatory behaviour by governments is, of course, not merely a historical phenomenon, since the possibility of predation is inherent in the institution of government. A large literature now exists which argues that predation is prevalent and well entrenched in developing countries. Predatory ruling groups in the developing world have included landowning elites in Latin America, ethnic minorities in Africa, and military or bureaucratic oligarchies in Asia. And in addition we have had any number of kleptocratic dictators in the developing world, such as Mobutu in Zaire, Trujillo in the Dominican Republic, Somoza in Nicaragua, the Duvaliers in Haiti, and Mugabe in Zimbabwe, who along with their coteries have systematically plundered and wrecked their economies for long periods of time (Bardhan 2000). Predation is therefore common, and an increasing amount of research now indicates that such activities bring about the presence and persistence of dysfunctional institutions, which generate poverty traps, impoverish a nation, and constrain economic progress (Hoff 2000, Hoff and Stiglitz 2001).

In our analysis therefore, we shall make a distinction between opportunism and predation. Williamson's (1985) concept of opportunism, while an important advance in terms of understanding human behaviour, has too broad a definition as it encompasses both economic behaviour as it occurs through markets and other forms of non-market action – which as we have noted above will have a major impact on economic outcomes. Thus we would distinguish between behaviour in which an agent attempts to get undue benefit out of a market transaction by misleading, distorting, concealing, lying or cheating. Such behaviour conforms to the traditional notion of opportunism. However, when non-market means such as embezzling or stealing are used – or mechanisms that are under the control of the state such as rules, regulations, policies, or outright coercion are utilized to encroach upon the entitlements and endowments of individuals to appropriate benefits which would not have otherwise been available through the market mechanism – we would term this predatory behaviour. Behaviour of the type undertaken by various types of dominant groups in developing countries, neo-patrimonial ruling elites, or autocrats such as Mobutu, Somoza and Mugabe, is most appropriately defined as predatory rather than opportunistic. Even in developed economies governed by the rule of law, predatory behaviour by significant market actors has been found to be common, as the examples of Enron, Madoff, and the sale of mortgage-backed securities by Wall Street firms, which they knew were 'doomed to fail' (Bloomberg News, 14 May 2010), have shown.

THE REPRESENTATIVE AGENT

The distinction between opportunism and predation is important, since the control of both such types of behaviour is necessary to permit an economic system to function in a productive manner and the control of each requires the presence of different types of institutions. Depending on whether opportunism or predation is the more dominant form of economic behaviour in a society, the extent of institutional change needed for a country to embark on a path of sustained progress will also be different. In particular, as we shall argue later, the control or elimination of predatory behaviour by entrenched interests who are in control of the machinery of the state, as is found in many developing countries, will not be amenable to small, incremental institutional reforms. One important conclusion that can be drawn from the discussion above on different types of human behaviour, all of which are clearly important from an economic point of view, is that the neoclassical assumption of a representative agent is not a very realistic one. Rather, society is populated by people who are driven by different types of economic motivation, and the manner in which an economy will eventually function will depend very much on what the dominant behavioural characteristics turn out to be. Thus where a society is populated by people, who on average behave like *homo oeconomicus* – with limits on their behaviour based on informal norms such as those specified by Adam Smith, Arrow and Williamson – the formal institutional framework required to bring about allocative efficiency and the social good as a consequence of their individual actions is likely to be quite minimal. On the other hand, if opportunistic or predatory behaviour is not uncommon, or dominant elites by their own example make such behaviour a social standard, then a deeper process of institutional change, with the consequent emergence of more elaborate formal and informal institutions, will be required to ensure that individual behaviour changes in a manner that will result in favourable economic outcomes.

Based on this empirical reality, Colander (2008) argues that a realistic model of the economy must take into account the fact that there is agent heterogeneity. Thus a macro-model must not only analyse the characteristics of the individual, but also permit a study of the structure and impact of the interplay that exists between large numbers of such heterogeneous agents. Colander indicates that in complex systems aggregate behaviour cannot be deduced from an analysis of individuals alone. Such a view is commonplace in other disciplines from biology to physics and sociology. So, for instance, the aggregate behaviour of systems of particles or social insects cannot be deduced from the characteristics of a 'representative' of the population. Complex systems involve emergent properties that cannot be understood from an analysis of the systems' components. Consequently, macroeconomics needs to move away from the microeconomic foundations proposed by neoclassical economics in which certain fundamental characteristics of individual human behaviour are postulated and models that explain macroeconomic performance are formulated on the basis of generalizing these characteristics to cover the population at large. As Hoover (2001) points out, macroeconomics deals with what he calls synthetic aggregates, such as real GDP and the general price level, which are fabricated from components that make them dimensionally distinct from their elements. Such aggregates exist objectively and independently of any individual human mind, and can be manipulated separately from any micro-foundations that they may have. The macro-properties of the economy, therefore, cannot be explained by referring only to the behaviour of individual actors – rational or otherwise.

While dropping the assumption of a representative agent who behaves like *homo oeconomicus* and accepting the reality that society consists of individuals who will behave under different criterion of self-interest may be fatal to neoclassical theory, it opens the way to a consideration of other more appropriate models of social interaction. One such model that can be borrowed from evolutionary biology, and is based on game theory, is that of an evolutionary stable strategy or ESS (Maynard Smith 1982, 1995). The ESS model is applicable whenever independent selfish entities interact with each other on the basis of a conflict of interests, but nevertheless the social organization within which they interact has properties of stability and comes to resemble a single organized whole. Dawkins (2006) defines an ESS as a strategy that, if most of the members of a population adopt it, cannot be invaded and bettered by an alternative strategy under the influence of natural selection. The logic of the ESS is that since each individual based on self-interest is trying to maximize their own success, the only strategy that will persist will be one which cannot be bettered by any deviant individual. Within this framework, the simple neoclassical model can be modelled as a Social Contract game. In this game, if all individuals behave in a rational self-interested manner and cooperate with each other, then each individual will be better off than if everyone defects. However, from a game theoretic point of view this is not a stable solution since in a society of cooperators it would pay an individual to defect.

A Social Contract game that assumes rational, cooperative individuals is therefore not an ESS. In any event, since we would argue that society does not consist of one type of representative agent but consists of actors who behave as simple self-seekers, altruists, opportunists or predators, social interaction needs to be modelled to take account of this variability in behavioural patterns. This is precisely what the ESS models in evolutionary biology try to do. Dawkins (2006: 70), describing a simple Hawk-Dove game (a hawk being an actor that fights hard and retreats only when seriously injured, and a dove being one that threatens but retreats and never hurts anybody), shows that based on any arbitrary set of payoffs, neither Hawk nor Dove is an ESS. However, depending on the value of the payoffs, a stable population is generated when a specific stable ratio of hawks to doves follows these respective strategies in the population. Of course, even in a population with only hawks and doves, the optimum strategy in terms of overall payoffs is if all members of the population agree to cooperate and behave like doves. But as we have noted above, this is not a stable situation because it is not immune to treachery from within. Dawkins states that computer simulations undertaken by various researchers show that the addition of other strategies such as 'Retaliator', 'Bully', or other conditional strategies does not change the conclusion that an evolutionary stable population (that is, one that is in some sort of homeostatic equilibrium) is one that has a mixture of individuals who will follow different strategies. The use of game theory therefore shows that actors with different behavioural characteristics of self-interest can interact and receive payoffs which will generate stable solutions. This indicates that the concept of a representative agent is not necessary for analysing the functioning of a market.

The theoretical and empirical critiques of the neoclassical model discussed above are fundamental and question its basic value to providing an understanding of the functioning of an economic system. Our discussion also shows that the empirical evidence on human behaviour, and the outcomes of this behaviour, does not provide any support for the neoclassical model even from a positivist point of view (Friedman 1953, Lucas 1986). Discussing this issue, Arrow (1986) points out that there are a great many areas of applied economics, and in fact major theories of macroeconomics, that are based on non-neoclassical assumptions about human behaviour. The quantity theory of money is one such major example. Given that money is not a direct source of utility within a strict utility maximization framework in which by assumption there is no uncertainty, there is no reason for people to hold on to money. Yet the stability of the demand function for money is an empirically proven fact, with money being held not simply as a means but as an end in itself. The

Keynesian model, with its assumptions of money illusion, wage and price rigidity, and 'animal spirits' that influence human behaviour, is another major example of a macroeconomic model that explains the functioning of the economic system in a different manner.

However, in spite of these difficulties, and because of its simplicity and the absence of an equally coherent, rigorously formulated alternative, the basic neoclassical model still holds sway in economic theory. To challenge this view, therefore, using the theoretically informed inductive approach adopted in this study, in Chapter 3 we will first consider the institutional economics view of the functioning of an economic system. This literature accepts the validity of the behavioural and other empirical evidence that we have discussed in this chapter and attempts to offer alternative hypotheses based on the available evidence. Based on an analytical review of this literature, we shall put forward certain working hypotheses of relevance to our study. Subsequently, in Chapters 4, 5, 6 and 7 these hypotheses will be tested against generalizations that have emerged from the empirical and historical evidence on the origins of modern economic growth, and the sources of recent economic growth both in the developed and developing countries. Through this approach we will attempt to assess whether the neoclassical model, or the alternative institutionalist model, is a better tool for understanding the economic performance of nations, and if the latter provides a better basis for development theory, policy and practice.

3. The old and new institutional economics

The old and new institutional economics literature, particularly the former, is vast. In this chapter, therefore, we shall only consider the major themes and major studies which form part of this literature. Following Williamson (2000), we would also note that the new institutional economics operates at two levels. The first is the macro level, which deals with the institutional environment or rules of the game. The second is the more micro-level, dealing with the structures of governance within which transactions occur and the management of these transactions. Since our focus in the book is to assess whether this body of thought provides an alternative model of the functioning of the economic system as compared with the neoclassical model, and whether this model is a better basis for understanding the problems of growth and development, this chapter will limit its review to those studies where the approach or findings are relevant to the institutional environment or institutional change at the macro level. Micro-level studies will only be considered where it is believed that they will contribute to our understanding of the macro-level.

In the previous chapter we noted that both the classical liberal thinkers, and their protagonists in the Marxist and historical schools, recognized the role of institutions in the functioning of the economic system. However, they saw this role as being a secondary one, with hard resources such as land, labour and capital being the primary determinants of wealth creation in a country. Menger ([1883]1963), although very much part of the marginalist school of that period, was one of the early economists who gave greater consideration to the origin and presence of various institutions in a society. The question that he sought to answer was this: how can one account for the emergence and continuation of functional institutions such as markets, money and private property? His answer was that such institutions were the unintended consequences of purposive actions by individual economic agents behaving in a self-interested manner. A harmony of interests amongst agents resulted in the necessary functional institutions emerging spontaneously and developing in an organic manner. This evolutionary view or invisible hand theorem of the evolution of institutions such as markets, money and private property was echoed by Hayek (1945, 1973). Thus while Menger identified the need to study the institutional order of a society separate from the question of resources, he nevertheless broadly followed classical liberal thought in arguing that the institutions required for the smooth functioning of the economic system would emerge automatically. In spite of this, however, Menger did also recognize that a large number of social structures were not the result of natural processes, and emerged as a consequence of the purposeful activity of humans directed specifically towards the establishment and development of such structures (Menger [1883]1963: 131). In this sense, he was one of the first thinkers to accept that viable institutions could be constructed and did not necessarily have to emerge through an endogenous or evolutionary historical process.

OLD INSTITUTIONALISM

With the onset of the neoclassical marginalist revolution, the development of institutionalism remained limited and outside the mainstream. The major works of the early period, now referred to as old institutionalism, were those of Veblen ([1899]1949) and Commons (1934). Veblen disagreed with the neoclassical view that economy activity was driven by individuals attempting to maximize utility. He argued that economic behaviour was motivated by what he termed conspicuous consumption and conspicuous leisure. By this he meant expenditures that were in excess of what was required for physical comfort, and were determined by a desire to emulate what was considered to be the conventional standards of decency in a particular society ([1899]1949: 102). Convention and habit were therefore much more important in explaining economic behaviour than utility maximization.

Although Veblen did not put forward any formal conceptual structure to justify his views, there are two propositions in his writings that are of considerable relevance to the model of institutional change being developed in this book. First, he rejected the neoclassical view that human action was motivated by a benign or rational self-interest. On the contrary, he maintained that antagonism, conflict of interest and predation were key to understanding human behaviour and the evolution of economic organizations in society. In his model, the ruling class in any non-primitive society was the leisure class. The emergence of this class required a predatory habit of life to develop. Thus he stated, 'When the predatory habit of life has been settled upon the group by long habituation, it becomes the able-bodied man's accredited office in the social economy to kill, to destroy such competitors in the struggle for existence' ([1899]1949: 14), and consequently 'aggression becomes the accredited form of action' ([1899]1949: 17). In other words, the ruling classes were predatory, and they maintained their dominance in society through a mixture of direct and indirect coercion. Second, Veblen argued that there was an interactive relationship between human attitudes and institutions, with a continuous process of Darwinian natural selection and selective adaptation occurring between these two forces. Therefore he stated that, 'Institutions are not only themselves the result of a selective and adaptive process which shapes the prevailing or dominant types of spiritual attitude', but also 'changing institutions in their turn make for a … further adaptation of individual temperament and habits to the changing environment through the formation of new institutions' ([1899]1949: 188).

Commons (1934) shared Veblen's view that a conflict of interests was central to understanding economic relations between agents. However, because there was a relationship of mutual dependence between man and man, this conflict needed to be resolved and a new harmony of interests created. To achieve this and produce order out of conflict, society needed institutions. Commons defined institutions as the 'working rules of collective action' (1934: 6). These rules of collective action had the capability of inducing cooperative individual action (1934: 701). Commons argued that the principles of conflict, dependence and order were the dominant characteristics of human activity and it was necessary to identify which economic activity embodied all three constituents, as this – rather than the categories identified by orthodox economics such as commodities, labour, desires, etc. – should be the ultimate unit of economic investigation. The activity that he identified as containing all the three elements stated above was a *transaction*, or the transfer of legal control over resources. According to Commons the categories being investigated by classical economic theory, such as *commodities* or *individuals*, reflected the relations of man to nature. However, our concern is the relation of man to man. In this relation *ownership* and the transfer of ownership are central, because ownership means the power to control and restrict supply (Commons 1934: 5, 57). Therefore instead of starting with individuals, we must start with transactions between individuals, and the expected repetition of these transactions, as 'each transaction is in itself a possible harmony of interests out of a conflict of interests and a collective regulation of the conflict' (1934: 242). Thus within this framework, the resolution of conflict through the intervention of existing institutions or the invention of new ones was key to obtaining the necessary degree of cooperation between human beings so that order could be maintained and efficiency realized.

This vision raises the question of how the necessary institutions or rules of collective action come into being. Commons' answer to this was that although 'there is a great variety of institutions and sanctions … the general principle common to all of them is custom and the derived habitual assumptions', which according to him underpinned all human relations (1934: 701). He argued that custom was more powerful than the individual or the state and this was because of habit. Individuals do not start *de novo*, rather in the process of growing up they learn to fit themselves to custom. Whatever habitual assumptions they have acquired or taken for granted will gradually lead their minds to becoming institutionalized, such that collective action would now control individual action and collective opinion control individual opinion. Commons classified habitual and customary assumptions into three categories – technological, proprietary, and ethical. Technological assumptions were related to what was useful to produce or the methods and materials that must be used for production; proprietary assumptions controlled the bargaining over the acquisition of profit, interest, rent or wages; and ethical assumptions arose from the current customary procedures for deciding conflicts of interest. The latter were akin to the 'class consciousness' of Karl Marx and the 'instinct' of Veblen (1934: 699).

Thus, within this framework, conforming to custom was necessary to make a living, avoid punishment by society, and operate in an environment that gave security of expectations. But custom, precedent, statute, and habitual assumptions, were not something immutable to Commons. They were 'working rules', 'indicating ... thereby their temporary and changing character conforming to the evolution of economic, political, and ethical conditions' of society (1934: 705). The classical economists were, therefore, mistaken in their view that rights – such as those to life, liberty, property, reputation, etc. – were 'natural rights'. Instead these were all customs, which might 'appear to be natural, unchangeable, inalienable, though they are artificial, collective, transitory, forfeitable' (1934: 703). To illustrate this, Commons gives the example of slavery in the United States. In this case what were considered 'natural rights' in 1856 became 'unnatural', consequent to the proclamation of 1863, and the subsequent emancipation of slaves resulted in wiping out some four billion dollars worth of property value. Since the working rules of society are neither natural nor immutable but transitory and changeable, the question then arises as to how they are to be enforced. To explain this, Commons argued that enforcement would be done by the state, which had a monopoly over violence and was the constituted authority for this purpose. However, the hierarchy of officials who would undertake this task were once again normally guided by working rules and habitual assumptions. Therefore, not only does the formal law itself emerge out of custom, precedent and common law, but the judiciary, who are constituted to interpret the law, are also generally guided in their decision-making by custom, precedent and habitual assumptions. Commons even believed that modern economic relations between agents did not pass from custom to contract, they only passed from primitive customs to business customs. Therefore, even the competitive forces commonly observable in markets were just another means of enforcing custom.

Drawing on the views of the old institutionalists, and focusing on the concept of 'embeddedness', Polanyi (1944) and Polanyi, Arensberg and Pearson (1957), further elaborated these ideas from an anthropological point of view. Polanyi through his detailed research of the functioning of markets throughout history argued that human economic relations have always been embedded in the broader context of human society. Historically, the economy has not been an autonomous entity, it has instead been subordinated to politics, religion and social relations. Thus Polanyi (1944: 57) states that 'in this framework the orderly production and distribution of goods was secured through a great variety of individual motives ... Among these motives, gain was not prominent. Custom and law, magic and religion, cooperated in inducing the individual to comply with rules of behaviour, which eventually ensured the functioning of the economic system'. However, this situation changed with the emergence of the capitalist system, with the market now coming to dominate the economic system, and this was of overwhelming consequence for the whole organization of society. Polanyi states that 'it means no less than the running of society as an adjunct to the market. Instead of the economy being embedded in social relations, social relations are embedded in the economic system' (1944: 60), but to him this dominance of the market did not imply that a flimsy principle such as self-interest could provide the basis for its functioning. On the contrary, he maintained that for self-regulating markets to function society must be shaped in such a manner so as to allow the system to operate according to the laws of the market – and this required an appropriate framework consisting of customs, laws, regulations and the economic role of the state. The core of Polanyi's argument was that there were certain organizational structures, customs, laws, etc., that provided an institutional framework for the functioning of a market economy, and these institutions were generalizable over many time/place contexts. They therefore needed to be taken account of in any theoretical analysis of a market-based system, because apart from the motive of self-interest, these institutions had the capacity of shaping human behaviour in consistent ways.

Based on the discussion above, we can summarize the main differences between the old institutionalist view of the functioning of the economic system and the neoclassical model. First, the harmony of interests view of human behaviour was rejected in favour of one dominated by a conflict of interest. This of course opens the way to opportunism and predation in human relations. Second, economic agents were not seen as being rational utility maximizers. Rather, their actions were seen as being motivated by custom, habit and instincts, all of which were embedded in a particular social setting thereby making any generalized theorizing difficult. For analytical purposes, therefore, society could not be reduced to an aggregation of representative economic agents who behaved in a similar manner. On this point, however, Polanyi (1944) and Polanyi et al. (1957) disagreed with the old institutionalists. Their view was that the functioning of the market economy did require certain types of organizational structures, laws, etc., and these were generalizable over time and place. Thus such institutions needed to be taken account of in any theoretical analysis. Third, institutions were seen as being fundamental to the functioning of the economic system, their role being to resolve conflicts of interest and promote the human cooperation necessary for efficient production. This implied that the nature of institutions would have a direct and fundamental influence on the productivity and capacity of a society to create wealth. Fourth, the institutions themselves were seen as being the working rules of collective action. They were, therefore, structures that could be constructed through human action and had the capability of being changed depending on the changing conditions in a society. These differences – in particular that of rejecting the view of man as *homo oeconomicus* for the purposes of economic analysis – resulted in an inability on the part of the old institutionalists to develop an alternative formal framework to that of neoclassical economics. Thus commenting on the old institutional economics, Coase (1984: 230) states, 'the American institutionalists were not theoretical but anti-theoretical … Without a theory, they had nothing to pass on except a mass of descriptive material waiting for a theory'. In its initial theorizing, this is the major weakness that the new institutional economics set about to rectify.

NEW INSTITUTIONALISM

The new institutional economics maintains that institutions are central to understanding economic phenomena and explaining economic performance. It argues that besides market prices, economic activities are coordinated by several other institutions that should also be studied as a result (Langlois 1986). However, unlike the old institutionalism and in common with the neoclassical model, it agrees that individual behaviour is ruled by rational choice in the sense of wealth maximization and the pursuit of economic benefit. Explaining this view, Bates (1995) states that the new institutional economics applies to non-market institutions the same form of reasoning that neoclassical economics applies to markets (i.e. how rational individuals might employ non-market institutions to achieve optimal solutions, particularly where there is market failure). This provides the rationale for entities such as the law, property rights, bureaucracies, and other non-market structures. Thus when markets fail, Bates argues that rationally acting individuals will cause non-market social institutions to arise. Giving examples of this process, Bates (1995) indicates that where there are production externalities, the new institutionalism's solution is the creation of property rights; where public goods exist, state institutions will be required to transcend the limits of individual rationality and achieve socially desirable outcomes; where there is imperfect information and costs of acquiring information, social processes to minimize costs such as contractual agreements beneficial to both parties, will emerge; and, where fundamental uncertainty exists, the new institutionalism proposes that governance structures, such the firm, will be created wherein long-term relationships can be established and economic decisions withdrawn from the market.

While there are several themes or variants within the new institutional economics, Furubotn and Richter (2005: 34) indicate that the mainstream view is the transaction cost approach of Coase (1937, 1960), Williamson (1975, 1985), and North (1981, 1990). Since this theme is the most relevant from the point of view of the macro-level perspective of this book, we shall limit our consideration to this body of analysis. There are, of course, some differences between the perceptions concerning human behaviour amongst the various protagonists in this line of thinking. Coase (1960), for instance, proposes a greater degree of rationality than Simon (1965, 1979) or Williamson (1985). Nevertheless, the general approach within this framework is one which holds that all economic phenomena occur in an environment in which incomplete information, limited rationality, and opportunism, rule everywhere. Unlike the economic universe assumed by neoclassical economics, these factors are taken to be the fundamental characteristics of the world we live in. They make transactions costly, and generate uncertainties, which then prevent a market-based system from automatically giving the right signals required to achieve an optimum allocation of resources. In such a world, some framework or 'institutions' would be required to impose constraints on human interaction and provide an order within which exchanges could be structured (North 1990).

Thus, the new institutionalism argues that markets and the price mechanism cannot, and do not, exist in a vacuum. Rather they are embedded in a specific framework of formal rules and informal constraints, one which North (1990) defines as being the institutions of a particular society. Formal institutions include both the political and economic rules that govern the decision-making structures of the system, such as constitutions, judicial laws, and regulations. The informal constraints are the customs, norms, and conventions that have emerged out of the culture of a society. They also include self-imposed codes of behaviour that are based on religious beliefs, ideas, and ideologies. These rules and constraints form the institutional framework of a society and define a set of payoffs to political and economic activity. Where the framework generates a set of incentives favourable to productive activities, good economic performance is likely to result. Where the incentives or payoffs are unfavourable to productive activity, the economy is likely to be dominated by rent-seeking, opportunism, and predation.

The institutions of a society, particularly the formal rules, have costs of functioning. Coase (1937) named these costs 'transaction costs'. Therefore, in addition to the normal costs of production for labour, capital or technology, which are taken account of within the neoclassical framework, there are the additional costs of running the economic system (Arrow 1969). These include the costs of information, such as the cost of discovering what the relevant prices are, and since uncertainty is inherent in any exchange transaction, there are costs associated with the conclusion of contracts, as well as monitoring and enforcement. In Furubotn and Richter (2005: 53) we find an elaboration of what these transaction costs are:

- *Search and information costs*: these include the costs of gathering information on prices, costs of communication, and costs incurred in finding a suitable party with whom to conduct a market transaction.
- *Bargaining and decision costs*: outlays made to obtain legal and other advice, and to draft, negotiate and conclude a contract, would be covered under this category.
- *Supervision and enforcement costs*: these are costs involved in safeguarding and enforcing the contractual provisions agreed upon.

Transaction cost theory takes into account the fact that many of the actors in a modern economy are not just individuals, but also organizations that are legally constituted entities and within which transactions occur. Therefore the functioning of a market, and its outcomes, is governed not only by individuals maximizing utility, but also by the actions of economic organizations governed by a legal framework, such as the modern corporation. As a consequence of these transaction costs, Coase (1937) argued that the market may not be the best mechanism to conduct an exchange, because the costs of making that exchange may be greater than the gains the exchange might bring. Further, as 'what are traded in markets are not physical entities but the rights to perform certain actions, and the rights which individuals possess are established by the legal system' (Coase 1992: 717), in a world of positive transaction costs, the legal system will have a profound effect on the working of the economic system.

Coase (1960) showed that where it was costless to transact, a re-arrangement of legal rights through the market would occur whenever this would lead to an increase in the value of production. Thus when there were zero transaction costs, the initial institutional arrangements or the nature of property rights did not matter, since within the framework of competitive markets private bargaining would costlessly result in all the gains from trade being realized and allocative efficiency being achieved. However, where transaction costs were positive, the initial delimitation of legal rights would have an effect on the efficiency with which the economic system operated. As Wallis and North (1986) have indicated, in the real world the costs of transacting will be very significant. They estimate that 45 per cent of the national income of the US economy is devoted to transacting. Since the nature of the institutions in an economy will determine the extent and level of these transaction costs, clearly they will have enormous power to influence the efficiency of the system, and consequently will either encourage or inhibit economic growth and development.

At the level of formal rules, since the state has the monopoly over coercion and embodies all the rules that specify and enforce property rights, to understand the basic incentive structure of the economy, it is necessary to analyse the nature of the state. North (1981: 21) argues that there are essentially two types of models which explain the existence and nature of the state. The first is a contract theory of the state, which emerges out of classical liberal thinking. This theory assumes that there is an equal distribution of violence potential amongst all agents. Therefore, they cede these rights to a Hobbesian state so that the initial contracting can result in the development of efficient property rights and gains from mutually beneficial exchange can occur. The second is a predation theory of the state. This view, which emerges from Marxist thinking, sees agents as having unequal violence potential and unequal power. The state then becomes an agency of an individual or group, whose function it is to specify a set of property rights that maximizes the revenue of the group in power, irrespective of its impact on the wealth of society as a whole. A contract-based state would obviously put in place a set of property rights with incentives that were favourable to productive activity and economic growth. The opposite would occur in a predatory state.

North (1981), using the Coasian framework of transaction costs, extends the contract theory of a state described above into a neoclassical theory of the state. His objective is to try and explain why throughout history states have tended to generate and enforce inefficient property rights that have in turn affected economic performance. North's model is built on an exchange view of the relationship between the ruler and the constituent public, with the ruler providing protection and justice in return for revenue. Using this framework, he argues that the model has two constraints that are likely to lead to inefficiencies. First, there is the competitive constraint under which the ruler will avoid offending powerful constituents who may challenge his rule. This will result in a property rights structure that is favourable to these groups regardless of the effects on efficiency. Second, there is the transaction cost constraint under which the collection of taxes involves costs of measurement, monitoring and collection. Because of these, efficient property rights may lead to a higher national income but lower tax revenues accruing to the state. The ruler may then prefer to grant monopoly rights which might make tax collection easier. Both these constraints will lead to inefficient property rights that will have a negative impact on incentives and economic growth. Thus even within a neoclassical institutionalist framework, once we admit the possibility of positive transaction costs, there is no guarantee that formal rules will be put in place, which ensure that efficient solutions will be achieved.

The formal rules we have discussed above, however, while important, only make up part of the sum of constraints that shape individual choices. As emphasized by the old institutionalists, informal rules in the form of customs, conventions, norms, etc. play a significant role in influencing and ordering human behaviour. In many stateless primitive societies, for instance, peace and order are preserved through informal constraints and without any formal institutions. Evans-Pritchard's classic (1941) analysis of the Nuer tribe in Eastern Africa showed that the deterrent effects of providing compensation within the tribe, and the threat of a blood feud which would affect all family members in case of a transgression by any one of them, were adequate to preserve order, control self-interest, and prevent inter-family cattle raiding. Denzau and North (1994) argue that under conditions of uncertainty an individual's interpretation of the environment will reflect their learning. Decision-making will be based, at least in part, on mental models based upon the myths, dogmas, customs and ideologies that form the cultural background of an individual. By mental models we mean the internal constructs and representations that individual cognitive systems create in order to interpret the environment. If this is so, then one could expect that individuals with common cultural backgrounds and experiences would reasonably share convergent mental models, ideologies and informal constraints. North (1990: 85) gives an example of how ideas and beliefs that emerge out of culture can have a powerful influence on subjective preferences. He states that the abolition of slavery in the United States was not the consequence of decision-making based on some rational choice outcome. Rather it was the result of a growing conviction in the northern states about the immorality and unacceptability of this institution. In sum, therefore, the formal and informal rules, the incentive structures that they create, and the transaction costs that they generate, have a powerful impact on the efficiency of an economic system and social outcomes.

THE VISIBLE HAND

Based on the discussion above on the old and new institutionalism, it is evident that there are essentially two views on the role of institutions in the functioning of a market-based economic system. The classical/neoclassical view originating in the works of Adam Smith ([1776]1904), and later elaborated upon by Menger ([1883]1963) and Hayek (1973), argues that self-interest and the functioning of the market mechanism or 'invisible hand' will result in a self-regulating and self-equilibrating system that will lead to an efficient allocation of resources. Further, the harmony of interests between economic agents would ensure that any institutions required for the smooth functioning of the system would emerge automatically or spontaneously. On this basis

Hayek (1973) argues that all social institutions, including the market itself, are part of a spontaneous order that has not been designed by anyone, but has arisen instead out of our human cultural evolution.

The institutionalist view, on the other hand, while accepting the Hayekian (1945) position that knowledge is inherently dispersed amongst individuals – and therefore markets are the best way to coordinate decentralized decision-making based on localized knowledge – states that since bounded rationality, opportunism and transaction costs are ubiquitous, there is no guarantee that the price mechanism will result in self-equilibrating markets that will yield efficient solutions. Further, unfettered markets cannot resolve the problems of market failure caused by externalities, public goods, information imperfections, etc. Therefore contrary to the classical/neoclassical view, markets, to function efficiently, require the 'visible hand' of formal institutions, laws, rules, regulations and systems of enforcement. These provide a framework to: correct the inherent factors that can cause market failure; mitigate the negative impact of transaction costs; address the consequences of human behaviour as it really is. Informal institutions, such as trust and codes of conduct, can of course play an important role in facilitating and improving the functioning of formal systems. However, in today's complex world where most transactions are not at arm's length, they cannot replace the need for formal systems. Going beyond the functioning of a market alone, Hodgson (2006: 2) in fact argues that institutions are necessary to facilitate all social interaction. By constraining and enabling behaviour, they permit ordered thought, expectation and action, whereby form and consistency are given to human activity. For instance, the rules of language enable to communicate and the rules of traffic enable vehicular movement to occur more easily and with greater safety – but both language and the rules of traffic are human constructs, suggesting that the required institutions for the smooth functioning of the economic system are unlikely to arise spontaneously. Instead they will have to be constructed through conscious decision-making and human intervention, and in the absence of appropriate formal and informal frameworks, natural or spontaneous forces are more likely than not to result in dysfunctional institutions, low-level equilibrium situations, and market failure.

INSTITUTIONAL CHANGE

If institutions, and the incentives that they generate, are the underlying determinants of economic performance, an understanding of how institutional change occurs and the manner in which more efficient institutions are established in a society, is the next issue that we need to consider. The evolutionary hypothesis on the emergence of institutions, both economic and social, states that they arise spontaneously out of human cultural evolution (Hayek 1973, Menger [1883]1963). Contributing to this view Alchian (1950) argues that competition, as a ubiquitous and powerful force, will weed out inferior institutions and perpetuate those that can better solve human problems. However, such a functionalist view cannot explain the observed existence and persistence of dysfunctional institutions in many parts of the world. North (1981, 1990) gives us an alternative neoclassical-inspired institutionalist view of this process. According to him, institutional change occurs due to changes in relative prices or preferences. Starting from an initial situation, changes in population growth, technology, the costs of information, etc., will, as a consequence of the ongoing maximization efforts of agents, change the relative prices of various inputs and resources. This endogenous process will then result in new bargains and new contractual relations.

Thus North argues, for instance, that the plagues and famines of the 14th century resulted in an era of abundant land and scarce labour, shifting the relative bargaining strength from landlords to peasants. This led to rising wages, increasingly liberal terms for tenants, a breakdown of the master–servant aspect of serfdom, and eventually an end to servile obligations (North 1981: 134). Similarly, Hayami and Ruttan (1985) argue that the rise in rice prices caused by the expansion in international trade in 19th century Thailand led to a significant change in the relative price of labour to land, resulting in a major transformation of property rights. Traditional rights in human property, in the form of slavery, were replaced by more precise private property rights relating both to land and labour. Conceptualizing these outcomes, North states that the final institutional framework arrived at will depend on two factors. First, there is the relative bargaining power of the participants and how the free rider problem is addressed in a particular context. Second, since formal rules are nested in a hierarchy that includes informal rules such as customs, traditions and conventions, institutional change will be path dependent, or dependent on the nature of the initial institutional matrix in a society. Let us consider these two issues.

The neoclassical model implies that changes in individual costs and benefits will result in automatic changes in behaviour. However, the free rider dilemma, as defined by Olson (1965), indicates that economic agents motivated by individual self-interest will not incur the costs of participating in large group action, because the individual benefits of a favourable outcome to such an action can still be received by being a free rider. It is therefore not in the interests of an individual urban worker or farmer to participate in an appeal, or to riot and incur potential danger to life and limb, to change property rights, although such a change will yield direct benefits to that person. But large group action does occur and is a fundamental force for change, indicating that the neoclassical model cannot predict either when or why such an action may occur. To overcome the collective action problem implicit in the free rider dilemma, individuals have to go beyond the immediate calculus of the costs and benefits of an action. North (1981: 53) argues that ideologies and beliefs can provide just such a basis to overcome individual self-interest. Ideologies are linked to our moral and ethical judgements of fairness and they provide us with a world-view to facilitate decision-making. Thus ideology can overcome the free rider problem and provide a basis for large group action. However, in an historical sense – since collective action motivated by ideologies is the exception rather than the rule – North states that the free rider dilemma will have the following implications for institutional stability and change:

- *The free rider dilemma accounts for the stability of regimes*: the high costs to an individual of opposing the coercive forces of the state will usually result in apathy and acceptance, no matter how oppressive the regime may be. It is hard to overcome the free rider problem in organizing a large group to defend itself against a concentrated interest (Olson 1965).
- *A ruler has no free rider problem*: institutional change will therefore come from rulers rather than constituents.
- *Radical changes in the form of revolutions are more likely to be palace revolutions*: these will be undertaken by the ruler's agents, a competing ruler, or a small elite.

The second factor that new institutionalists argue as having an important influence on the trajectory of institutional change is path dependence. We noted above that if there are zero transaction costs, the initial institutional arrangements do not matter (Coase 1960). A change in relative prices or preferences will induce an immediate restructuring of institutions so that optimum solutions can be achieved. However, in a world where there are imperfect markets characterized by transaction costs and increasing returns to institutional arrangements, such restructuring is not likely to occur. North (1990: 94), borrowing from the literature on technological change, points out that there are four self-reinforcing mechanisms which will make institutional change occur incrementally through marginal adjustments, with a long-run trajectory that is not easy to reverse (i.e. it is path dependent). All four mechanisms have externalities and increasing returns associated with them. They are: significant set up or fixed costs; learning effects; coordination effects with other economic agents; and expectations of increased prevalence. These mechanisms will result in a lock-in situation where any exit is difficult; inefficiencies will result from the initial adoption of poorer institutions; and the phenomenon of small events will cumulatively lead to a particular path. A consequence of these factors is that multiple equilibria can occur – namely, a similar set of formal institutions and organizations, which have been set up to exploit the created opportunities, will yield different solutions depending on the initial conditions. North gives the example of Latin America, where in spite of adopting post-independence constitutions based on the British/United States institutional tradition, most of these countries reverted in due course to the bureaucratic centralized control that they had inherited from earlier Spanish rule.

In sum, therefore, the new institutional economics literature reviewed above sees institutional change as an endogenous evolutionary process. However, given the free rider problem, path dependence and the importance of the initial conditions, it is impossible to predict how or when such a change will occur. This is a major deficiency of the theory and reduces its value as a coherent hypothesis of institutional change. Further, because of its focus on endogenous change, it only recognizes the role that ideas and ideologies generated internally within a society can play in overcoming domestic collective action problems. It ignores the fact that very significant economic and political structures have been established in the international arena since the end of the Second World War, and based on these supra-national institutions, international action has become an increasingly significant force in the world today. Thus the ideas and ideologies that underlie the activities of these international institutions, and by definition are exogenous to a particular society, can equally facilitate or bring about institutional change in that society. As Toye (1995: 63) states, 'externally imposed change can be much faster, and this is why reforms to institutions are so often externally driven'.

NEW INSTITUTIONALISM AND POLITICAL ECONOMY APPROACHES

Neoclassical economics has no theory of institutions. Exchange is seen as occurring through spontaneous markets. However, the model of the economic system as it emerges from the institutional economics literature argues that institutions are necessary to resolve conflicts of interest between individuals and bring about the cooperation that is necessary for mutually beneficial exchange to occur. Markets are not spontaneous, but are embedded in an institutional framework consisting of formal and informal rules. This framework is central to economic performance because it determines the payoffs of the system and thereby decides whether economic agents will behave in a productive or predatory manner. Although the old institutionalists put greater emphasis on informal rules and institutions such as customs, conventions and habits, both streams of the literature agree that such rules play a major role in influencing human behaviour and the manner in which the economic system will function.

In terms of the emergence of institutions and institutional change, both strands of the literature see this as an endogenous process that occurs as a consequence of developments within a social order. The old institutional economics argues that institutions will emerge out of habit, custom and precedent. Until recently, as discussed above, the new institutional economics view was that institutional change occurred as a consequence of changes in relative prices, with the final outcome depending on how these changes affected the relative bargaining power of the groups or classes that controlled the assets whose prices had changed. In both cases therefore, institutions – both formal rules such as constitutions and laws, and informal constraints – are seen as emerging and changing in an adaptive, incremental and evolutionary manner. By linking institutional change to relative prices consequent to the wealth maximization efforts of agents, and by modeling the state as a revenue maximizer, the new institutionalism claims that it has extended neoclassical theory in a manner which enables it to reflect the real world more accurately. Let us consider this issue.

The neoclassical model has a determinacy in the sense that, given its assumptions, it provides certain predictable outcomes which can be tested. The question is whether by borrowing its tools new institutionalism has given institutional theory a similar determinism and predictive capacity or not. The central issue here, as admitted by the new institutionalists, relates to the collective action problem implicit in the bargaining between different groups that results in institutional change. Bardhan (1989) argues that changes in relative prices may change the costs and benefits of collective action for different classes and groups, but they cannot predetermine the balance of class forces or the outcome of social conflicts. Contrary to the historical examples given by North (1981), and Hayami and Ruttan (1985), Bardhan refers to the case of 16th and 17th century Poland, where an expansion of the grain trade played an important role in the relapse into serfdom. He also indicates that it can be debated whether the enclosure movement in 18th century England came about because enclosed farming was more efficient than open field farming, or whether it occurred because the redistributive effects of enclosures in favour of landowners made collective action on their part easier.

Thus even where it is evident that a relative price change will lead to both parties being better off, the core bargaining problem still remains, because disputes may arise over how the potential benefits are to be shared, and these may result in a breakdown of the necessary coordination required for a mutually beneficial solution to be achieved. Coase's famous (1960) example of a single railway line passing through a valley, in which there are a multitude of small farmers, brings out the essence of this problem. The railway line generates revenues for its owners, but also inflicts costs on the farmers in the form of smoke, soot and noise. Coase shows that in the absence of transaction costs any form of property rights would result in an efficient allocation of resources being achieved. Depending on whether the property rights favoured the farmers or the railway, one party would compensate the other to adjust for the negative externality inflicted by the railway line on agriculture, resulting in a reduction of the number of trains. Through the creation of a new institution, in this case property rights, the market imperfection can be addressed, and a movement made from an inefficient position to the Pareto frontier.

However, as Bates (1995) points out there are an infinite number of points on the Pareto frontier between which economic agents cannot be indifferent because different solutions will result in different distributional outcomes. There will therefore be disagreement as to which point should be chosen. The problem can be formulated in game theoretic terms (Bardhan 1999). The institutional innovation may shift the bargaining frontier outwards thus creating potential gains for all parties. But in the process of this occurring, the payoff for the weaker party may go up due to the better 'exit' and 'voice' options created by the institutional change, resulting in the stronger party losing out in the new equilibrium. Giving the example of land rights, Bardhan explains why inefficient institutions exist and land reform is resisted by large landlords, although there is plenty of evidence to show that arrangements such as leasing out land to small farmers can lead to more efficient production options that are beneficial to both parties. First, the social and political externalities that accrue to large land ownership will generate rents that are characterized by increasing returns. Second, it may be the relative rather than the absolute gain from an institutional change that matters, because this affects the relative bargaining strength of the two parties. As a consequence of these two factors distributional conflicts will occur, resulting in change being resisted and dysfunctional institutions persisting. Bardhan further states that because of the bargaining problem, the usual neoclassical division between equity and efficiency cannot be maintained because the distributional implications of a particular institutional arrangement will determine whether such a solution comes into existence or not. This then leads to the possibility of multiple equilibria and indeterminacy in the system.

The use of neoclassical tools and modes of reasoning, which focus on individual costs and benefits and changes in relative prices, therefore do not provide institutional theory with any useful explanatory or predictive power. Historical outcomes are dependent on initial conditions, and how various institutions interact with each other, and this of course is uncertain and unpredictable. As Bates (1995) argues, the creation of economic institutions takes place not on a *tabula rasa*, but within the context of a pre-existing set of institutions in which some players are already endowed with greater power than others. Thus 'behind every Pareto optimal outcome ... arrived at by marginal adjustments among maximizing agents devising institutional solutions to problems of market failure, lies a previous act of coercion' (1995: 47). In other words, the marginalist choices studied by new institutionalists take place within structures which are part of an existing political arena in which the state, as the agency of enforcement, plays a central role. Issues of free riding, the presence of concentrated interests, and generally the absence of a level playing field between the parties, therefore need to be understood in order to predict outcomes – and this of course implies the non-determinacy and non-dependency of outcomes on economic rationality or maximization based on rational choice.

Based on these considerations, Bates concludes that in order to establish where a certain set of institutions has emerged from, or to find out which set of property rights will prevail – in Coase's example above, whether favouring the rights of the farmers or the rights of the railway – one needs to look at the structure of politics. This suggests that the nature of property rights will largely be determined by the nature of the political institutions. In recognition of these issues, more recent new institutionalist writings seem to be moving in the direction of a more political economy view of institutions. North, Wallis and Weingast (2009), for instance, now argue that the state cannot be modelled as if it were an individual (i.e. a revenue-maximizing ruler) as this misses its essential nature. They now hold that the state is an organization and must be modelled as such. In its default form, which North calls a 'natural state', its purpose is to bring about a balance of violence amongst elites so that a social order can emerge which combines economic, political and military interests. The power of the state can then be used to limit the access to resources whereby the dominant coalition can earn rents, and these rents will then be used to create a credible commitment among elites to support the current regime. Thus North et al. (2009: 14) state that 'the political system is not exogenous to the economic system, since the political system is a primary actor in the economy. Similarly, the economic system is not exogenous to the political system either, since the existence of economic rents structures political relationships'.

These recent institutionalist writings are more consistent with the view developed in Chapter 2 that predation is not an uncommon characteristic of the relationship between individual agents and is certainly quite commonly observed in the behaviour of dominant groups and the state. It also suggests that there is a reversion towards the old institutionalist and Marxian view wherein inequalities in the bargaining power between agents and the central role played by violence, in determining institutional and economic outcomes, are emphasized. Using the history of Western Europe since the 10th century to elaborate on this Kohn (2005: Ch.5), for instance, argues that violence is the basis for both predation and the maintenance of peace and order. Violence affects economic activity by altering the environment relating to security of possessions and freedom of disposal. Historically, specialists in violence have controlled governments. This was a predatory class of kings, lords and the nobility, whose profession was violence. Nobles relished war because that was what they did. However, waging war required resources, and this resulted in predation and exactions from the nobles' subjects. But this predation, and the violence that underpinned it, were both constrained by law and custom.

Kohn (2005: Ch.18), describing the manner in which feudalism developed in Europe after the collapse of the post-Roman Carolingian empire, indicates that while in principle the rights of kings and rulers was unlimited, in practice they were unable to impose their will on their vassals or subjects and they were expected to rule according to custom. The weakness of territorial governments during this early period permitted local associational structures to emerge for self-help, mutual protection, and self-rule at the local level. These structures included artisan guilds, merchant associations, *polder* boards to maintain dykes, village associations in mountainous areas, and of course the city governments of northern Italy and north-western Europe. In many cases territorial rulers co-opted such organizations to act on their behalf and delegated authority to them. Thus while rulers had prerogatives, subjects and associations of subjects also had rights. In such a decentralized framework, rulers themselves had an interest in respecting law and custom because their continued dynastic rule relied on the acceptance by vassals, subjects, associations, and rivals, of their legality and legitimacy. This situation led to a constant struggle between prerogatives and rights, with the effectiveness of constraints on a ruler depending on the bargaining power of the various parties involved. Kohn (2005: Ch.23) further argues that the existence of associations of subjects, albeit with limited rights, by promoting social capital and lowering the cost of joint action against predation and arbitrary rule, played a major role in preventing free-riding and facilitating collective action.

The acceptance of a more political economy-centered approach in the macro-theory of institutionalism will of course give the system greater indeterminacy because the outcomes are now taken to depend on the bargaining strength of the parties involved – and this depends on a number of variables that will include wealth, military strength and historical circumstances. Nevertheless, the theory still offers a number of important insights into the process of economic development and institutional change. Following our theoretically informed inductive approach, it is therefore possible to compare these insights with the predictions of neoclassical theory and to test them against the generalizations that emerge from the historical and empirical evidence. Some of these major insights are outlined below.

- First, while the pursuit of economic benefit may be central to human motivation in a generalized sense, the type of behaviour that individual agents or organizations exhibit in order to achieve this objective is not necessarily dominated by a simple or benign self-interest. Given that a conflict of interests is fundamental to human relations, self-interest will result in opportunistic or predatory behaviour on a scale which is significant enough to affect economic outcomes. This will lead to rent-seeking and so needs to be taken account of in any explanation of the functioning of the economic system.

- Second, institutions – both formal and informal – matter. They are the underlying determinants of economic performance because they determine the incentives and payoffs of the system. Where the institutional framework generates a set of incentives that is unfavourable to productive activity, economic activities will be dominated by rent-seeking and predation. To control such predation and enable a self-regulating market-based system to function, a 'visible hand' of rules, regulations and institutions that will encourage productive activity is required.

- Third, the trajectory of institutional change depends on the outcome of bargaining between economic and political agents. Since a ruler or dominant elite in control of a state represents a concentrated interest, a resolution of the collective action problem, in particular the free rider dilemma, is central to enabling institutional change to occur in any society. Consequently, ideas and ideology matter because they can play a key role in overcoming the free rider problem and facilitating collective action. Ideas and ideology are therefore a fundamental force in institutional change. In their absence, institutional innovations are not likely to occur, unless they are initiated by the ruling elite. The ideas and ideologies that motivate ruling elites are therefore also important in influencing the process and content of institutional change.

- Fourth, given the important role that ideas and ideologies can play in inspiring institutional change, fundamental change does not necessarily have to be brought about through an endogenous process. Exogenous forces, particularly in today's globalized world where international action plays a significant political role, also have the potential of bringing about change, so long as there is a common consensus on the ideas and ideologies that underlie such interventions.

In the following chapters we shall consider the validity of these propositions through an assessment of the available empirical and quantitative evidence, as well as through case studies and historical analysis.

4. Development strategies and performance: an overview

This chapter provides an overview of the performance of all developing countries and also considers whether the few developing countries that have achieved high levels of growth in the past 25 years or so have done so on the basis of neoclassically determined strategies or not. The purpose is to assess whether variables associated with mainstream growth theory, or the insights that emerge out of the institutional economics literature – and in particular, the role of institution-related factors – can provide a better explanation for the variable performance that has been observed. In this context the development strategies being proposed by the major international financial institutions, and the East-Asian model of development, will also be discussed.

The table below gives the per capita GDP growth rates of major economies and regions between 1950 and 2001.

As can be seen, between 1950 and 1973, the period after the end of the Second World War and up to the oil shock of the early 1970s, there was similarity in the growth rates amongst developing countries, and between these and that of the United States. The African region had some relative under-performance compared to other regions, while there were much higher growth rates in Western Europe. Post-1973, however, the average world growth rates collapsed by around 50 per cent, with African growth declining to almost zero. The only region which showed an increase in growth rates compared with the

Table 4.1:   Per capita GDP growth rates 1950–2001

	1950–73	**1973–2001**
Western Europe	4.05	1.88
United States	2.45	1.86
Asia (excl. Japan)	2.91	3.56
Latin America	2.58	0.91
Africa	2.00	0.19
World	2.92	1.41

Source: Maddison (2006: 643, Vol. HS-8, Table 8b)

previous period was Asia (excluding Japan). This suggests that the model of development being followed by most developing countries in the two decades since 1950 had fundamental weaknesses, and after showing some initial promise, exhausted its possibilities. In comparison to this, the strategies followed by the Asian economies resulted in high and increasing growth rates over the entire period, particularly since the early 1970s. Let us consider this further.

The table below disaggregates the per capita GDP growth rates achieved by the major developing country regions between 1975 and 2005.

The major trends that can be observed for this period are as follows:

- East Asia and the Pacific have continued to have high levels of growth.
- South Asia has seen a major acceleration of its growth rate.
- Latin American growth, although positive, has remained at low levels.
- Middle Eastern and North African growth has remained at low levels, although there seems to have been some acceleration during the 2001–2005 period.
- Sub-Saharan Africa had negative growth between 1975 and 1995. However, there seemed to have been some turnaround after the mid 1990s, with an acceleration in growth after 2000.

Based on these observed trends, we can now consider the reasons for these variations in growth rates and review the efficacy of the underlying growth strategies being followed.

Table 4.2:   *All developing country regions: per capita GDP growth rates 1975–2005*

	75–80	**81–85**	**86–90**	**91–95**	**96–00**	**01–05**
East Asia & Pacific	5.26	6.12	5.76	9.10	5.63	7.06
South Asia	1.03	3.14	3.89	3.01	3.59	4.65
Latin America & Caribbean	3.31	–0.95	–0.43	1.61	1.53	1.21
Middle East & North Africa	–0.20	2.41	–1.20	1.18	1.91	2.78
Sub-Saharan Africa	–0.06	–1.60	–0.21	–1.64	0.79	1.79

Source: Arbache et al. (2008), based on World Development and African Development Indicators

DEVELOPMENT STRATEGIES

In terms of the development strategies being followed in the developing world, the period between 1950 and today can broadly be divided into two time periods – pre- and post-1980. Thinking during the early period was dominated by the post-revolutionary economic experience of the Soviet Union as well as the models of development expounded by economists such as Arthur Lewis, Nurkse, and Rostow. These ideas were formalized into growth models, such as those of Harrod-Domar and Mahalanobis, which gave primacy to investment and capital formation as fundamental sources of growth. Given low levels of domestic savings and the weakness of the domestic entrepreneurial and business classes, the state was seen as a prime mover in bringing about economic development, mobilizing resources and investing these in the process of industrialization. An integral part of this state-led strategy was the development of a large government-owned public sector; the utilization of a wide range of regulations and administrative controls to direct the domestic economy; and the putting in place of high tariff barriers to encourage the growth of import substituting industries. As the data above indicate, with a few exceptional countries and brief time periods, this strategy did result in positive, though mediocre, growth rates during the period from 1950 to 1970. However, the considerable worsening of the world economic situation after the oil shock of the early 1970s, declining growth rates in most developing countries, and the superior performance of the East Asian economies – a region in which export-oriented rather than inward looking policies were being implemented – did eventually call into question the validity of this development strategy. This was further reinforced by a major seven country study conducted by the OECD (Little et al. 1970) that brought into focus the negative impact on long-term growth of the import-substituting state-led strategies being followed in most developing countries. In particular, this study showed that many of the industries established under such a policy regime had a negative value-added when their output was re-valued at world prices. Industrialization of this kind therefore made a negative contribution to the national incomes of these countries.

As a consequence of this debate, by around 1980 there was a fundamental change in the development paradigm. The new consensus was that in order to achieve sustainable growth developing countries should follow market-oriented strategies based on the neoclassical model and implement policy prescriptions derived from it. This shift was epitomized by pronouncements in the *World Development Report 1983* (World Bank 1983), which indicated that successful development entailed 'getting prices right'. It was now being argued that the economic environment should be such that the prices of goods had to reflect their scarcity value or opportunity cost and the factors of production should be priced according to their marginal productivities measured at international prices. A consequence of this shift was that from the early 1980s onwards developing countries, supported by major aid and financial support programmes under the auspices of the World Bank and IMF, began to undertake structural adjustment and economic reform programmes to liberalize markets and reduce state intervention in economic activities. Underlying these programmes was the concept that developing countries would be eligible to receive substantial amounts of additional concessional assistance so long as they agreed to a set of conditionalities which required them to undertake a policy reform package inspired by the neoclassical model.

A considerable body of evidence is now available to make an assessment of the structural adjustment programmes carried out between the early 1980s and the early 1990s, as well as the efficacy of World Bank/IMF policy advice based on the neoclassical model (Killick 1995, 1997; Mosley et al. 1995; Schadler et al. 1993; World Bank 1994). Chakravarti (2006) has reviewed and summarized this evidence and has found that while the assessments undertaken by the international financial institutions themselves indicate that the economic reform programmes had some degree of success all the studies undertaken by independent researchers show that these programmes had, in fact, been failures, both in terms of encouraging developing countries to adopt more neoclassically-oriented macroeconomic policies and in promoting growth. Burnside and Dollar (1997), for instance, considering a sample of 56 developing countries over the period 1970–1993, found that there was very little correlation between aid and policy and that aid had no systematic impact on the macroeconomic policies being pursued by the countries in the sample. Furthermore Easterly (2000), analysing 155 poverty spells in 65 developing countries over the period 1980–1998, found that structural adjustment lending had no systematic effect on growth or poverty reduction throughout the period being considered.

In spite of this evidence showing no clear association between the structural adjustment programmes, aid and policy, the late 1980s and early 1990s did in fact see the beginnings of a new trend towards the adoption of a better economic policy stance by low-income countries. Sachs and Warner (1995), for instance, identified 35 countries that undertook macroeconomic and trade liberalization between 1985 and 1994. These included several countries in Africa, such as Benin, Cameroon, Ghana, Kenya, Mali, Uganda and Zambia. Burnside and Dollar (1997) also confirmed this trend. However, as the data in Table 4.2 show, these incipient policy changes did not seem to have had any perceptible impact on African growth rates, which continued to remain negative during this period. In comparing developing country regions therefore, on the one hand we have the evidence from Africa, which by and large was pushed by the international financial institutions to follow the structural adjustment approach, but which continued to experience low growth. On the other, we have the experience of the East Asian region, which as we noted continued to have high growth rates, starting around the mid 1970s. In order to draw some conclusions which would be of value to development theory and practice, it would thus be useful to contrast the development strategies followed by these two regions.

THE EAST ASIAN MODEL

Until recently, the East Asian region was the exception to the general pattern of poor long-term growth exhibited by most developing countries. Starting from similar per capita income levels as other developing countries in the 1960s, these countries adopted development strategies that resulted in high rates of capital accumulation, which ultimately is the only proximate basis for the achievement of high and sustained levels of growth. In 1965, investment levels in this region were similar to those in Latin America. However, between 1965 and 1990 both savings and investment increased sharply in the East Asian economies, far outstripping the performance of other developing country regions. The domestic savings/GDP ratio increased from about 17 per cent in 1960 to over 37 per cent in 1990, making this region the only group of developing countries in which gross savings exceeded investment. By 1990, investment rates in this region were nearly double the average for Latin America and significantly higher than those in other developing regions. The most remarkable aspect of the increase in investment rates was the high levels of private investment achieved. From about 15 per cent of GDP in the early 1970s, private investment rose to 22 per cent in the mid 1970s, and then levelled off at a rate of about 18 per cent of GDP for most of the next fifteen years. By comparison, private investment in other low- and middle-income countries averaged about 11 per cent of GDP over the same period.

In order to understand the recipe for this success, the World Bank undertook its first in-depth assessment of the policies used in eight High Performing Asian Economies (HPAEs) in 1993 (World Bank 1993). This study, and the subsequent debate, reached two major conclusions, with important implications for the validity of the neoclassical model and its use as a basis for development policy and practice. First, the World Bank study found that the HPAEs had undertaken a large number of policies to intervene in markets and alter market signals. To explain this massive government intervention in markets, the study accepted that developing countries could face significant market failures in resource allocation for various reasons. These included capital market deficiencies; a lumpiness of investment leading to scale economies; the technological interdependence of investment decisions; difficulties in appropriating knowledge and skills, etc. All of these called for government interventions to promote efficiency through measures to coordinate investment and counteract externalities. Thus 'market friendly' interventions that sought to correct generic failures – such as good macroeconomic management, generalized skill creation, selective policies in support of areas such as exports where large externalities are present, etc. – were appropriate and consistent with neoclassical theory. Second, the study concluded that the East Asian countries had gotten the basics right in terms of adhering to orthodox policy prescriptions in order to maintain macroeconomic stability. Budget deficits were held at levels that could be prudently financed and inflation was kept under control. Between 1961 and 1991, the average rate of consumer price increase for these economies was 7.5 per cent per annum. Exchange rate over-valuation was avoided, with countries moving gradually from initial fixed-rate regimes to freely floating competitive exchange rates. The stability of the real exchange rates in this region was in sharp contrast to the over-valuation of rates observed in Africa and Latin America. Finally, when macroeconomic stability was threatened due to external shocks, governments in the region undertook quick and flexible policy responses based on orthodox solutions to restore balance and maintain growth.

This World Bank interpretation of the policy package underlying East Asian success was subsequently scrutinized by a large number of researchers, who argued that the Bank's view was contrary to the facts. Wade (2004), analysing the role of government in Korea, showed that the interventions were not just to remedy market failures but also to directly influence resource allocation. Thus to promote the development of industries such as automobiles, electronics, petrochemicals and other heavy industries, the range of interventions included subsidization and the control of credit, influencing the macroparameters of investment choice, investing in technology, modulating international competition through tariffs and other measures, and providing industry-specific assistance packages. Similarly Amsden (1989), in describing the policy measures undertaken in late industrializing countries such as Japan, Korea, Taiwan and Brazil, which successfully industrialized their economies, indicated that underlying this success was a developmental state that amongst other measures established development banking institutions, undertook local content management, selectively opened markets to foreigners, and encouraged the establishment of large national firms.

Stein (1995) points out that even in Singapore, which has been hailed as a model of *laissez faire*, the government between 1965 and 1979 undertook a large number of measures, including direct interventions, in support of a strategy of export-oriented industrialization. These included concessional tax rates and accelerated depreciation for export companies; compulsory saving schemes; keeping wages down through subsidised housing and immigration;

and starting new public enterprises in manufacturing. Thus by the early 1980s, there were more than 450 state-owned enterprises accounting for almost 25 per cent of GNP. Hughes (2001) on the other hand – while agreeing that there were close linkages between government, large corporations and the banking system – from a neoclassical perspective has argued that these policies brought about the emergence of an inefficient form of 'crony capitalism' in the East Asian economies. She states that this cronyism resulted in large-scale unproductive investments and mindless support for capital flows that in turn played a significant role in precipitating the East Asian financial crisis of 1997–1998.

The consensus that emerged from this debate has been that while there could be no doubt that the East Asian economies followed the orthodox path in terms of macroeconomic policies, particularly in maintaining fiscal discipline, competitive exchange rates and an outward orientation, the facts indicate that they diverged from the neoclassical model in terms of microeconomic interventions and interference in the investment decisions of firms (Rodrik 1996). Commenting on the World Bank's analysis, Lall (1996) points out that once one accepts that there are significant market failures, it cannot then be argued that only generic policies may be required. Since different industries have different technological characteristics, there are no theoretical grounds to hold the view that such failures can be remedied by a single generic policy. Rather, both generic policies and selective industrial policy interventions are likely to be required. With the benefit of hindsight, the World Bank (2001a) eventually reconsidered these issues. Stiglitz (2001), writing in this collection, agrees that almost all economies in this region had some form of government intervention in markets, with specific industrial policies being an important part of their growth strategies. So what we do know about these countries is that government policy not only acted to address generic market failures, but also acted to influence the allocation of resources by changing market incentives, and that this policy package was associated with high growth rates. Commenting on the 'crony' critique, Stiglitz notes that while cronyism and a lack of corporate governance are of course matters of great concern these are not unique to East Asia, as massive frauds and corporate failures in the US have shown in the past few years. Furthermore, the extent to which such problems are inherent in fledging capitalist systems and can have negative consequences for allocative efficiency and productivity is difficult to gauge. In any case subsequent events, which showed a strong recovery in East Asia taking place after the financial crisis had been brought under control, indicated that the East Asian model was not fundamentally flawed, and that the neoclassical critique of this model has been based on a superficial understanding of the factors underlying East Asia's long-term economic performance.

The successful use of interventionist polices by the East Asian economies has provided empirical support to the theoretical view that where there are significant knowledge and information imperfections, coordination problems, and other distortions which can be termed 'market failures' in the neoclassical sense, as is the case of countries in the early stages of their development, strategies based on deductive abstract theories are of little value. Instead inductive theories of economic development based on the concrete model of countries that have industrialized in similar circumstances are more useful (Amsden 2004: 290). In East Asia's case the relevant model was that of Japan, and this model was in fact emulated by the other governments in the region. As Wade (2004) indicates, the Japanese were the first to recognize that international competitive advantage could be deliberately engineered by a capitalist developmental state operating through a committed economic bureaucracy – in Japan's case this constituted a network of government organizations led by the Ministry of International Trade and Industry. Chang (2002) goes further to argue that this view is, in fact, generalizable to the process that the advanced countries of today went through during their early periods of industrialization. Thus, between 1721 and the repeal of the Corn Laws in 1846, Chang states that Britain implemented a highly aggressive infant industry programme which included protection, export subsidies, and lowering the tariffs on industrial inputs, to promote domestic industry. Free trade was only adopted in 1860, when the country's industrial superiority was unquestionable. Similarly, the United States adopted protectionism after the end of the Anglo-American war in 1814. From then until the Second World War, the United States was the most protectionist country in the West, except for Russia (Chang 2002: 17, Table 2.1). Based on this historical evidence, he argues that free markets are not the best mechanism when it comes to accelerating the process of economic development and achieving high rates of growth.

In view of East Asia's success, some researchers such as Stein (1995) have suggested that this model could also be reproduced in other regions such as Africa. However, as Rodrik (1996) indicates, it first needs to be answered why trade protection, industrial policies, subsidized credit and other interventionist policies, which had been used widely in most developing countries since the 1950s, failed almost universally everywhere except in East Asia. Although as a consequence of the Uruguay Round of trade negotiations and the agreements on Trade Related Investment Measures (TRIMs), Trade Related Aspects of Intellectual Property Rights (TRIPs) and the General Agreement on Trade in Services (GATs), the scope for undertaking most of the micro-level policies undertaken by the East Asian governments is now severely circumscribed, it is nevertheless of historical and academic interest to understand how East Asia avoided the rent-seeking activities and corruption that typically accompany such *dirigiste* policies. The fundamental issue here is that when market failure occurs on a large scale, it is generally agreed that the only way to correct this is through government intervention. However, as the experience of most developing regions in the 1960s and 1970s showed, government intervention can lead to severe 'government failure' with even greater negative consequences for growth and development. So the question arises as to what the special characteristics were of the East Asian state that enabled it to correct market failure and play the role of a successful developmental state?

Rodrik (1996) has no clear explanation for this except to state that a combination of strong leadership and a well-functioning bureaucracy had an important role in achieving this goal. Amsden (2004: 286) is more explicit in stating that the ruling elites in these countries undertook the institutional engineering that was necessary to put in place the high quality institutional framework required to bring about industrialization and high growth rates. Both Rodrik's and Amsden's analysis, therefore, provide empirical support to the working hypotheses that emerge out of the institutional economics literature, stated in Chapter 3, that the behaviour of the state depends on the beliefs, ideas, and ideologies of the ruling elites in control of the state. In East Asia's case these beliefs ensured that the elites overcame their natural tendency towards opportunism, predation and rent-seeking, and enabled them to put in place a high quality governance and institutional framework that included measures to maintain the security of property and contractual rights; a policy environment that strongly encouraged private enterprise and the development of knowledge-based assets; the development and maintenance of stable financial institutions; and an efficient and relatively non-corrupt bureaucracy. This last factor in particular has been stressed almost universally, with agreement that the high degree of bureaucratic competence that existed in these countries played a critical role in the success of the coordinated market interventions and micro-level industrial policies implemented. However, what is not emphasized in this consensus is the fact that the bureaucracy itself, as an important organization with its own collective interests, was equally inspired and motivated by the same beliefs and vision as the ruling elites, and this ensured that it efficiently implemented the nationally agreed developmental policies and strategies.

AFRICAN ECONOMIC PERFORMANCE

Let us now consider African economic performance. In spite of evidence from the East Asian economies, and the empirical studies mentioned above showing the limited efficacy of the structural adjustment programmes of the 1980s and 1990s, the international financial institutions led by the World Bank still use the neoclassical model as a key basis for development policy and practice. In the case of Africa, they argue that although there may have been initial resistance to the adoption of policy prescriptions based on the neoclassical model, market-based reforms and policy reform did eventually come about once the process came to be owned and led by the developing countries themselves (Levy 2004), and that this change underlies the recent trend towards higher growth rates. In support of this view the association is made between the improved policy stance, a trend that commenced in the early 1990s, and the recent acceleration in the growth rates of a large number of African countries (Arbache and Page 2008, 2008a). This evidence needs to be reviewed more closely in order to understand the factors underlying the higher growth rates observed recently, because we know that the World Bank abandoned the conditionality-based structural adjustment approach and adopted what was termed Poverty Reduction Strategy Programmes (PRSPs) in 1999. The PRSP approach is discussed in greater detail below. At this stage, however, we just need to note that the fundamental difference between this and the earlier structural adjustment approach is that the new programmes mainly focus on encouraging developing countries to prepare poverty alleviation programmes and increase what is termed 'pro-poor' spending. The policy dialogue on macroeconomic issues, which was central to the structural adjustment programmes, of course continues within the PRSP framework, but given the new emphasis on ownership and leadership of the developing countries themselves, aid is no longer tied to a set of conditionalities that requires an improved policy stance.

In terms of the history of the region, 34 colonies representing about three quarters of Africa's population became independent between 1956 and 1968. Although at independence the political constitutions adopted by these countries were pluralistic, by the mid 1970s they had almost universally been replaced by authoritarian structures with neo-patrimonial systems of governance. This transition was in some sense not surprising, since most African independence movements were dominated by emergent nationalistic petty bourgeois groups who were captive to ideas that opposed anything associated with colonialism – and in particular private business or the export sector. Bates, in his (1989) study of African agricultural policy, describes the two main features of such regimes. First, the leaders engaged in bureaucratic accumulation, acting to enhance the wealth and power of those who derived their incomes from the public sector; and second, they also acted on behalf of private groups such as the military or ethnic groups, rather than as representatives of the majority of the population, and undertook measures to redistribute wealth towards such factions. Consequently, African governments soon came to be dominated by a narrow political leadership who implemented policies to heavily tax any dynamic sector of the economy, and also significantly increased the transaction costs facing all private economic activity (Ndulu and O'Connell 1999). Elaborating of how African economic policy reflected the class interests of the elites who controlled governments, Ndulu and O'Connell indicate that where the leaders had important political roots in private economic activity, such as smallholder agriculture – as did Kenya's Kenyatta, Botswana's Khama and Masire, and Cote d'Ivoire's Houphouet Boigny – the policy towards agriculture, and the private sector in general, was more favourable.

In the first few decades after independence, therefore, African governments – unlike those in East Asia – did not play the role of a capitalist developmental state, actively encouraging the accumulation of capital and private sector-led industrialization with an outward export orientation. Rather private enterprise was viewed with suspicion and a plethora of controls and regulations were put in place that prevented this sector from functioning efficiently. Robinson, in his (1999) theory of a predatory state, argues that one clear causal channel through which development facilitates the extension of political power from small elites to the rest of society is by its impact on collective action. Development policies by improving infrastructure, literacy, communication and urbanization, make it easier for groups to engage in successful collective action and thereby reduce their costs of contesting power. Based on this proposition he develops a formal model which explains why many absolute dictators such as Mobuto of Zaire, the Duvaliers of Haiti, and Trujillo of the Dominican Republic, amongst others, followed non-developmental policies to ensure that no opposition group – such as an educated middle class, a strong local business community, or even a well-functioning bureaucracy – could emerge that would then challenge their hold on power.

Thus in spite of being in power for a long time, the Duvaliers did not build any roads in Haiti; Trujillo avoided building any roads in the Dominican Republic which could integrate the economy; and Mobuto is famous for a remark on this subject that explained the underlying thinking behind such behaviour. In response to a request from President Habyarimana of Rwanda for armed support to help fight insurgents, President Mobuto is quoted as saying 'I told you not to build any roads ... building roads never did any good ... I've been in power in Zaire for thirty years and never built one road. Now they are driving down them to get you' (Robinson 1999, quoted from *Jeune Afrique* 1991). The logic of holding on to political power, therefore, clearly had a significant influence on the behaviour of African ruling elites and made them establish predatory rather than developmental systems of governance. One of the strongest indicators of the impact of such policies on the private sector has been relatively high level of capital flight from this region as compared with other parts of the world. Collier, Hoeffler and Pattillo (2004) estimated the capital flight ratio, which is the ratio of capital flight to the total of all privately owned capital, for the period 1980–1998. They found that for Sub-Saharan Africa this ratio increased from around 16 per cent in 1980 to a high of about 35 per cent in 1989, and then declined somewhat towards the end of the 1990s. During the same period the ratio reached a maximum of about 10 per cent in Latin America and South Asia, two other regions of the developing world where capital flight was important. The flows out of East Asia were insignificant.

The second aspect of the East Asian recipe for success was the maintenance of orthodox and stable macroeconomic policies. Let us consider how Africa fared in this respect. Ito (1997) examined this issue by drawing on various World Bank studies that compared groups of countries from East Asia and Africa with similar endowments between the mid 1970s and early 1990s. These were Nigeria and Indonesia; Cote d'Ivoire and Malaysia; and Ghana, Tanzania and Thailand. Comparing Nigeria and Indonesia, he found that Indonesia adopted prudent fiscal and monetary policies that kept inflation low, and adopted a flexible exchange rate policy in response to oil price changes in the mid 1980s. In Nigeria, on the other hand, no such policies were followed and the exchange rate was adjusted only in response to crises. Comparing Ghana and Tanzania with Thailand, Ito found that in Thailand a stable exchange rate policy was maintained throughout the period, with a gradual depreciation of the currency. Private investment was actively encouraged through a favourable economic environment and supported by strong banks. In contrast, Ghana and Tanzania experienced huge swings in their exchange rates with an appreciation of the real exchange rate by more than 100 per cent in the early 1980s. Private investment was controlled in both these countries, and even actively discouraged in Tanzania. From this evidence we can see that African governments followed unstable and poor macroeconomic policies during the period under consideration and this undoubtedly made a significant contribution to the poor economic performance observed.

In spite of this poor policy and growth performance in the first few decades after independence, and the failure of conditionality-based structural adjustment programmes in the 1980s and 1990s, as we have already noted African economic performance did begin to improve in the mid 1990s. Between 1996 and 2007, out of the 46 countries classified within the Sub-Saharan Africa category, 26 had GDP growth rates of 4 per cent per annum or higher. While this is a hopeful sign, African countries have had several periods of growth acceleration in the past, followed by periods of deceleration – so a closer analysis to assess if any fundamental changes have occurred this time around needs to be made. In terms of economic fundamentals, Arbache and Page (2008) conclude that between the 1985–1994 period and 1995–2005, there is only modest evidence of improvements. They found that there were no significant changes in the savings/GDP, investment/GDP, and private investment/ GDP ratios between these two periods, with the levels of all these variables being low compared with East Asia, even in the latter period. In fact, the average gross fixed capital formation/GDP ratio for Sub-Saharan Africa of

Table 4.3:   Savings and investment rates 1995–2005

1995–2005 average (%)	Sub-Saharan Africa	East Asia
Savings/GDP	17.47	38.45
Investment/GDP	17.69	32.77
Private Investment/GDP	13.11	19.27

16.5 per cent between 2000 and 2006 was lower than that for the region during the earlier 1980–1989 period, when it averaged 18.5 per cent (World Bank 2008: Africa Development Indicators 2008–2009, Table 2.22).

Furthemore, Arbache et al. have found that although there was some increase in the foreign trade/GDP ratio between 1985 and 2005, indicating that the African economies became more open, the public debt/GDP ratio also increased substantially, showing a worsening fiscal situation.

Given the poor performance of these key economic ratios, what had then changed to bring about the higher growth rates? To understand this it is necessary to analyse a broader set of variables that goes beyond what is considered relevant within a neoclassical framework. First, the external circumstances facing Africa were more favourable after 1995. The world economy had been increasing at a rate of about 3.2 per cent per annum since the mid 1990s, global trade was expanding sharply, and there was a significant increase in foreign direct investment flows to Africa. Further, between 1999 and 2007, the average terms of trade index for Sub-Saharan Africa improved by about 60 per cent, with an obvious positive impact on growth rates. Second, on the political front, Ndulu and O'Connell (1999) describe how this landscape had begun to change, particularly after the fall of the Berlin Wall in 1989. Between 1988 and 1992, 33 out of Africa's 42 non-democratic regimes had measurably increased civil liberties, and by 1994, 16 of these countries had held meaningful multi-party elections. As a consequence, between the early 1990s and 2007, there was a significant improvement in the polity indicators – which measure the degree of political rights in a country – of almost half the previously authoritarian regimes, with democratic transitions occurring in over 14 countries including South Africa (World Bank 2008: African Development Indicators 2008–2009, Table 13.5). A polity score of 3 or higher is associated with the presence of democratic institutions. Third, both macroeconomic management, and the institutional and governance environment, seem to have improved in a large group of Sub-Saharan African countries. This is evidenced by the fact that the number of these countries with World Bank Country Policy and Institutional Assessment (CPIA) scores of 3.5 or higher increased from five in 1997 to 17 in 2006 (excluding oil exporters). The CPIA measures standards of macroeconomic management, public sector management, the inclusiveness of policies, and the quality of institutions. It has a range from 1 to 6, both for the overall score and the sub-components, with a score of 3.5 or above considered by the World Bank to indicate good performance. There is also a strong positive correlation between a country's CPIA score and its polity indicator (World Bank 2008: African Development Indicators).

The relationship between economic growth and institutional and governance-related indicators is considered in detail in the next chapter. Nevertheless it is of interest here to outline the performance of these indicators in the sub-group of African economies mentioned above to show that high growth has been associated with significant changes in *these* variables rather than those considered important by neoclassical economics such as high rates of investment. The table below summarizes changes in important economic, political and governance-related variables for 24 of the African economies which had growth rates of 4 per cent and above between 1996 and 2007. The two small island economies of Sao Tome and Cape Verde have been excluded from the analysis. The table is intended to indicate the direction of change in the respective variables over the past decade or so. The (+) sign indicates improvement, as well as the achievement of a level indicating above average performance in that particular variable over the period being considered. A (++) indicates that an above median country score or a high level score has been achieved over a longer period of time. A blank or a (–) sign indicates that the score for the respective variable has either remained constant or worsened over the period being considered. Botswana, Namibia and South Africa are not part of the low-income group of countries who are supported through the concessional window of the World Bank – the International Development Association (IDA), and therefore the World Bank, does not calculate CPIA or other scores for them. However, given the favourable state of their policy environment and institutions, it is safe to assume that they would have received high scores in any such estimation. The column on 'Governance' is based on the World Bank's governance indicators database. The overall 'Governance' indicator is a composite of six sub-indicators that measure voice and accountability, political stability, government effectiveness, regulatory quality, rule of law, and control of corruption. Because of the importance of corruption in assessing economic governance the performance in this area is reported separately, although it is part of the overall governance indicator as well.

From the table we can see that six of the 24 countries with high growth rates were oil exporters. All the countries in this group except Nigeria, which saw some improvements, had poor macroeconomic management, poor CPIA scores, high levels of corruption and poor governance. The high growth found in these countries was therefore probably a consequence of the high demand and high prices for oil during this period and consequently this could well see a reversal during the current world-wide recessionary environment. The

Table 4.4:   Economic and political governance indicators

Country	Democratic institutions	Polity score >3	CPIA >3.5	Macro-mgmt >3.5	Governance	Corruption
Benin	+	++	+	+	++	++
Botswana	++	++	+	++	++	++
Burkina Faso			+	+		
Ethiopia				+		
Gambia						
Ghana	+	+	+	++	++	++
Liberia	+	+			+	+
Mali	+	++	+	+	+	+
Mauritania						
Mozambique	+	+	+	+	+	+
Namibia	++	++	+	++	++	++
Rwanda			+	+	+	+
Senegal	+	+	+	+	+	+
Sierra Leone	+	+		+	+	
South Africa	++	++	+	++	++	++
Tanzania			+	+	+	+
Uganda			+	+	+	+
Zambia	+	+		+	+	+
Oil exporters						
Angola	−	−			−	−
Congo, Rep.	−	−			−	−
Chad	−	−			−	−
Eq. Guinea	−	−			−	−
Nigeria	+	+		+	−	−
Sudan	−	−			−	−

Sources: African Development Indicators 2008–2009, World Bank 2008; World Bank Governance Indicators website

remaining 18 countries, however, provide findings which seem to confirm some of the important elements underlying the East Asian success discussed earlier. In 15 countries or almost four fifths of the total we find that good macroeconomic management was being practised, with significant improvements in the policy environment taking place during the period being considered. In 2006, 12 of the 18 countries had CPIA scores of 3.5 or more. At the institutional level, while five countries had high and stable levels of good governance indicators pre-dating the mid 1990s, the period itself saw significant improvements in the standards of governance and the control of corruption in a further eight countries. Finally, apart from the three countries that had democratic systems in existence prior to the period under consideration, the period itself saw improved and high level polity scores, with transitions to democratic institutions occurring in another eight countries. All in all, therefore, the picture that emerges from this recent high growth episode in Sub-Saharan Africa (excluding the oil exporters) is that this acceleration was not random but associated with significantly improved economic and political governance. While there was little change observed in some of the standard economic variables associated with high growth, such as high savings and investment, the improved institutional framework and more favourable environment for private investment seem to have fundamentally changed the efficiency and productivity of the economic system.

CURRENT APPROACHES TO DEVELOPMENT

We shall now consider the current approaches being followed by developing countries under advice from the World Bank, the IMF, and other donor agencies. The failure of structural adjustment programmes to bring about sustained economic growth, and in particular to bring about a reduction in poverty levels, caused a re-think of the approaches to development in the latter part of the 1990s. Also underlying this re-assessment were new empirical findings suggesting that factors such as income and asset inequalities, and institutional and governance related variables, were important determinants of development outcomes. The first statement on this new approach can be found in the *Comprehensive Development Framework* (World Bank 1999). The CDF states that development strategies have in the past put too much emphasis on macroeconomic considerations while ignoring what are termed structural, social and human agendas. The structural factors include good and clean government, transparent regulatory systems, an effective legal and judicial system which protects human and property rights, a well-organized financial system, and a vigorous commitment from leaders to fight corruption. The human pre-requisites focus on the provision of adequate education programmes, particularly universal primary education and comprehensive health care. Finally, the physical pre-requisites include the provision of adequate water, energy, roads, telecommunications, and attention to the environment. Within this framework, the private sector is seen as the engine for growth. Subsequent to the adoption of the CDF by the World Bank and IMF boards, the Bank further elaborated its content by the preparation of the *Poverty Reduction Strategy Sourcebook* (World Bank 2000).

The development model outlined in the *Sourcebook* treads familiar neoclassical ground on the need for macroeconomic stability, fiscal prudence, a competitive exchange rate and a liberal trade regime. However, it also presents a new perspective on development in two areas. First, it states that since past economic growth had a limited impact on poverty, government expenditures and external assistance flows need to focus on what is termed 'pro-poor' spending. This mainly concerns the social sectors and social safety nets. Second, the importance of systems to ensure good economic and political governance, as essential pre-requisites for growth and poverty reduction, is emphasized. This requires an architecture of the state which include participatory, free and fair electoral processes; the protection of civil liberties; open and transparent public expenditure systems; the control of corruption; and an independent judicial system. The model outlined in the *Sourcebook* is therefore a combination of policy prescriptions derived from neoclassical theory, along with an explicit recognition that society requires an institutional framework which limits predation and encourages both private and public actors to act in a productive manner. Since the adoption of this approach by the World Bank, almost all low-income countries have prepared Poverty Reduction Strategy Papers (PRSPs). Indeed many countries have now prepared second and third generation PRSPs. In most cases, these documents have become the core of their national development strategies, and the central basis around which external assistance from the international donor community is being provided. The analysis below, therefore, considers the extent to which the PRSPs in practice conform to the model of development outlined in the CDF and the *Sourcebook*.

Chakravarti (2006: 125) conducted a detailed analysis of ten first and second generation PRSPs, mainly from Africa and Latin America and found that in all the countries, except one, private investment was expected to increase but had nevertheless remained at relatively low levels compared to what was achieved in the East Asian economies. This was despite the fact that all the PRSPs stated that encouragement of the private sector was very important, and four of the ten countries had attempted to propose well-specified private sector development strategies, with policies which included the creation of a favourable legal and regulatory environment, undertaking the privatization of public assets, and providing incentives to attract foreign investment. This weak commitment to private investment and the private sector in general had been confirmed by another 27-country study of PRSPs (USAID 2004). This had found that while all countries saw the private sector as a key actor in achieving poverty reduction, in 20 of the 27 considered, there was an inadequate specification of the indicators by which it could be assessed whether the investment climate was improving or not. In the area of economic governance, Chakravarti (2006: 133) stated that in five of the ten countries studied, specific measures to improve bureaucratic efficiency were laid out. The others only contained general statements about the intent to reform the bureaucracy and make public expenditure more transparent. The treatment of corruption, however, was the area of greatest concern in the PRSPs, because in many ways the manner in which a government deals with this issue will be an indication of the quality of its economic governance. While all the PRSPs identified corruption as a serious problem, none of them contained a meaningful analysis of its causes or specified a well-defined strategy to combat it. The general approach taken was to focus on the implementation of new or more transparent public procurement regulations and assume that this would tackle the problem of corruption in its totality.

Since political governance has been given a major emphasis in the CDF and *Poverty Reduction Sourcebook*, let us consider what the PRSPs propose in this area. All ten countries studied indicated that human rights were guaranteed by their constitutions. In only four of them, however, can we find a more detailed account of current practices; the efficacy of existing systems to ensure civil liberties and free and fair elections; and the measures being undertaken to strengthen the independence of the judiciary, undertake legal reform, and improve the rule of law. In this respect, the African PRSPs in the sample provided a particularly poor example of a concern for civil liberties, with three of the four countries considered having no discussion on fundamental rights or freedoms. In five of the countries significant programmes to strengthen the independence of the judiciary and the rule of law were outlined. These included the establishment of more transparent and merit-based systems for the appointment and elevation of magistrates and judges; a revision of the civil and penal codes; a simplification of legal procedures; and the training of judicial officers. In the area of political governance therefore the PRSPs are a mixed bag. While the new trend by governments to explicitly discuss political governance and internal political processes with the international community is a favourable development, and the judicial reform measures being proposed by several countries are significant, nevertheless the content of the PRSPs in general do not come up to the standards specified in the CDF or *Sourcebook*.

The social sector or 'pro-poor' public expenditure programmes are the main strength of the PRSPs. All the documents have comprehensive programmes covering education, health, social safety nets, agricultural development, water, sewerage, and infrastructure. The consequence of these programmes is that public expenditure, both capital and recurring cost, is expected to increase sharply in the medium term. In a significant proportion of countries, social sector spending is expected to reach two thirds of the total recurring budget. Since there is little scope in these countries for additional measures of taxation, government savings or increased domestic borrowing, it is evident that the higher expenditures inspired by the PRSPs will have to be

Table 4.5:   Sub-Saharan Africa: aid dependency ratios

	Aid/GNP (%)		Aid/Gross Capital Formation (%)	
	2000	**2006**	**2000**	**2006**
Sub-Saharan Africa	4.1	6.0	21.5	27.1
Latin America	0.2	0.2	1.2	1.2

Source: World Development Indicators 2008

financed entirely from new external resources. The sources of this funding would either have to be debt relief under HIPC and similar programmes, or higher levels of aid from bilateral and multilateral agencies. In fact, this is exactly what has happened since the inception of the PRSPs, as the data on aid dependency for the Sub-Saharan African region show.

Table 4.5 shows Sub-Saharan Africa's high and increasing dependence on aid over time as compared with other developing country regions such as Latin America. This trend is confirmed by the statistics on the relationship between aid and gross capital formation, which show that between 2000 and 2006, on average, the percentage of capital formation financed by aid increased from around 21 per cent to over 27 per cent in this region. This dependence is exemplified by several countries in East and Central Africa, where aid/gross capital formation ratios of between 70 and 120 per cent are commonly found (Table 4.6).

The analysis above indicates that while in theory the poverty reduction approach embraces a view of development that goes beyond the neoclassical model, and many low-income countries now do seem to recognize the importance of institutional and governance-related variables, nevertheless the core content of the PRSPs shows a reversion to old-style development thinking

Table 4.6:   Aid/gross capital formation 2006 (%)

Burkina Faso	83.3
Ethiopia	53.0
Ghana	28.1
Malawi	89.1
Mozambique	122.0
Tanzania	77.0
Uganda	69.9
Zambia	57.9

Source: African Development Indicators 2008/09, World Bank

which fundamentally argued that development was a matter of mobilizing and investing additional resources. This reversion is evident from the current nature of the dialogue between developed and developing countries which focuses on the Millennium Development Goals (MDGs). One of the main points in this dialogue has been to suggest that poverty levels (based on $1/day at 1990 prices) can be cut by half by 2015 if the level of aid is doubled. Underlying this proposition is the old Nurkse/Harrod-Domar notion that higher levels of aid automatically will translate into higher rates of per capita GDP growth and the only factor that can put a limit on the appropriate level of aid to a country is its absorptive capacity. As a consequence, several estimates have emerged in the literature in recent years proposing various levels of aid as a means of achieving the MDGs (see Anderson and Waddington 2007, for a summary). The discussion on the role and importance of institutional and governance-related factors in achieving sustained growth has receded into the background. Thus even the MDGs, which have many laudable goals, are inadequate in this respect. Of the multitude of targets in the MDGs, there is only one (No. 12) that states that there should be a commitment to good governance. However, even this reference is devoid of any content, and unlike the other MDGs, none of the indicators that need to be achieved are specified.

The PRSP approach has therefore confused rather than clarified what the main thrust of a country's development efforts should be and what the main content of the dialogue between developed and developing countries needs to focus on. This conclusion will become all the more evident in the next chapter, which considers the recent empirical evidence on the relationship between institutional and governance-related factors and economic growth.

5. Institutions and governance: the new empirical evidence

The application of the principles of neoclassical theory to the problems of growth and development is to be found in the neoclassical growth model. The approach assumes that all countries are on the same production function, so that differences in physical capital, labour, and human capital, generate the differences in output (Solow 2001). This vision has been fundamental to mainstream development thinking for the past 60 years. Based on this framework, it is possible to elaborate a series of propositions that lend themselves to empirical testing. The empirical literature testing the neoclassical growth model consists of studies that use either growth accounting techniques based on a Cobb-Douglas or similar neoclassical production function, or cross-country regressions, that have variables that are generally utilized to reflect factor accumulation as independent parameters to explain variations in GDP growth rates. One of the earliest studies is that of Abramovitz (1956). Considering the sources of increase of national income in the US between 1870 and 1953, he found that while net national product per head increased by 400 per cent during this period, productivity per head rose by 250 per cent. Based on this finding Abramovitz concluded that the main source of growth of output was not the labour or capital input per capita but the 'complex little understood forces which cause productivity to rise'. Subsequent work by Young (1995), and Collins and Bosworth (1996), with data refinements including proxies for human capital, has reversed these findings. They found that most of the contribution to GDP growth, particularly the high rates seen in the East Asian economies, came from high rates of physical and human capital accumulation, rather than from productivity growth. At the wider cross-country level as well, the Barro (1989) regressions, as well as the survey conducted by Levine and Renelt (1992), have confirmed that when considering variations in GDP growth rates the positive correlation between GDP growth and the share of investment in GDP is the most robust finding. Levine and Renelt found that for a sample of 119 countries over the period 1960–1989, the investment/GDP ratio could explain about half the variation in growth rates.

GROWTH ACCOUNTING STUDIES

In this section we review the findings referred to above in the context of a simple neoclassical specification, where potential output is a function of:

F (K, L, H; A)

where K is physical capital, L is labour, H is human capital, and A is the residual representing total factor productivity. In the standard model, the residual is assumed to represent the exogenously occurring technical progress. As Solow (2001) elaborates, if A(t) or factor productivity over time is considered in purely technological terms, given the usual assumption of similar access to common technical knowledge in all economies, one would expect this value to be broadly similar for all countries. The assumption that common technologies are available worldwide is based on the observed fact that most of the world's new vintages of capital are produced in a small number of R&D intensive countries, with the rest generally importing the equipment embodying these technologies or their designs (Eaton and Kortum 2001). However, if the values and path of A(t) are empirically found to vary substantially from one country to another, this would suggest that the shape of the production surface varies from country to country, and that the transformation of inputs into outputs is heavily influenced by other factors than those specified in the neoclassical production function. As Khan and Villanueva (1991) indicate, the neoclassical residual or multi-factor productivity is in fact a catch-all variable which captures all the influences on increases in output for given levels of inputs. These include technical progress, improvements in education and training, and other endogenous variables such as macroeconomic policies, which can bring about a more efficient use of existing capacity or a more efficient allocation of resources. If this is so, the efficiency differences between countries are more likely to be caused by non-technological rather than technological differences. Such a finding would of course have serious implications for the resource-based neoclassical vision of economic growth, and would open the way for alternative models where non-technological factors, such as policies and institutions, may have a more significant influence on GDP growth. Thus Solow (2001: 287) concludes that 'the non-technological sources of differences in total factor productivity may be more important than the technological ones. Indeed, they may control the technological ones, especially in developing countries'. Since this is an empirical question, let us now consider some of the evidence in this area.

Collins and Bosworth (1996), using a standard neoclassical production function, have decomposed the growth of output per worker into the contributions of the growth of physical capital per worker, the growth of education per

Table 5.1:   Contribution of total factor productivity to growth of output

(% points per year)	Growth of output per worker		Contribution of total factor productivity (TFP)	
Region	**1960–94**	**1984–94**	**1960–94**	**1984–94**
United States	1.1	0.9	0.3	0.7
Other industrial countries	2.9	1.7	1.1	0.7
East Asia	4.2	4.4	1.1	1.6
Latin America	1.5	0.1	0.2	–0.4
Middle East	1.6	–1.1	–0.3	–1.5
Africa	0.3	–0.6	–0.6	–0.4

Source: Collins and Bosworth (1996: 158–159)

worker, and a residual representing the growth of total factor productivity. Table 5.1 summarizes this information for various regions of the world for the periods 1960–1994 and 1984–1994.

The data above show that there are significant regional variations in the contribution of TFP to the growth of output per worker, and there is no tendency for any convergence between the developing world and the levels obtaining in industrial countries over time, except perhaps in East Asia. In the industrial world the contribution of TFP has averaged around 40 per cent for the whole period, rising to almost 80 per cent in the US during 1984–1994. In East Asia there seems to have been a rising trend, with the contribution of TFP increasing to about 40 per cent in the most recent 1984–1994 period. In Latin America, the Middle East and Africa, on the other hand, and particularly in the latter, the negative effect of A, the residual, can be seen to have overwhelmed the positive contribution of physical capital and human capital. This resulted in zero or negative growth rates of output per worker. Clearly, in these developing country regions, inputs in the form of the traditional factors of production are not being converted into outputs as expected, because the transformation process is dominated by non-technological factors that are not taken account of in the neoclassical model.

This conclusion is reinforced by the study undertaken by Ndulu and O'Connell (1999) in which they conducted a similar growth accounting exercise to compare Sub-Saharan Africa with other developing countries. Applying a Cobb-Douglas production function to data for the period 1960–1994, they decomposed the growth of output per worker for 21 African and 45 other developing countries. Such a comparison is particularly interest-

Table 5.2:   Decomposition of growth of output

	21 Sub-Saharan countries		45 Other developing countries	
(%) Growth	1960–94	1973–94	1960–94	1973–94
GDP per worker	0.39	–0.44	2.07	1.42
Physical capital	0.60	0.33	1.19	1.04
Human capital	0.23	0.26	0.39	0.44
Residual	–0.44	–1.02	0.46	–0.07

Source: Adapted from Ndulu and O'Connell (1999: 45)

ing because Africa has had the worst economic performance amongst all the developing country regions. Therefore, if it is found that the poor performance is again due to the residual, this undermines the neoclassical argument that factors of production are the key determinants of economic growth.

Table 5.2 clearly brings out that while physical and human capital make their expected contribution to the growth of output per worker, in Sub-Saharan Africa's case, this contribution is overwhelmed by the influence of the residual, with the value of this factor being the main cause of negative per capita growth rates during 1973–1994. These data are consistent with the findings in Chapter 4, which showed that the reasons for the acceleration of growth rates in this region after 1996, and particularly after 2000, could not be found in higher investment levels. Rather, the causes of earlier slow growth, and the current acceleration, were to be found elsewhere, most probably in non-technological variables such as institutions, and factors related to economic and political governance.

The enormous variance in the contribution of total factor productivity as compared to the contributions of physical and human capital is further elaborated upon in a major study by Hall and Jones (1999). Using the usual growth accounting techniques and a Cobb-Douglas production function, they decompose output per worker into three components – the contributions of physical capital intensity, human capital per worker, and productivity. The data set is for 1988. It covers 127 countries and the results have been presented as ratios to US values.

Table 5.3 shows that output per worker in the developing world ranges from about 40 per cent of the US level in Latin America, to between 3 and 8 per cent of US levels in selected African and Asian countries. This large variation is mainly accounted for by the variability of A, or the residual, which is supposed to reflect productivity. While capital intensity and human capital levels compare favourably between the developing world and the United States,

Table 5.3:   Contributions of capital, human capital and productivity:
ratios to US values

Country	Y/L	$(K/Y)^{\alpha/(1-\alpha)}$	H/L	A
United States	1.000	1.000	1.000	1.000
West Germany	0.818	1.118	0.802	0.912
United Kingdom	0.727	0.891	0.808	1.011
Hong Kong	0.608	0.741	0.735	1.115
Japan	0.587	1.119	0.797	0.658
Mexico	0.433	0.868	0.538	0.926
Argentina	0.418	0.953	0.676	0.648
USSR	0.417	1.231	0.724	0.468
India	0.086	0.709	0.454	0.267
China	0.060	0.891	0.632	0.106
Kenya	0.056	0.747	0.457	0.165
Zaire	0.033	0.499	0.408	0.160
Correlation with A (logs)	0.889	0.248	0.522	1.000

Source: Hall and Jones (1999: 91)

being between 70 per cent to 80 per cent or more of US levels for capital intensity, and 40 per cent to 50 per cent or more for human capital, the contribution
of productivity ranges at between 10 and 25 per cent for the selected Asian and
African countries in our sample. This large variation in the productivity of the
transformation process between developed and developing countries re-
affirms our earlier observation based on data from Collins and Bosworth
(1996) that the two regions are not on the same production surface. Hall and
Jones (1999) emphasize that although the residual is traditionally taken to
reflect technical change, it could in fact be a reflection of the policy environment, or more generally a measure of our ignorance, containing all the
elements contributing to growth other than factor accumulation per se. The
data in Table 5.3 giving the correlation between A and the other variables
support this conclusion. Here we find that the residual has a very high correlation with output per worker at almost 0.9. However, its correlation with
human capital and capital intensity, and the latter in particular, is comparatively low, indicating that variables which are generally included in the broad
definition of the factors of production are not the key determinants of the level
or rate of growth of output per worker in most low-income countries.

Caselli (2005), summarizing the key findings of the growth accounting literature, states that it is now generally agreed that:

Income = F (Factors, Efficiency).

The consensus view is that 'efficiency' plays a large role, accounting for at least 50 per cent of the differences in per capita incomes. Studies that use a standard factor-only model to test for variance decomposition find that 34 to 39 per cent of the variance can be explained by differences in factor inputs, and that after controlling for factor accumulation, country-specific effects play a large role in output differences. Caselli notes that the growth accounting method treats the multiplicative factor A as factor-neutral, implying that some countries use all of their inputs more efficiently than others. However, the wide variations in A suggest there are significant differences between countries in the efficiency use of labour and capital, and the substitutability of these factors with each other.

In Shen (1984) we find an attempt to assess the relative impact of the inefficient use of inputs and substitution between factors on input productivities in low-income countries. He stated that if inefficient use of inputs, or X-inefficiency, is fully reflected in a lower wage rate, then this factor has no independent significance in the analysis. But the situation is different if the substitution mechanism breaks down – which is often the case in less developed countries – because wage rates exceed marginal productivities or inappropriate technologies have been chosen. In such circumstances both labour and capital become inefficient. Holding scale and technology constant, Shen estimated X-inefficiency for a sample of 18 countries. Based on the assumption that the technology employed in the US is the best practice technology, he used data from 2000 plants in Massachusetts to estimate the capital and labour inputs required to produce one unit of output in each industry. He then compared the labour input and capital input in the average plant in each sample country with its image plant in Massachusetts. Grouping the estimates from the 18 countries by per capita income, Shen found that the differences in input usage between the United States and the countries with the next highest per capita income were clearly dominated by a substitution relationship, with the production isoquant sloping downwards and to the south-east. However, a comparison between countries in the high-income category (which includes the US) and those in the low-income groups showed that the latter use more labour and more capital per unit of output. This illustrated that low-income countries failed to adopt the optimal factor combination corresponding to their factor prices, and consequently used their factors of production inefficiently.

Liebenstein (1989), theorizing on X-inefficiency, states that in a competitive market such inefficiencies cannot exist because competition ensures that minimum cost technologies will be adopted. The existence of these inefficiencies therefore indicates that the environment or the institutional setting – which includes historical factors, the regulatory framework, organizational structure and effectiveness – has a significant impact on the presence or absence of competition and the manner in which inputs are converted into outputs. The findings discussed above indicate that the empirical evidence is at odds with the outcomes predicted by neoclassical theory, and that this theory does not provide us with an adequate framework to understand the problems of growth and development. In Chapter 3 we discussed the alternative view of the functioning of an economic system, termed institutional economics, that focuses on variables that reflect the institutional structure of a society. As we noted, the central theme that emerges from this vision is that for economic agents to engage in productive behaviour their property and contract rights need to be protected from violation and predatory activities. This requires governance and institutional frameworks that promote the dispersion of economic and political power, guarantee the presence of an independent judicial system, and ensure the maintenance of the rule of law. Based on this line of thinking, a substantial body of empirical research is now available which considers the relationship between a broad range of economic and political variables and economic performance. The main findings of this literature are summarized below. The purpose is to assess whether or not institution-related variables provide a better explanation for the observed cross-country variations in growth rates, as compared to variables that reflect factor accumulation.

CROSS-COUNTRY REGRESSION STUDIES

The cross-country empirical evidence reviewed in this section has been divided into two tables. The first set of studies (Table 5.4) focus on the impact of a wide range of economic and political variables on GDP growth rates. The independent variables used include those which are part of the standard neoclassical specification for predicting growth paths, such as initial income, proxies for human capital, and the investment/GDP ratio. However, a number of other variables which reflect the institutional framework and the nature of economic and political governance in a society are also part of the specifications. These include measures that reflect the protection of property and contract rights, the quality of the bureaucracy, the maintenance of the rule of law, and the extent of corruption. Some of the studies considered use composite indices to measure the nature of these variables. Thus Knack and Keefer (1995) use the commercially available International Country Risk Guide (ICRG) and Business Environment Risk Intelligence (BERI) indices, and

Easterly and Levine (2003) estimate an Institutional Index based on the World Bank's governance indicators. Since some researchers such as Sachs (2003) have questioned the relative importance of institution-related variables in explaining economic performance, many of the more recent studies have included variables that reflect geography, health, and endowment-related factors in their specifications. The purpose is to assess the relative impact of each of these factors on economic performance. Strictly speaking, econometric analysis of the type discussed in this section does not show causality between the independent and dependent variables. It only shows the degree of association or correlation. However, where such correlations may exist with a high degree of statistical significance, it can justifiably be claimed that the independent variables in question provide a better explanation for observed variations in the dependent variable, as compared to any other set of variables.

In view of the known correlation between many of the independent variables chosen in these studies, and GDP per capita or its growth rate – the dependent variable in most cases – some researchers such as Acemoglu, Johnson and Robinson (2002), and Easterly and Levine (2003), use the technique of introducing instrumental variables into their equations to enhance the quality of their results. Instruments are variables that have a strong relationship with the independent estimators, but clearly no connection with the dependent variable. The purpose of such variables is to overcome the problem of multicollinearity and provide improved information on the direction of causation. In the studies mentioned above, data on European settler mortality has been used as an instrumental variable, replacing many of the institution-related variables in the estimation process. This has been done because settler mortality is correlated with institution-related variables, but clearly has no connection to current levels of GDP or its growth rate.

The second table (Table 5.5) consists of those studies that specifically attempt to assess the impact of democracy on economic performance. Here again the standard variables used in neoclassical growth analysis are included in the specifications. However, the focus is on measuring the relative impact of measures which are indicative of the nature of the political system, in particular the extent of democracy present in a country. Thus Barro (1996) uses a Democracy Index based on Gastil's political rights country classification. Other studies, such as Persson and Tabellini's (2007), use the Polity IV data set codes to assess the extent to which a country is a democracy or non-democracy.

All the studies reviewed above find that there is a strong relationship between economic growth and variables representing institutional quality and the protection of property rights. These include the rule of law, the quality of the bureaucracy, the absence of corruption, the expropriation risk, and the enforceability of contracts. Thus all the research using regression techniques

Table 5.4: *Impact of economic and institutional variables on economic growth*

Study and coverage	Major independent variables	Main findings
Mauro (1995) Study covers GDP growth rates and investment rates on 70 countries over the period 1974–1989.	**Economic:** Initial GDP, human capital proxies, government expenditure. **Institutional:** Nine indicators of institutional efficiency including bureaucratic efficiency, corruption, efficiency of legal system, orderly political process, political stability.	• Corruption has a strong negative association with the investment rate. • Bureaucratic efficiency index is significantly and robustly associated with growth rates, after controlling for other variables.
Knack and Keefer (1995) Impact on per capita GDP growth in 97 countries over the period 1974–1989.	**Economic:** Initial GDP, secondary education as proxy for human capital, government consumption. **Institutional:** An ICRG Index, which includes rule of law, expropriation risk, corruption, quality of bureaucracy. A BERI Index, which includes contract enforceability, risk of nationalization, bureaucratic delays. Various indicators of political stability included, such as revolutions and assassinations.	• Inclusion of the institutional variables increases the explanatory power of the growth regressions, with the ICRG Index having a similar effect to the secondary education (human capital) variable. • Security of property and contractual rights is found to be a significant determinant of growth.

Table 5.4: Continued

Study and coverage	Major independent variables	Main findings
Barro (1996) Panel data from 100 countries over the period 1965–1990 are used to test for the conditional convergence of per capita income.	**Economic:** Initial GDP, initial human capital, life expectancy, fertility, inflation, government consumption. **Institutional:** Rule of law index.	• The rule of law index based on ICRG is positively and significantly related to growth. A one rank improvement in the underlying index is associated with a 0.5 percentage point increase in the per capita growth rate.
Alesina (1997) Data on GDP growth for 100 countries over the period 1970–1989.	**Economic:** Initial income, human capital, investment/GDP, openness, initial inequality. **Institutional:** Socio-political instability, corruption, protection of property rights/contracts, democracy, civil liberties.	• Coefficients for rule of law, corruption, bureaucratic quality, protection of property/contracts, are all strongly significant. • Democracy and civil liberties have no clear associations. • Political/institutional variables taken together explain about half the cross-country variance in GDP growth.
Bloom and Sachs (1998) Study covering 77 countries over the period 1965–1990, considers the role of geography in explaining the observed growth gap between Africa and the rest of the world.	**Economic:** Initial income, trade openness, government deficit. **Institutional:** quality of institutions. **Geography:** Various geography and demography variables including land area in tropics, coastal and inland population density, population growth rate, life expectancy.	• Two thirds of Africa's growth shortfall compared to other regions is due to various aspects of tropical geography, demography, and public health. • One third of the variation in growth of per capita incomes is due to economic policy and institutional quality related variables.

Table 5.4: Continued

Study and coverage	Major independent variables	Main findings
Hall and Jones (1999) Data cover 127 countries over the period 1986–1995. Aggregate production function approach used to understand differences in output per worker.	The estimated production function includes a social infrastructure measure, which is a combination of two indexes: the first is based on the ICRG index and includes the rule of law, corruption, bureaucratic quality, risk of expropriation and government repudiation of contracts; the second is a measure of the openness of the country based on the Sachs-Warner index (1995). Index ranges from 0 to 1.	• A difference of 0.01 in the social infrastructure index is associated with a 5.14 per cent variation in output per worker. Applying this to the observed range of variation in social infrastructure, it is found that this accounts for much of the differences in output per worker between countries.
Kaufmann, Kray and Zoido-Lobaton (1999) Study uses per capita GDP data for 1997 and 1998 in a sample of 173 countries, to analyse income variations.	**Institutional:** Six aggregate governance indicators constructed out of 300 governance measures covering civil liberties, free elections, independence of media, quality and independence of bureaucracy, rule of law, corruption, market friendly policies. **Other:** Historically motivated instrument variables used in other key studies.	• Strong positive association between each of the six aggregate governance indicators and per capita incomes, infant mortality, and adult literacy.
Kaufmann and Kray (2002) Per capita GDP data from 26 countries in Latin America and the Caribbean.	**Institutional:** Six aggregate governance indicators, and historically motivated instrument variables used in other key studies.	• Strong causal link running from better governance to higher per capita incomes, but weak link in the opposite direction (i.e. higher incomes do not guarantee good governance in the long run).

Table 5.4: Continued

Study and coverage	Major independent variables	Main findings
Rodrik, Subramaniam and Trebbi (2002) Study considers variance in per capita incomes, output per worker, and factor productivity in a sample of 140 countries.	**Economic:** Indicator representing trade openness and integration with world economy. **Geographic:** Indicator represented by variables such as area in tropics, distance from equator, prevalence of malaria, and access to the sea. **Institutional:** Institution variable using European settler mortality as an instrument, and rule of law index.	• Half the variance in per capita income levels is accounted for by the three variables used, with the institutional variable accounting for most of the difference. • The institutional variable is found to be an important determinant of factor accumulation and productivity, while international integration and geography are not influential.
Acemoglu, Johnson and Robinson (2002) Urbanization in 1500 and per capita incomes today are compared for a sample of colonies, based on data from Maddison (2001).	**Economic:** Urbanization in 1500 used as a measure of early prosperity. Various instrument variables used for testing the hypothesis. **Institutional:** Security of property rights – from Political Risk Service; constraints on the Executive – from the Gurr Polity III data set.	• Higher urbanization in 1500 has a significant negative correlation with lower GDP today and the current level of institutional development. Maddison's (2001) data show that many colonies in Asia and Latin America were richer than the United States between 1500 and 1700. The reversal of fortunes occurred mostly in the late 18th and early 19th centuries. This reversal cannot be explained by the 'geography' hypothesis.

Table 5.4: Continued

Study and coverage	Major independent variables	Main findings
Easterly and Levine (2003) The relative impact of institutions, policy and endowment-related indicators on per capita income levels in 72 former colonies is considered.	**Economic:** Endowment indicators including European settler mortality, latitude, land-locked situation, crop and mineral variables. Policy variables including inflation and openness. **Institutional:** Institutional Index based on Kaufmann et al's (1999) aggregate governance indicators.	• Simple regressions show that endowment indicators significantly explain both the cross-country variations in GDP and differences in institutional development. However, at the two stage least square level, the Institutional Index significantly explains economic development, with endowments not explaining development beyond their ability to explain institutional development. • The policy indicators are not significant after taking account of the impact of institutions.
Sachs (2003) Review of previous major studies on the role of tropics related variables in explaining cross-country growth differences.	Measure of malaria risk added to a vector of institutional quality variables used in other key studies.	• Geography, human health, and environmental variables have a direct and significant effect on per capita income levels. They do not operate through institutions. This is shown by the fact that the malaria risk variable is statistically significant, thus explaining why malaria-prone regions – mainly the tropics – have lower per capita income levels compared with non-malarial regions.

Table 5.4: Continued

Study and coverage	Major independent variables	Main findings
Glaeser et al. (2004) GDP per capita data for up to 71 countries over the period 1960–2000 are used.	**Economic:** Initial GDP, initial human capital, life expectancy, fertility, inflation, government consumption. **Institutional:** eight institutional variables taken for the Polity IV data base including, expropriation risk, government effectiveness, measure of autocracy, judicial independence, constitutional review process, etc. **Other:** European settler mortality and malaria risk used as instruments.	• Variables reflecting assessments of institutional quality, such as risk of expropriation and government effectiveness, have significant coefficients. However, those representing constraints on the executive, such as judicial independence, show no relation to growth. • Settler mortality and malaria risk are highly correlated and both are strong independent predictors of the current level of institutional quality and constraints on the executive. • Assessing countries in different groups, the study finds that: – initial levels of schooling are a strong predictor of institutional outcomes. – those with high initial human capital have grown twice as fast. – stable democracies have grown slightly faster than autocracies. – autocracies have a much higher dispersion of growth rates.

shows that much of the observed cross-country variation in per capita income levels can be explained by differences in institutional quality. Hall and Jones (1999), using the production function approach, also come to the same conclusion. They find that differences in their social infrastructure index, which is essentially a measure of institutional quality, account for much of the variation in output per worker across countries. One study – Kaufmann, Kray and Zoido-Lobaton's (1999), additionally finds that measures of good political governance such as free elections, the degree of civil liberties, and the independence of the media, have a strong and positive association with per capita income levels. Extending their earlier findings, Kaufmann and Kray (2002) conclude that the empirical evidence clearly shows there is a strong causal link between better governance and higher per capita incomes.

While accepting the importance of institutions, three studies in our review emphasize the key role of variables that are more consistent with the neoclassical view of growth and development. Bloom and Sachs (1998) and Sachs (2003) argue that various aspects of tropical geography, and human health-related variables, have a significant effect on per capita incomes. This impact is direct and does not operate through the quality of institutions. Glaeser et al. (2004), on the other hand, do find that institutional quality has a strong effect on per capita income growth rates, but that the institutional outcomes themselves are determined by the initial level of schooling in a country (i.e. the initial human capital levels are a strong predictor of future growth rates). Disputing this point of view, we have Rodrik, Subramaniam and Trebbi (2002), Easterly and Levine (2002), and Acemoglu, Johnson and Robinson (2002). This group of studies also considers the relative importance of geography-related variables and institutional quality for economic growth and arrives at a different set of conclusions. Rodrik et al. (2002) find that geography is not influential and that institutions are the most important determinant of productivity and factor accumulation. Acemoglu et al. (2002) show that a higher level of prosperity in 1500 A.D. is associated with a lower current level of institutional development, as well as a lower per capita GDP today. This 'reversal of fortunes' cannot be explained by the hypothesis that emphasizes geography-related variables, because these variables have remained constant over time.

The 13 studies summarized in Table 5.4 constitute the core of the cross-country empirics undertaken in recent years that have tried to understand the variables accounting for differences in per capita income levels and variations in growth rates. Apart from the studies by Sachs (1998, 2003), all the other researchers using different methodologies come to similar conclusions. In sum, therefore, it is reasonable to conclude that the overwhelming weight of empirical evidence shows that institution-related variables and institutional quality are key to determining developmental outcomes and that sustained growth in developing economies is not based on the parameters that neoclassical theory considers central. More specifically, and contrary to what neoclassical theory professes, good institutions are much more important than high levels of resource flows.

DEMOCRACY AND ECONOMIC GROWTH

The primary focus of the studies reviewed in Table 5.5 is the relationship between democracy and economic growth. The studies included in Table 5.4, such as Barro's (1996), which explicitly consider democracy variables, are therefore also included here.

The evidence in the studies reviewed in Table 5.5 indicates that there is no strong association between democracy and growth. However, the transition from autocracy to democracy does seem to have some growth-enhancing effect, particularly in low-income countries (Persson and Tabellini 2007, Rodrik and Wacziarg 2005). Certainly there is no evidence that autocracies, on average, perform better than democracies, and as Rodrik's (1999) results show there is much greater randomness in the growth rates of autocracies, with democracies being better able to absorb the negative impact of shocks. In spite of this inconclusive evidence, many would argue that since the necessary conditions for security of property and the protection of contractual rights, such as the rule of law, independence and quality of the bureaucracy, etc., are exactly the same as those for a lasting democracy, there are adequate grounds for the bias in development policy and practice to be in favour of the establishment of competitive economic and political systems. In the section below, therefore, we shall consider this issue in the context of the recent experience of India and China. These two countries have totally different political systems – one is a democracy and the other a one-party state. By using a more detailed case study approach, and establishing what the common characteristics are between the two, it should be possible to identify which of the institutional variables identified in the cross-country empirical studies provides a more fundamental basis for sustained growth and high levels of economic performance.

INDIA AND CHINA

Starting in the early 1980s, India and China joined the club of high growth Asian economies. Considering their prior poor performance, and the considerable differences between these two countries at the political and institutional level, this acceleration of growth rates requires some explanation. An analysis

Table 5.5: Impact of democracy on economic growth

Study and coverage	Major independent variables	Main findings
Barro (1996) Study uses panel data from 100 countries over the period 1965–1990 to test for the conditional convergence of per capita income.	**Economic:** Initial GDP, initial human capital, life expectancy, fertility, inflation, government consumption. **Political:** Democracy index using Gastil's political rights classification.	Growth increases with increased democracy at low levels of democracy, but the relationship turns negative once a moderate amount of political freedom has been attained. The turning point is about half way along the democracy scale.
Barro (1996a) Study considers the relationship between democracy and growth rates of per capita GDP in a sample of 100 countries over the period 1960–1990.	**Economic:** Standard variables used in growth analysis such as initial income, investment ratio, various human capital measures, government consumption, black market premium. **Political:** Democracy index based on political rights indicator compiled by Gastil.	The democracy coefficient in the growth equation is moderately negative but not statistically significant. However, the results also indicate that there is a non-linear relationship between democracy and growth. The middle level of democracy is the most favourable to growth, whereas the lowest and highest groups do not have significantly different growth rates.
Rodrik (1999) GDP data from 90 countries over the period 1970–1990.	**Political:** Countries divided into two groups – autocracies and democracies.	No strong determinate relationship between level of political participation and long-run growth rates. However, the coefficient of variation for GDP growth rates is much higher for autocracies as a group, as compared with democracies (i.e. more risk and randomness of growth rates in autocracies). Countries with greater freedom experience lower declines in growth when faced with shocks.

Table 5.5: Continued

Study and coverage	Major independent variables	Main findings
Rodrik and Wacziarg (2005) Per capita GDP growth data for 154 countries from 1950–2000 are used.	**Political:** Polity IV codes used to assess whether a country is a democracy or has gone through regime change.	New democracies grow 0.87 percentage points faster that those having no regime change. The growth effect of democratic transitions is even more significant and has a large magnitude in sub-samples only considering low income, ethnically diverse, or Sub-Saharan African countries that experienced sustained democratization between 1950 and 2000.
Persson and Tabellini (2007) Panel data set on per capita income growth and nature of political regime, for over 70 countries over the period 1960–2000.	**Political:** Regime classified as democracy or non-democracy based on whether the Polity 2 variable in the Polity IV data set is positive.	The transition from autocracy to democracy is on average associated with a growth acceleration of about one percentage point.

of this issue can be found in Keefer (World Bank 2007: Ch.7). From the mid 1960s to the end of the 1970s, India had real per capita GDP growth rates of under 1 per cent. After 1980, this increased to about 3.5 per cent per annum, with a further and significant acceleration commencing in the early 1990s. Likewise, prior to 1980, China had average per capita GDP growth rates of about 2.5 per cent. After this date, however, growth accelerated, reaching three times this level in a few years. Keefer explains this improved performance in terms of two factors. First, using a sample of 193 countries over the period 1980–2004, he shows that the presence of a large market with enormous opportunities, and an abundance of cheap labour, attracted high levels of investment in spite of the existence of average-level governance indicators. In both India and China he also finds that the market size managed to offset weak governance and have a major influence on attracting foreign investment, in comparison to other countries with smaller markets and similar levels of governance. Second, although in terms of the World Bank's indicators of governance, both China and India currently have just average levels compared to the rest of the world – coming into the 50th percentile of countries – these are better than average when compared to other developing countries with similar levels of income. Furthermore, this average level hides the fact that there were major improvements in both governance and the macroeconomic policy stance in both countries around 1980, as compared with the previous decade. In particular, and in spite of very different political underpinnings for secure governance, both China and India implemented significant changes in internal checks and balances to limit arbitrary behaviour by political leaders.

Commencing in 1980, India has experienced significant changes in the manner in which its economic and political system functions. On the economic front, there has been a major shift away from the old state-dominated and state-regulated *dirigiste* system. On the political front, the institutional frame-work has evolved into one which is more supportive of an open and democratic society. (These changes are considered in detail in Chapter 7.) In this section, therefore, we shall only summarize some of the salient features that are of relevance to our argument. The 1970s in India represented a period of significant deterioration in the policy and governance environment. Major banks were nationalized, private industry was subjected to wide-ranging licensing and control regulations, and the role of state-owned enterprises was expanded. Checks and balances in the political arena declined with the split in the ruling Congress Party and the dominance of Indira Gandhi, the new Prime Minister. Following major unrest in the country in 1973–1974, the government declared a state of emergency in 1975. In 1976 the 42nd amendment to the Constitution was passed which effectively removed the judicial oversight of the executive. The defeat of the Congress Party in the 1977 elections led to a reversal of this process. At the economic level some liberalization did take place, and on the political front repressive legislation, including the 42nd Amendment, was repealed. The 1980s saw the beginnings of an improved macroeconomic policy environment. This incipient trend was strongly reinforced after 1991, when an aggressive policy of liberalization was adopted to free economic activity from the restraints established in the 1970s. Licensing was removed, quantitative restrictions and tariffs on imports were reduced, current account convertibility was introduced, and the country opened up to foreign investment. At the governance level, the ICRG indicators covering bureaucratic quality, the rule of law and corruption improved during the 1990s. An indication of the significant impact that the reform programme had on the efficiency of investment, and the productive efficiency of the economy in general, is given by the time path for the incremental capital-output ratio. This declined from over seven in the 1975–1980 period to around four in the mid 1980s, and then further to between three and four during 1993–1995 (Lal and Natarajan 2001).

When China's economic growth accelerated in the early 1980s the conventional features associated with private markets were absent. There was no property or contract law, no secure property rights, and no independent court system. Therefore, in a formal sense, economic returns remained at the mercy of political predation, with the consequent negative incentive that this has on economic agents to engage in productive activity. As has been widely observed in Africa and Latin America, such political dominance results in rent-seeking and patronage based systems as well as poor economic growth. So how did China avoid these problems and achieve economic success? Montinola, Qian and Weingast (1996) argue that once the economic reforms commenced in 1979–1980, property rights were no longer completely insecure or without political foundations. On the contrary, because of political decentralization, fiscal autonomy, the market-oriented ideology of the Communist Party, and the opening up of the economy, the system had significant limits on the discretion of both the central government and that of governments at various levels. Montinola et al. call this framework 'market preserving federalism', because by limiting the discretionary authority of the national government and encouraging competition amongst sub-national governments it brought about a balance of power, and a credible commitment to the system from whoever might be in power, without elections and a separation of powers as was the case in the West.

Montinola et al. (1996) describe the three main elements of the new system as it emerged in the 1980s. First, as part of the market-oriented reforms, there was a considerable decentralization of authority and the ownership of assets. Commencing in 1979, a substantial proportion of the state-owned enterprises controlled by the central government was transferred to local governments. Provincial and local governments were also given wide-ranging authority within the market environment, including setting the prices for most goods except those considered to be of national importance such as energy or grain. As a consequence, by 1985 enterprises controlled by the central government contributed only 20 per cent of industrial output, with the rest coming from provincial, county and township enterprises. Meanwhile the share of foreign investment administered by the provinces increased from 35 per cent in 1985 to 68 per cent in 1992. In 1979, the first four Special Economic Zones (SEZs) were also established. Over time, the two which were most success-ful – Guangdong and Fujian – gained greater autonomy to pursue economic reform aggressively and take their own economic decisions locally on tax rates, incentives, and foreign investment. Second, economic reform brought about a major expansion of township and village enterprises (TVEs). By 1993 these accounted for 30 per cent of industrial output. Township and village governments had the right to the profit from their own enterprises. Although strictly state-owned the incentives facing these enterprises were quite different, in that they were not bailed out like other state enterprises if they made a loss and therefore had to make a profit. TVEs could also be leased out to individuals. As a result of these reforms, investment by private rural firms and TVEs increased to almost a third of total fixed investment in the 1980s. Third, from 1980 onwards fiscal reforms were introduced. Based on various formulas, a revenue-sharing system between central, provincial and city governments was established. The new fiscal autonomy gave sub-national governments greater independent authority over their own economies and established a positive relationship between local revenue and local economic prosperity.

Montinola et al. (1996) argue that these reforms were durable because they brought about the emergence of new circumstances and new forces that not only supported their continuance but also facilitated further reforms. For instance, the decentralization of authority resulted in the emergence of strong regional economic powers. Thus after Tiananmen Square in 1989, when conservatives tried to recentralize financial and investment powers, their attempts failed because of resistance from Guangdong and other provinces. At a political level, the commitment on the part of the central government was reinforced by the institutionalization of the Communist Party, and the intro-duction of checks and balances at the top by Deng Xiaoping after 1977. Deng governed by rules, clear lines of authority, and collective decision-making. Major decisions came to be dependent on agreements being reached between 30 or more top leaders. Concrete evaluation processes, including measures of gross output and investment, were used for cadre promotion. These political reforms changed the incentive structures within the Party and government. More autonomy at the local level translated into higher benefits for local cadres. The incentive to rise in the ranks by being beholden to senior leaders therefore became much less, as compared to the past. Another important factor supporting the reform process was that the majority of the Chinese people gained economically from the reforms. This of course made it much more difficult to reverse them. As a consequence of all these factors the reform process continued to gather pace, starting in the early 1980s.

After 1990 the model changed, with a greater emphasis on private investment – initially foreign, but then domestic as well (World Bank 2007). In 1997, the government privatized 250,000 small and medium enterprises, selling many of these to party members themselves. As a consequence, by 2005 private firms financed by foreign and domestic investment accounted for almost 60 per cent of manufacturing sales. By 1999 the private sector was recognized in the Chinese constitution as an integral part of the economy, and in 2004 the National People's Congress changed the constitution to declare that a citizen's lawful private property was inviolable. All these measures have enhanced the security and transferability of property rights. On the economic policy front, reform gathered apace as well. In 1994 fiscal federalism was formalized with the introduction of a tax administration system with a clear specification of national, local and shared taxes. Exchange rate liberalization was pursued gradually, such that by early 1994 a unified market-based exchange rate was adopted and trade account convertibility achieved. In sum, therefore, the aforesaid discussion indicates that, in spite of major differences between the political and economic systems in China and the West, over the past twenty-five years or so China has made fundamental changes to its institutional framework, such that security of property and contractual rights have been introduced into the economic system and checks and balances on decision-making into the political system. On the macroeconomic policy front, as in the East Asian economies, gradual liberalization has been undertaken, with stable and orthodox fiscal, monetary and exchange rate policies being consistently followed throughout the period.

SUMMARY OF THE EMPIRICAL EVIDENCE

In our discussion we have considered wide-ranging cross-country econometric evidence, and case studies from two of the largest developing countries, to establish what the key variables were that underpinned successful economic performance. This evidence has provided us with two basic conclusions. First, it has given support to the propositions hypothesized in Chapter 3 that insisted institutions matter. The studies reviewed showed that variables associated with good economic and political governance are far more important in explaining developmental outcomes as compared to the traditional factors of production associated with neoclassical theory. Successful and sustained economic growth requires that institutional frameworks need to be in place in order to control opportunism and predatory behaviour by individual agents and the state. Second, although democracy per se does not seem to be a requirement for good economic performance, many of the institutions which characterize a stable democracy are clearly fundamental requirements for sustained economic growth. These include the presence of checks and balances in the political system; the maintenance of the rule of law; the security of property rights; and the protection of contractual rights. The experience of China since the early 1980s – a communist country without the same political framework as Western democracies – confirms this conclusion. In particular, the experience of both India and China shows that a credible commitment by the state to control arbitrary power and strengthen those systems that will permit more consensual decision-making in the political arena is central to achieving sustained economic growth. Consistent with our methodology of taking an inductive approach, in the next chapter we shall consider the historical experience of Western Europe. The purpose of the analysis will be to identify the factors that underlie successful institutional change and to assess the extent to which these factors conform to the key variables identified in the empirical evidence reviewed in this chapter.

6. Institutions in economic history

Modern economic growth finds its origins in Western Europe. This chapter considers some of the key factors that underpinned the beginnings of this growth in Western Europe and compares these with the reasons why other parts of the world remained relatively backward and undeveloped during the same period. The purpose of this comparison is to understand how the necessary institutions that form the basis for successful economic growth emerged. Maddison (2006) provides us with data on per capita GDP levels and growth rates for the major economic regions of the world since 1000 A.D. These enable us to identify the historical time period when the divergence between Western Europe and the other major economies of the world at that time began. The Asian region includes areas of the near East that were under the Ottoman Empire and India.

The data below show that around 1000 A.D., the per capita income levels of all the major economic regions of the world were almost similar, with

Table 6.1: *Per capita GDP levels and growth rates – major regions*

Year	W. Europe	Asia (excl. Japan)	China	India
(1990 international dollars)				
		Per capita GDP		
1000	400	450	450	450
1500	774	572	600	550
1600	894	575	600	550
1700	1024	571	600	550
1820	1232	575	600	533
1870	1974	543	530	533
Average annual compound growth rates of per capita GDP				
1000–1500	0.13	0.05	0.06	0.04
1500–1820	0.15	0.00	0.00	– 0.01
1820–1870	0.95	–0.11	–0.25	0.00

Source: Maddison (2006: Appendix B, Tables B–21 and B–22)

Table 6.2:   Per capita GDP levels (1990 international dollars)

Year	Western Europe	China
1000	400	450
1300	593	600
1400	679	600
1700	1024	600
1820	1204	600

Source: Maddison (2006: Table 8–3, p. 629)

Western Europe having slightly lower levels of income caused by the economic collapse following the fall of the Roman Empire. Maddison argues that the economic ascension of Western Europe started in the 11th and 12th centuries, and gathered apace after the 14th and 15th centuries. On the other hand, after the 14th century China – the leading Asian economy – and the rest of Asia remained stagnant. Table 6.2 compares per capita GDP levels for Western Europe and China during this period. As can be seen, the two areas had similar levels of per capita income in 1300, but by 1820 while this had doubled in Western Europe incomes had remained stagnant in China. Underlying this divergence in the performance of per capita incomes in the two regions was the fact that in China both the population and total GDP increased by 2.8 times over this period. Consequently, per capita incomes remained constant. In Western Europe on the other hand, while the population almost doubled, total GDP increased by more than 3.6 times. Western Europe, therefore, had a somewhat lower rate of population growth and a much higher growth rate of GDP (Maddison 2006: 629).

Having established the time period during which the economic performance of Western Europe and the rest of the world began to diverge, we can now attempt to identify the factors underlying this divergence by considering the salient features in the economic histories of these regions. We shall first consider the major population centres and economies outside Western Europe between the 10th and 15th to 16th centuries. Japan is excluded from this analysis because our purpose is to compare Western Europe with those civilizations that seemed to show vibrancy and growth potential during the early part of the millennium, but then stagnated, and remained poor into the modern age. These were the Chinese Empire in the Far East, the Islamic world centred around the Ottoman Empire in the near East, and the Mughal Empire in India during the latter part of this period. The analysis of the Eastern Empires below is taken from a number of sources, but primarily based on the detailed economic histories found in the works of Jones (1981) and Landes (1998). Before considering each region in detail, however, it is first necessary to assess whether the available data support the argument put forward by Marxist historians and some other scholars (Frank 1998, Pomeranz 2000), that the non-European world was ahead of the western world prior to European conquest and that the poverty of these regions is a consequence of colonial exploitation.

The argument that the backwardness of what used to be called the 'Third World' is due to colonial exploitation is well known. The mechanisms of exploitation elaborated upon, and well documented in the literature, include direct plunder, forcible exactions, and a range of unequal trading, commercial and other economic relations, all of which resulted in a transfer of resources from the Third World to Europe. The question still remains, however, as to whether these regions were ahead of Western Europe at the advent of colonialism, as has been claimed by some scholars such as Bagchi (1982) and Chaudhri (1978) for India, and Pomeranz (2000) for China. Resolution of this issue will enable us to understand whether these regions had the potential to have developed independently, but whose advancement was retarded by colonial exploitation, or whether they were already static economies whose backwardness was made worse by colonialism. We shall first summarize the arguments presented that Maddison (1998, 2006) based on his laborious efforts and careful scrutiny of the data available from a wide range of sources. Additional data that may shed light on this issue are included in the sections dealing with the specific Eastern Empires.

Quantitative evidence to support the view that the pre-colonial societies of Asia were either at the same level or even ahead of Western Europe at that time emerged from the work of Bairoch and Levy-Leboyer (1981). They estimated that China was well ahead of Western Europe in 1800, and Japan and the rest of Asia were only 5 per cent lower than Europe. Frank (1998: 171, 284) cites Bairoch and Levy-Leboyer to suggest that around 1800, Europe and the United States, after initially lagging behind, suddenly caught up and overtook Asia both economically and politically. Pomeranz (2000: 16, 111) also cites Bairoch and Levy-Leboyer and comes to the same conclusion. Maddison (2006: 49) states that if they are right, then much of the backwardness of the Third World has to be explained by colonial exploitation, and much less of Europe's performance can then be due to centuries of slow accumulation, scientific and technological innovation, and organizational and financial prosperity. Both the underdevelopment of the eastern world, and the economic progress made by Europe, cannot then be ascribed to inherent forces, and the internal characteristics of these societies. However, as we can see from the data on per capita GDP in Tables 6.1 and 6.2, comparing Western Europe with India and China, Maddison comes to the conclusion that Bairoch and Levy-Leboyer, and the others who subscribe to their view, are wrong. He finds that Europe was already rich compared to other parts of the world before the

Industrial Revolution. This was a consequence of centuries of slow accumulation. As the data in Table 6.1 indicate, per capita GDP in Europe grew at a rate of almost 0.15 per cent per annum for the entire period from 1000 A.D. to the Industrial Revolution. India and China, on the other hand, exhibited growth rates that were not significantly different from zero during the same period. Commenting on Bairochl and Levy-Leboyer's findings, Maddison states that these were essentially guesstimates that were never properly documented and then used to support this position that the Third World had been impoverished by the rich countries (Bairoch 1967).

CHINA

China is the one civilization that many historians believe could have surpassed Europe. However, consistent with our earlier finding about the dangers of arbitrary rule, progress only occurred when there were relatively benevolent rulers, and decline and decay occurred when the rulers were exploitative or despotic. Thus during the Sung dynasty (960–1279) China saw considerable progress. Government regulation of commerce was reduced; merchant families and private businesses were encouraged; and a greater decentralization of decision-making was implemented by giving local officials in the civil service and the gentry more authority. As a consequence of these and other measures, there was a major expansion of rice cultivation and production and the population is estimated to have doubled during the 10th and 11th centuries. During the Sung dynasty, China had achieved such a sustained period of technological and economic progress that industrialization seemed to be a likely prospect. In textiles, the country had a water-driven machine for spinning hemp in the 12th century – five hundred years before England. In iron manufacture, the Chinese learned early on to use coke and coal in blast furnaces and were turning out as much as 125,000 tons of pig iron by the end of the 11th century, an amount equivalent to the entire production of Europe in 1700. Chinese inventions during this period included the wheelbarrow, the rigid horse collar, paper, printing, porcelain, the compass, and gunpowder. Maritime exploration and trade were also well developed. However, with the demise of the Sung dynasty and the establishment of the Yuan dynasty (1271–1368) under the Mongol leader Kublai Khan, economic and social progress reversed. Kublai Khan established a centralized government and became an absolute monarch, ruling through an aristocracy of Mongol lords. The Yuan dynasty was typified by over-taxation, exploitation of the countryside, and famines. Intrigue and succession struggles were common. All this led to rebellions, the eventual overthrow of the Yuan, and the establishment of the Ming dynasty (1368–1644).

The Ming period did not see China realizing its potential either. After initially expanding their navy, the Ming allowed even that to decay and retreated from the sea. A formal ban on maritime trade was extended to all maritime exploration after 1480. Jones (1981: 203) states that China became inward looking during the Ming period, with efforts on the part of rulers to redirect all energies back into agrarianism. The first Emperor, Hongwu, tried to create a rigid system of self-sufficient rural communities that would not engage in trade or have any need to interact with the urban areas. He also made efforts to curb the influence of merchant families and wealthy landlords. The variant of Confucianism adopted by the Ming reinforced an empty cultural superiority and justified the self-engrossment of the Celestial Empire in itself. Along with this intellectual xenophobia came an indifference to technology and a resistance to European science. As the 15th century progressed, there-fore, the country retreated into economic, social and technological backward-ness. The major industrial advances of the earlier period were allowed to descend into technological oblivion. Earlier inventions, such as the astronom-ical clock, were destroyed, and even important devices introduced by Christian clerics, like the Jesuit canon, were left in an undeveloped and noto-riously unreliable form. Coke and coal smelting fell into disuse and the iron industry regressed. Hemp spinning was never mechanized or adapted to the processing of other fibres such as cotton (Landes 1998). By the time the Manchu had taken over in 1644 China had descended into predatory despo-tism, with the state functioning mainly as a revenue pump in support of a small elite. Jones (1981: 209) estimates that the Chinese paid 24 per cent of their GNP to 2 per cent of their numbers in return for some semblance of protection and defence and the coordination of irrigation and flood control. The Manchu rulers, being foreign invaders, only further reinforced this military despotism.

In terms of the quantitative evidence, we have already presented Maddison's estimates on China above. These are based on his extensive analy-sis of the trends in population, total output and per capita product over the past two millennia (Maddison 1998). He indicates that apart from other source material, thanks to China's bureaucratic system and efforts to monitor economic activity for the purposes of taxation, there is a great mass of survey data that can be reliably used for statistical estimation. Based on this material, Maddison finds that Western Europe overtook China, the leading Asian econ-omy of that time, in the 14th century, and then continued to forge ahead slowly after that date. The static nature of China's economy is corroborated by the estimates of Rozman (1973), which show that there was no significant change in the proportion of urban population (as measured by the population in towns of 10,000 or over) between the 10th century and the beginning of the 19th century. This quantitative information suggests that colonialism cannot be blamed for China's initial backwardness. In this context, it also needs to be noted that European penetration in any case was low until the mid 19th century. It started in 1842 when the British captured Hong Kong with the intention of obtaining access to Canton for the opium trade. Other attacks by colonial powers followed to open up the interior of the country. By this time, however, China was already well behind Europe in terms of per capita incomes and economic performance.

ISLAM AND THE OTTOMAN EMPIRE

During the period we are considering, Muslim rule extended from the Mediterranean to India. Landes (1998: 54) states that initially Islam absorbed and developed the knowledge and ways of conquered peoples. There was little sign of the arbitrary seizure of commercial property by medieval Islamic governments. Far back in Islamic history, the judges of Cordova had protected private property against ministers and the caliph. Between 750 and 1100, Islamic science and technology far surpassed that of Europe. However, something then went wrong. Militant Islam became the dominant theme of Islamic thought and all scientific or secular thought began to be denounced as heresy by the religious zealots. For militant Islam the truth had already been revealed, and since there was no distinction between the religious and the secular, spiritual conformity was required in all spheres of thought. By the time the Ottoman Empire had established itself in the late 13th century, Islam had become a regressive force against social and economic change. In spite of this, however, the Ottoman Empire initially experienced a heady growth phase. This was led by able leaders, minority communities were encouraged to undertake commercial activities, and there was interaction and a willingness to learn from the neighbouring European civilizations – for instance, the Ottomans absorbed the use of canons, clocks, and shipbuilding from the West. The imperial capital at Constantinople grew from about 100,000 people in 1453 to over 500,000 by 1600. At this latter date it was larger than contemporary European cities: it also offered a large market and trading flourished in the city.

However, after this tolerant start, the Ottomans reverted to a more warlike and typical despotism, typified by arbitrary rule. Obscurantist thought, which discouraged inventiveness and the borrowing of western techniques and encouraged close mindedness, intolerance and intellectual regression, became the order of the day. Thus, for instance, the Ottomans continued to use obsolete shipbuilding technology in the 16th and 17th centuries, resulting in them being out-gunned and out-manoeuvred by ships of the European sailing powers. This resulted in their commercial activities being confined to land, while the Levant fleets of England, Holland and France operated in Ottoman territories under privileges of exemption from taxation and the jurisdiction of local courts. Ottoman obscurantism also meant that no precautions were taken against the plague, which remained endemic throughout their empire at a time when it was being eliminated in Europe. Between 1812 and 1814, one-third of the populations of Bucharest and Belgrade perished. It has been estimated that in a bad year the plague could cause the death of up to 150,000 people, forcing the closure of trade fairs and leaving the harvest uncut in fields and the cattle to starve in their stalls (Jones 1981: 181). In the area of commerce and industry, progress was restricted by the fact that the ruling Turkish ethnic groups had a distaste for such activities and believed themselves to be too superior to engage in any form of business. The sector therefore remained undeveloped, and as a preserve of minority communities, it was constantly subjected to arbitrariness and exactions by the authorities.

Over time, as the size of the Ottoman Empire grew, it became a conglomeration of opportunistic acquisitions which could not be administered uniformly. As Jones (1981: 180) notes, there was no political integration capable of matching the organization of the European nation states, which were also emerging and consolidating themselves during the same period. As a consequence, the empire remained a congeries of people with conflicting loyalties. This lack of political integration was compounded by the problems of heredity and succession that confronted every subsequent generation of Ottoman rulers. The system of having multiple spouses and concubines resulted in a proliferation of descendants, posing questions of legitimacy every time a ruler died. Intrigue and murder became common parts of palace life. Thanks partly to a change in the succession laws, sultans came to be reared and surrounded in the palace and harem by degenerates. This was partly responsible for the amazing succession of 13 incompetent sultans who reigned from 1566 to 1703. Included in this group were lechers like Murad III, who fathered 103 children, drunkards like Selim the Sot, and mental defectives like Mustapha, who was twice deposed for idiocy. Meanwhile, the Ottoman bureaucracy continued to run the state as an agrarian despotism. Christian subjects were bound to the land by an obligation of perpetual debt. The once vigorous Turkish warriors sank into a lethargy induced by unearned landlord incomes. More generally, the economic system came to rest on arbitrary seizure, confiscation, and a total insecurity of life and property rights. A typical example of this was the common practice by sultans of seizing the estates of their subordinates on their death and handing back only what they chose to to their families.

The historical narrative above is by necessity very limited. Yet it does suggest that the backwardness of the Ottoman Empire was primarily due to institutional factors which were inherent to that society – and in particular, the continued dominance of a despotic and decaying feudalism.

MUGHAL INDIA

Like the Manchu empire in China and the Ottoman empire in the near east, the Muslim dynasties that ruled India between the 12th and 18th centuries were military despotisms originating in invasions from outside the region. Between the 13th and early 16th century, northern India was under the control of Turkic invaders who established the Delhi Sultanate. The period was marked by instability and parasitic tax collection. During the period, 19 out of 35 sultans were assassinated. The Mughals, who became rulers of India in the early 16th century, were an offshoot of the great Mongol Khans who roamed the steppes of central Asia in earlier periods. In taking the reins of government, the new conquerors essentially left intact the cellular village structure of India, while remaining a distinct and separate warlord class. Jones (1981: 196), summarizing the research from various sources, indicates that through the land revenue system a very large proportion of total income – estimated by some to be up to one half – was taken away from the producers and shared amongst the tiny elite of parasitic rulers and their minions. This taxation, of course, did not finance any of the services that the emerging nation states of Europe were beginning to provide. As a consequence, the peasantry were left destitute. Giving an example of the voluptuous selfishness and conspicuous waste of both the Mughals and native princes, Jones cites the case of Asaf-ud-Daulah, ruler of Oudh, a province of the Mughal Empire. In 1782, Asaf-ud-Daulah had jewels valued at 8 million pounds sterling, 20 palaces, 7,000 servants, 1,500 double-barrelled guns, 1,200 elephants, 3,000 horses, 1,000 hunting dogs, 50 barbers, and much else.

In the absence of an enforceable legal code, as was the case in China and Turkey as well, whether or not a ruler ruled effectively depended entirely on his personal character. There were no constitutional checks on a ruler's behaviour, or that of the nobility or officialdom. Although land was held at the pleasure of the emperor, a significant part of Mughal territory was in effect ruled by intermediaries called *zamindars*. They formed a native aristocracy whose primary role was to collect taxes from the peasantry and remit these to the royal treasury. The Mughals did have some enlightened rulers such as Akbar (1542–1605), however their rule became more and more rapacious in the latter years of the dynasty. Aurangzeb (1659–1707) engaged in incessant warfare during his reign and sucked the tax base dry. Being committed to fundamentalist Islam, he introduced *shari'a* law throughout the kingdom and went out of his way to suppress any original or secular thought. After the death of Aurangzeb in 1707 the Mughal Empire began to disintegrate. Continuous internal rivalries and conflict enabled the British East India Company to expand its influence and eventually gain control after the Battle of Plassey in 1757.

In spite of this, India witnessed the beginnings of a mercantile economy during the Mughal period. During Akbar's reign, Ahmedabad became a thriving centre of trade in textiles and by some accounts was one of the largest cities in the world at that time. Other literature speaks of the burgher cities of Allahabad and Benares in the northern plains. Mughal India had a bigger industry than any other pre-colonial country of the world at that time. It was an exporter of a range of products including cotton textiles and silks. Apart from the textiles, a domestic handicrafts industry, mainly catering for the ruling elites – consisting of jewellery, footwear, swords and weapons, etc. – also existed. Bardhan (2001) adds that during the Mughal period, merchant systems, like those in Europe, with sophisticated credit instruments such as the *hundi* or bill of exchange, had developed to enable trade within the far-flung economy. However, these traditional instruments of exchange did not evolve into more complex rules and institutions of enforcement as happened in early modern Europe. Bardhan argues that the leap from a mercantile to industrial economy did not occur, because unlike in Europe the state did not act as a catalyst to enforce contract and property rights, and did not establish self-binding rules or a credible commitment not to make confiscatory demands. The domestic handicraft industry was of course eventually destroyed by the colonial relationship and cheap imports from Britain.

Maddison (1971, 2006: Appendix B, p. 252) confirms that there is little evidence to suggest that India had a dynamic economy in the period prior to colonial domination. Using data from the economic survey of Abul Fazl, the Mughal Emperor Akbar's vizier, carried out at the end of the 16th century, and an assessment of information from a number of other sources, he comes to the conclusion that farm output per head or rural consumption was at best probably slightly higher in 1600 than in 1900. Although a lack of data about India has constrained the debate about comparisons between this region and Europe during the pre-colonial period, a recent study by Allen (2007) – in which he has constructed a careful wage and price history of India for the period 1595 to 1910 – has provided some more firm conclusions. First, he undertakes an analysis of nominal wage trends. To ensure comparability, he converts all wages into grams of silver per day. For the period 1600 to 1850, which is of primary interest to us here, he compares the nominal wages of craftsmen and labourers in Europe with those in northern India – the latter region being broadly representative of India as a whole, with of course some regional variations. Based on the data Allen finds that:

- Starting at the beginning of the period, silver wages were much lower in India than in England. Even in the backward regions of Europe (Krakow and Milan), wages were double those in northern India. This divergence with north-western Europe widened over time, particularly after the mid 17th century.

- There was comparatively little trend in the Indian wage series, with some deflation in the second half of the 18th century. Wage inflation only became important after 1870.

Second, Allen proceeds to consider if higher nominal wages in Europe translated into a higher standard of living or not. For this purpose he first constructs an average consumption basket for a north European family, and then conducts a standard of living or welfare comparison based on labourer's wages in the two regions. This comparison shows that:

- In 1600 and the early 17th century, Indian workers came close to being able to afford the lifestyle of a European worker.
- Starting in the mid 17th, or early 18th century at the latest, however, Indian standards of living had fallen behind English levels, and by the mid 18th century Indian wages had slumped. This decline in wages, and the standard of living, is brought out more starkly when data on Western India and Bengal are included. During the same period, the standard of living in north-western Europe continued to rise steadily.
- To survive on such low wages, Indians shifted their diets to a subsistence budget consisting of inferior grains and spent very little on their clothing, utensils and housing. This latter fact is confirmed by observers of that period (Lockyer 1711: 258) as well as other scholars (Raychaudhri and Habib 1982).

As a confirmatory exercise, Allen undertakes the same comparison using an Indian subsistence basket and its equivalent counterpart in Europe. This comparison shows that:

- The highest earners in the two regions – London and north India – had incomes three to four times the subsistence requirements in the early 1600s.
- By the early to mid 18th century, the Indian welfare ratios had fallen to subsistence levels, whereas in north-western Europe they remained high and rose steadily.

Based on Allen (2007) we can therefore conclude that a comparison with Europe shows that India was a low-wage and rather static economy. During the heyday of the Mughal Empire (that is, the late 16th and early 17th century) the two regions perhaps had a similar standard of living. However, with the advent of despotic feudalism and incessant warfare under the later Mughals, starting with Aurangzeb, the economy of India went into decline. This was well before the advent of colonialism. As in the case of China, therefore,

India's initial backwardness cannot be ascribed to the exploitation that subsequently occurred under colonialism. Thus, considering all the three Asian empires discussed above, particularly that of China, although a mercantile economy did develop to some degree these did not advance into industrial economies because the nature of the state remained despotic and parasitic. China, India and Turkey continued to be governed by arbitrary feudal rulers who continued to exact as much as they could from their subjects. Consequently there was no development of a modern nation state, as occurred in Europe, which could support commercial development. We can therefore agree with Maddison (2006: 46), who concludes that the stagnation in these regions was primarily due to their indigenous institutions and the policies that were being followed by the ruling elites. This was of course reinforced in the latter part of the period under consideration by colonial exploitation and plunder.

WESTERN EUROPE

Let us now consider the experience of Western Europe. The analysis of early historical developments is taken from Kohn (2005: Ch.18). In the early Middle Ages, the conditions in Europe were similar to those in other parts of the world. The region was poor and there was little technology. After the collapse of the Western Roman Empire in the 5th century, local administrators, governors and military leaders became kings, dukes, and lords of their respective territories. For a brief period during the 9th century the post-Roman Carolingian empire again re-united most of Europe. However this soon disintegrated and Europe was then rapidly at the mercy of weak territorial governments. Feudalism in Europe around 1000 A.D. was consequently highly decentralized, with a hierarchy consisting of a king on top, then great lords or vassals with their fiefs, down through their subordinates to the knight at the lowest level. A ruler's ability to impose his will on subordinates was limited, as some of the great lords themselves commanded significant military forces. This was compounded by the widespread construction of stone castles, which given the existing military technology, were difficult to breach. Superior forces, therefore, could not suppress defenders easily. The authority of early medieval rulers was further weakened by the role of the church. When the Roman Empire collapsed, the church remained intact and rich in both wealth and land. Indeed by 900 A.D. it controlled up to a third of the cultivable land in Europe. The 'Investiture Controversy' with German rulers in the 11th century eventually resulted in the Pope successfully asserting his claim to be the sole channel of God's authority on earth. After this kings were reduced to mere secular rulers who could no longer claim a quasi-sacred status. As a consequence of all these developments the relationship between a ruler and his subjects within European feudalism came to be based on law and custom and these constrained him from ruling in an arbitrary manner.

The weakened authority of territorial rulers created sufficient space in the 11th and 12th centuries for the emergence of autonomous cities dominated by a newly wealthy merchant class. The increasing wealth of these cities enabled them not only to organize their own military defences, but also to purchase their 'freedom' or right to govern themselves from local lords in return for the payment of an appropriate tribute. The initial impetus towards self-government occurred in the cities of northern Italy, the Low Countries and the Baltic. These included Venice and Genoa in Italy; the Flemish cities of Bruges, Ghent, Antwerp and Brussels; and the city leagues in Germany (prior to the Hanseatic League). In these cities we find the origins of the political and economic institutions that underlie modern economic growth. Maddison (2006: 54) summarizes the reasons for the economic progress of the Venetian Republic. Venice was the most successful of the North Italian city states. It was dominated by a merchant capitalist elite who created a republic with political and legal institutions that guaranteed property rights and the enforceability of contracts. The republic's revenues were generated by a well-organized system of excise levies and property taxes based on cadastral surveys. It was also a pioneer in the developing banking, accountancy, foreign exchange and credit markets. As a consequence of all these factors, by 1171 Venice had become one of Europe's major commercial centres, and with 66,000 inhabitants, was one of the three largest cities of Europe.

In terms of industries, the biggest enterprise in Venice was the Arsenal. This was a public shipyard created in 1104 that employed thousands of workers. Apart from shipbuilding, the other industries included silk and velvet products, glass blowing, book production, and sugar manufacture based on plantations in Cyprus and Crete. Between the 11th and 13th centuries, once the Christian counter-attack on Islam had begun and Europeans took control of the Mediterranean, Venice played a major role in reopening the economy of the region to Western Europe. In spite of the Crusades, through skilful diplomacy it also continued to maintain trading relations and concessions with the Ottoman Empire. Major trading relations were also maintained with Flanders and the other commercial centres of northern Europe, primarily through the regularly held Champagne fairs. By the end of the 13th century, Venice had defeated the Moroccan fleets and opened the straits of Gibraltar as an alternative sea route to northern Europe. The experience of Venice, and its political and economic institutions, typifies that of the cities of the Low Countries, as well as those of the Hansa towns of the North Sea and Baltic. From the 12th century onwards the leading cities of the Flanders and Brabant – such as Bruges, Ghent, Antwerp, Leuven and Brussels – became major centres of commercial and industrial activity: Flanders was the centre of the European woollen textiles industry and by the 15th century Antwerp was a major centre for international banking, giving loans to rulers such as Henry VIII and Charles V. Its bourse provided a model for the London Exchange.

At the macro-political level, the fundamental differences between the system of governance in Asia and the emergent mercantilist societies in Europe are evident from the discussion above. The Asian empires continued to be ruled as military despotisms, with elites extracting huge surpluses from their subjects to finance their incessant wars and their lavish lifestyles based on extravagant levels of consumption. No institutional frameworks, laws or customs emerged to limit the arbitrary powers of rulers and establish certain rules of the game which could provide a more consensual basis for the manner in which a society was governed. Security of property and contractual rights, which as we noted in Chapter 5 are essential for investment and economic expansion, were unknown. Arbitrariness continued to be the hallmark of decision-making and policy. Thus the Ming court could decide in 1480 that there would be no further Chinese maritime exploration, or one of the Tughlak monarchs that pre-dated the Mughals could decree that Delhi should no longer be the capital of the kingdom and should be emptied of every single inhabitant. In Europe, however, there was a greater dispersion of power and a recognition of the constraining role of law and custom which a ruler could ignore only at his peril. This was the case even in more centralized monarchies such as that of England. For instance, one of the key reasons for the revolt of the barons, which eventually led to the Magna Carta, was the imposition of a series of arbitrary taxes by King John to finance his war against France. A further important consequence of the dispersion of political power was that regressive and incontrovertible system-wide decisions could not be imposed by some central authority. For example, in spite of the dominance of the Catholic Church during this period, and the pretensions of the Holy Roman Empire, no commanding focus of authority was universally accepted (Jones 1981: 109). Thus mercantile Italian towns such as Amalfi, Naples, Bari and Venice continued their trading activities through the Byzantine Empire, and the disapproval and pressure of the Pope did not change this behaviour or the attitude of the people in these towns (Pirenne 1953).

To complement the macro-level analysis, it is useful to understand the micro-level mechanisms and contractual systems which influenced commercial behaviour and permitted an expansion of trade in Europe during the early medieval period. In Kohn (2005: Ch.16) we find an historical analysis of this issue. To expand activities beyond arm's length trading, European merchants needed agents who took their goods to far-flung places. This opened up the possibility of malfeasance. The expansion of trade also required credit to be extended to strangers. This then raised the problem of default and the need for some mechanism to be in place that would ensure the security of contracts and payments. Kohn argues that the merchant associations that existed in most cities and territories during this period played a key role in addressing these problems. First, they acted as a third-party enforcer to guarantee relationships between their own members and between members and outsiders. To fulfil this function, merchant associations used both formal systems of order such as laws and courts and informal mechanisms based on social norms and reputation. In 1245, for instance, the Count of Champagne gave the right to Roman, Tuscan, Lombard and Provencal merchants to hold their own courts. In the Italian cities of the same period, many had a *mercanzia* court which could handle disputes between local and foreign merchants. Informal norms, particularly reputation, also played a crucial role in enforcing good commercial behaviour, particularly by distant agents whose performance was difficult to monitor. In this arena again merchant associations acted as reputation networks, providing information on the actions and behaviour of agents abroad. For example, Venetian officials stationed in overseas trading colonies provided regular information on trading conditions to their associations back home and the Italian *mercanzia* supplied its members with information on transportation costs, prices and market conditions in foreign markets. All this facilitated the monitoring of agents by their principals and encouraged distant agents to act in a scrupulous manner.

Second, since cross-territorial enforcement mechanisms were weak, merchant associations took on the important role of guaranteeing the good behaviour of their members in their relationship with merchants from other associations. Kohn indicates that by the 13th century such guarantees were commonly used throughout Europe, and took two forms. The first consisted of the principle of the joint liability of a 'nation' of traders. Collective responsibility was implicit in medieval European culture: for example, residents of a village or city had joint responsibility for the payment of taxes and many civil and military duties were communal concerns. The extension of this principle to the trading activities of merchants was therefore not surprising. From about the 12th century onwards, merchants trading at the Champagne Fairs were held collectively liable for the debts of any member of their respective associations. The goods of all members of a particular association therefore served as security for the debts of each one of them individually. The second form of guarantee was the use of reprisals. This practice permitted an unsatisfied creditor to seize the property of any member of a debtor's merchant association. To exercise this right an aggrieved merchant required an authorization from an appropriate local authority, such as a *lettre de marque*. Kohn notes that the use of such reprisals had, in fact, became a hazard for any merchant travelling abroad with his goods.

In Greif (2006) we find a more detailed analysis of how formal mechanisms based on the principle of joint liability, which he calls the community responsibility system, facilitated trade and interaction between the various merchant communes in Europe. Under this system

> a local community court held all members of a different community legally liable for default by any one involved in contracts with a member of the local community. If the defaulter's communal court refused to compensate the injured party, the local court confiscated the property of any member of the defaulter's commune present in its jurisdiction as compensation. A commune could avoid compensating for the default of one its members only by ceasing to trade with the other commune. When this cost was too high, a commune court's best response was to dispense impartial justice to non-members who had been cheated by a member of the commune. (Greif 2006: 340)

Using the example of Genoa, Greif argues that based on this formal mechanism Genoese merchants felt secure to expand their trading horizons using non-Genoese agents. Over time the greater use of these mechanisms, in this case third-party enforcement through courts, permitted market development by making impersonal exchange more secure. In his view this was one of the key factors underlying the expansion of trade and commerce in Europe.

To elaborate on how the micro-level factors discussed above were important in explaining the historical success and expansion of European trading, Greif (1998) undertakes a comparative analysis of the institutions governing trading activities of two communities trading in the Mediterranean during the 11th and 12th centuries. These were the Genoese traders of northern Italy and the Maghribi traders from the Muslim parts of the Mediterranean. Both the Genoese and Maghribi had comparable naval technology and traded similar goods. However, during the 12th century expansion of trade in the Mediterranean, the Genoese traders saw a major expansion of their activities whereas the Maghribi trade remained relatively stagnant. The Maghribi traders were Jewish merchants. However, they lived in the Muslim world – and in terms of cultural background, and the institutional framework used by them to facilitate trade and exchange, they had similarities with other Muslim traders and emergent mercantile communities in the east (such as the *vanias* of western India or the *chettiars* of southern India). Greif (1998: 91) shows that given the close social relations within the community, the Maghribi traders used the threat of collective punishment by their own community to keep the agents entrusted with their goods honest. The use of such informal mechanisms of enforcement, however, ensured that trade could only remain in the hands of their extended community and limited the extent to which the Maghribi could expand their trading activities. On the other hand, Greif (2006: 252) states that in Europe by the late medieval period kin-based social structures were no longer the centre of institutional complexes. Rather, non-kin based, self-governed, and interest-based social structures – such as communes, guilds, fraternities, and associations – had become progressively more important. In the absence of nation states, these self-governed communes and structures exercised their powers through their own local courts. By the use of such formal mechanisms, as we have discussed above, the Genoese, as well as the Venetians and other European trading communities, successfully expanded their trading activities. In due course there was a further evolution of commercial and legal systems in Europe based on individualistic rather than collectivist forms of behaviour and these of course provided the basis for future mercantile and capitalist development.

The discussion above provides us with some understanding of the factors underlying the divergence in the economic performance of Western Europe and the Asian empires from the early Middle Ages onwards. Focusing on the issue of institutional frameworks, Jones (1981: 89) adds that unlike in Asia, beyond the efforts of the local communities themselves, the medieval authorities in Europe also began introducing institutions to protect trade by their subjects, both from internal disorder and external disruption. At first it was actually necessary for lords or kings to take action in support of their subjects. For example, in 1315 Edward II ordered the bailiffs of the Abbot of Ramsey to seize goods belonging to men who were under the lordship of the Court of Flanders, because the latter had failed to act upon complaints about the seizure of goods belonging to the king's cousin. At a later stage they began to guarantee trade arrangements under public seals of papal, episcopal, royal, or municipal authority. Thus European princes were generally able to impose sufficient order for the prosecution of trade. This process was subsequently reinforced in the 15th and 16th centuries as the military power of feudal aristocracies declined and that of nation states under royal governments increased. One of the major attributes of the new nation states was that taxation was substituted for confiscation as the main source of revenues, and with this transformation, the establishment of the right to hold property, free of risk from arbitrary seizure, became a more integral part of the institutional framework of society. France was perhaps the only exception to this rule. The pre-revolutionary French tax system was notoriously iniquitous, confiscatory and arbitrary. The crown rented out the right to levy taxes on farmers and those who obtained this right were then allowed to extract just about any amount of tax from a certain region, so long as they paid the agreed fixed rent to the crown. Nevertheless, taking Western Europe as a whole, the region experienced key developments during this period that facilitated the expansion of the mercantilist and capitalist system. In contrast, no developments of this kind have been found in the history of the Islamic or Asian empires we have discussed.

The comparison between the Asian empires and early mercantilism in Western Europe indicates there are various political factors which underpin economic growth. For a viable private market economy to develop, a sovereign or government must not merely establish a relevant set of rights with institutions to enforce these rights, they must also make a credible commitment to abide by these systems. By a credible commitment we mean that once a ruler has agreed to a set of rules they will be constrained to obey these rules and there is no leeway for them to violate commitments already made (North and Weingast 1989). Clearly if a sovereign has the ability to alter property rights arbitrarily to their own benefit, the expected return and incentive to invest will decline. Thus the fundamental political dilemma that needs to be resolved for a country to make progress is that a government strong enough to protect property rights is also strong enough to confiscate the wealth of its citizens. The institutional economics literature argues that the only way to resolve the problem of self-seeking rulers and predatory behaviour is for self-enforcing mechanisms to be established that will then govern policy choices and political decision-making. Following Samuel Rutherford's famous (1644) dictum 'Lex Rex' or the Law is King rather than the King is Law, Barzel (2002) argues that the best way to do this is through the establishment of a rule of law state. Such a state can perform the function of a third-party enforcer on both the ruler and the citizenry. However, in order to strengthen self-enforcement, the powers of the enforcer need to be divided as well. This leads us to the concept of a separation of powers between the executive, the legislature, and the judiciary, as propounded by Montesquieu in the *Spirit of the Laws* (1748). Elaborating on how this can be achieved, Weingast (1995) states that such a decentralization of political authority can only occur through an historical process wherein a strong consensus develops amongst the citizens of a country about what is right and true and just. Such a consensus will then be embodied in its institutional framework and reflected in its constitution (written or unwritten), laws, and the regulatory structures that govern the functioning of that society.

The manner in which various countries of Western Europe arrived at these governance structures is complex and beyond the scope of this book. However, the fundamental processes by which arbitrary power and predatory rule came to be constrained, and the rule of law established, have been summarized by Kohn (2005: Ch.18). He argues that by the 14th century the custom that the imposition of new taxes or exactions by a ruler required some form of consent from his subjects was widely recognized. This gave an incentive to rulers to establish or encourage the emergence of some mechanism of consultation that would bring together the representatives of tax payers on whom the burden of any exactions would fall – the wealthy, commercial and landed interests. This tendency complemented the natural evolution that had been ongoing in all these societies since the 11th century for all kinds of social, interest-based, political or other associations to be formed by subjects. Consequently, by the 15th century almost every territory of Europe had established some form of representative assembly, leading in some sense to what can be termed medieval constitutional government. In this system there were several institutional constraints on the power of a monarch. These included representative assemblies, independent judiciaries (such as the Royal Council of legal scholars in Castile), the church, city or municipal governments, and various types of popular associations. In due course European monarchs did try to reassert themselves, leading to a clash between them and the emergent forces. This eventually led to the demise of feudal rule and the firm establishment of the political and economic institutions that underlie modern economic growth.

To get a better idea of how the process described above eventually resulted in the creation of rule of law states that would protect the property and contractual rights of their citizens, we must undertake a more detailed historical consideration of English and Dutch institutional evolution. Since England was the first medieval kingdom where steps were taken to restrict arbitrary monarchical power, and Britain was the first country to embark upon a sustained industrial expansion, it is the best example to analyse in order to arrive at an understanding of how the economic and political institutions that underpin modern economic growth came into being. However, since the Netherlands provides the first example of a large state in the modern era in which monarchical power was abolished, sovereignty was vested in a legal entity rather than the person of the monarch, and a rule of law-based system was established, a review of how these systems came into being can only strengthen our understanding of West European institutional evolution.

ENGLISH INSTITUTIONAL EVOLUTION

In Britain's case the starting point for an analysis of how a consensus emerged in society about the need to control absolutist monarchs and protect property rights, and how self-enforcing institutional systems were established, would be the Magna Carta. This document was drawn up after the defeat of King John by the English barons at Runnymede in 1215. At a political level, under clauses 14 and 16 of the Magna Carta, a Great Council consisting of the most powerful men in the realm was created. At an economic level, the Magna Carta had clauses protecting the property rights of merchants. These provisions protecting property rights became part of English common law in due course (Rosenberg 1986). The Great Council created under the Magna Carta was, in effect, Britain's proto-parliament. From the point of view of a decentralization of political power, the most important innovation to be found in this institution was that the Council permitted its members to renounce their allegiance to the king and pledge their allegiance to the Council itself in pressing circumstances. Although King John repudiated the Magna Carta soon after the barons had left London, the precedent that there could be centres of power other than the monarchy had been established. In 1258, Henry III had to agree to the Provisions of Oxford under which the Great Council of 15 barons was given the power to oversee the business of government and meet at least three times a year to monitor performance. While the powers of the Council remained limited and dependent on the good will of the monarch until the Tudor period, nevertheless as a consequence of these institutional developments, the absolutist Anglo-Norman monarchy had effectively been abolished and over time the power of Parliament increased. Under Edward I, Parliament became more representative. In the Model Parliament of 1295 there were less members from the nobility and more from the emerging gentry class. Thus the term house of 'Commons' emerged. By the Act of 1430, the franchise for voting in House of Commons elections was extended to any person who owned freehold property worth 40 shillings or more. These changes in franchise were a reflection of the growing power of the emerging propertied middle classes.

In spite of these developments, however, the English system was by no means self-enforcing in that monarchs still had the ability to unilaterally alter the terms of any agreement and in fact continued to behave in an arbitrary manner. Such behaviour was particularly common when it came to imposing taxes or new regulations to raise resources for the crown, and in the arbitrary seizure of property. This clash between the crown and wealth-holders came to a head in the early 17th century when the Stuarts became the rulers of England. Unlike the Tudors, they proclaimed their divine right to rule and were looking to become absolutist monarchs like their fellow rulers in France and Spain at that time. However, Parliament's powers had also been increasing during this period. It had, for instance, become the only body permitted to lawfully raise taxes. Clause 61 of the Magna Carta was widely used by supporters to proclaim Parliament's supremacy over the king. The subsequent period of English history during which there was armed conflict between the crown and Parliament is well known. The major events include the civil war, the execution of Charles I in 1641, the establishment of the Commonwealth under Oliver Cromwell and its subsequent collapse, the restoration of the monarchy, and finally the Glorious Revolution of 1688. From the point of view of the institutional evolution of Britain, this period, which culminated in the Glorious Revolution, is central, and has been subjected to detailed analysis by various researchers. In the discussion below we shall therefore summarize findings by North and Weingast (1989) and Weingast (1995) showing that by the last decades of the 17th century Britain had established a self-enforcing constitutional arrangement that credibly committed the state to protecting property rights and preserving markets. North and Weingast (1989) argue that these institutional forms permitted successful economic growth to occur in early modern England, leading in due course to the Industrial Revolution.

The fundamental problem which the institutional changes that occurred in the latter half of the 17th century sought to solve was the exercise of arbitrary and confiscatory power by the crown. The immediate background to this is to be found in the revenue problems of the Stuarts. At the beginning of their reign, about half of all the crown's revenues came from the land. To meet the debts of his predecessor Elizabeth I, James I (1603–1624) had to sell a significant proportion of the crown's landholdings. Most of the remaining lands were then sold by his successor, Charles I (1625–1641). The sale of these assets obviously made the revenue problem even more endemic. New sources of revenue therefore had to be found to sustain the king and his government. To achieve this end, the Stuarts used the following methods:

- Increasing the rates of existing taxes or imposing new ones.
- Obtaining forced loans from moneyed interests by using threats – the repayment of these loans was unpredictable and the terms of the original agreements were never kept. For instance, a forced loan of GBP 100,000 taken in 1617 would not be repaid until 1628.
- The sale of monopolies – the creation of such monopolies involved circumventing existing rights, which disrupted existing markets in these commodities and adversely affected existing economic interests in the targeted activity.
- Confiscating goods for so-called 'public purposes' and paying below market prices for them.
- Arbitrarily seizing property from citizens. For example, in 1640 the government seized £130,000 worth of bullion which had been placed for safety in the Tower of London by several merchants.

The activities described above indicate that there was a fundamental clash of interests between the king and wealth holders. As a consequence, Parliament and the common law courts, which represented wealth holder interests, attempted to fight these efforts. Thus in 1628 Parliament sent a petition to Charles I seeking redress on a number of issues including: taxation without Parliament's consent; forced loans; arbitrary interference with property rights; arbitrary arrest; a lack of enforcement of habeas corpus; and imprisonment contrary to the Magna Carta. However, these efforts by and large failed because the crown ran the government and had in place institutional mechanisms that enabled it to successfully implement its policies and measures. North and Weingast (1989) have identified three institutions that were central to the king's power. First, the crown had the royal prerogative. Under this it could issue royal proclamations and ordinances without recourse to Parliament. Such rules and regulations were enforced by prerogative courts, thereby bypassing the common law court system. Second, on issues concerning prerogative, the Star Chamber had the final say. The Star Chamber, which combined legislative, executive and judicial functions, played a key role in the enforcement of the crown rules. Third, the crown directly funded and ran the government. All employees, in effect, served at the crown's pleasure. This power was used by the Stuarts to control the judiciary. Thus judges, such as Chief Justices Coke (1616) and Crew (1628), were openly dismissed for ruling against the crown. In due course this resulted in a judiciary that by and large supported the crown. North and Weingast (1989: 813) have stated that the effect of these institutions was to combine executive, legislative and judicial powers in the crown and enable it to act in an arbitrary manner.

The institutional changes which followed the Glorious Revolution were designed to address this problem of arbitrary power. First, the Revolution Settlement brought about parliamentary supremacy. The divine right of kings was abolished forever, and no longer could a monarch claim to be above the law. Second, a permanent role for Parliament was established in the management of government. In particular, it gained a central role in the decision-making on government finances. It now had exclusive authority to raise taxes, veto power over expenditures, and the right to monitor how funds were used. Third, the prerogative courts were abolished and the prerogative powers were reduced and made subject to common law. Fourth, judges could now only be removed by the action of Parliament. This ensured the independence of the judiciary from the crown. North and Weingast argue that these new institutional arrangements were made self-enforcing as a result of two factors. The most important factor was that as a consequence of the successful dethroning of Charles I and James II a credible threat of removal had been established. This limited the crown's ability to ignore the new arrangements and act in an irresponsible or arbitrary manner again. The second factor was that as part of the settlement parliamentary interests agreed to raise enough tax revenues to put government finances on a firm footing. This arrangement removed one of the major reasons underlying the exercise of arbitrary power by the monarch. A major consequence of these institutional changes was that the power of wealth holders over government increased dramatically and private rights became much more secure. As evidence of the increased security of private rights, North and Weingast (1989: 824) point to the fact that in the decades following the Glorious Revolution there was a major expansion of private capital markets. Drawing accounts with the Bank of England – an early form of demand deposits – increased from modest levels in the 1690s, to a million pounds by 1720, and two million pounds by 1730.

DUTCH INSTITUTIONAL EVOLUTION

Prior to the establishment in 1581 of the Dutch Republic, the state that preceded the modern Netherlands, the area of the Low Countries consisted of a number of duchies, counties and bishoprics under the overall sovereignty of the Hapsburg rulers in Spain. Within this overall political framework, by the late Middle Ages, Amsterdam and the other major Dutch cities came to be run by a newly emergent rich merchant class. Since rulers did not have enough income to pay their mercenaries or army, they needed financial assistance from the up and coming merchant classes in the cities. This class could therefore induce sovereigns to grant municipal charters and city rights establishing the autonomous right of cities to run their own internal administrations. Over time the richer merchant families became a closed oligarchical group that was able to reserve all major government offices in the towns and cities for themselves and had the right to choose a city's councillors. In the Dutch provinces this elite group came to be called the regents or *vroedschappen*. Their increasing power during the period was exhibited, for instance, by the fact that Philip the Good (1396–1467), Duke of Burgundy, undertook measures during his rule to promote their role while diminishing the influence of the medieval city guilds.

Under the sovereignty of the ruler, the provinces themselves were governed by an assembly called the Provincial States. This body consisted of representatives of the nobility and the cities in that province. Thus, for instance, the Estate of the County of Holland had ten representatives from the nobility and representatives from each of the 18 cities in the province. The city representatives were chosen by their city councils. In 1463 Philip the Good created the States General, which was a parliamentary body that brought together representatives from all the provinces and cities within the Duchy of Burgundy. Since its first meeting was convened to consider a request from Philip for a loan to finance a war against France, it has been suggested that his main motive for establishing the States General was to put in place a more institutionalized method of obtaining financial support from the merchant elite and to ensure the support of the regents for the succession of his son. Over time, with the increasing prosperity of the provinces in the Low Countries, the power and influence of the merchant classes represented in the Provincial States and the States General increased. In 1568 continued heavy taxation by the Hapsburg rulers to finance their military adventures, and the persecution of Protestants under the Spanish Inquisition, finally led to a revolt of the Dutch provinces under the leadership of William I of Orange. This led to the commencement of the Eighty Years War, and in 1581 the States General, through the enactment of the Act of Abjuration, formally declared the independence of the Dutch provinces of the Low Countries from the Spanish king, Philip II.

Under the Act of Abjuration the States General declared the throne vacant, and quoting ancient rights, deposed the ruler for having violated the social contract with his subjects. In continuation of this anti-monarchical trend, in 1587 the States General assumed sovereignty itself, making the seven United Provinces into a Republic. In spite of the ongoing war with Spain, the free trade spirit supported by the Protestant ethic resulted in great prosperity for the Dutch Republic. The County of Holland was, for instance, the wealthiest and most urbanized region of Europe at that time. It also had the largest merchant fleet in the West. In the absence of a monarch or ruler, the States General had a chief executive or Stadtholder. This Stadtholder was generally a prince from the House of Orange. However, he did not have a royal prerogative, and from a legal point of view, was a servant of the States General. The de facto powers of this position were nevertheless considerable and these led to serious conflicts between the regents and other representatives of the merchant class and the Stadtholder. Thus some Princes of Orange, such Maurice and William II, attempted to rule as dictators, replacing entire city councils to increase their power. In reaction to these events, the regents in several provinces refused to appoint new Stadtholders, and this action led to the First Stadtholderless period (1650–1672) and the Second Stadtholderless period (1702–1747). The position of the Stadtholder was eventually abolished in 1795 after the Republic was over-run by Napoleon's forces and it became a French dominion. In 1813, after the defeat of Napoleon at Waterloo, the Netherlands reverted back to being a kingdom under the House of Orange-Nassau. However feudal despotism was at an end and in 1848 it became a modern-style democratic constitutional monarchy.

This discussion of Dutch history from the 14th to the mid 17th century shows how the arbitrary rule of monarchs and the princely class was restricted. The emergence of a strong merchant class in the Low Countries resulted in the establishment of institutions that would facilitate a much wider dispersion of political power and the development of a rule of law-based system. By the early 17th century it was well established in the Dutch Republic that rulers did not have any supremacy, and that the laws enacted by the parliament of the country – the States General – were the highest laws.

INSTITUTIONS AND ECONOMIC GROWTH

The wide range of empirical studies considered in Chapter 5 showed that institutional variables such as the rule of law, quality of the bureaucracy, absence of corruption, expropriation risk, and enforceability of contracts have a strong relationship with economic performance. Of these variables the security of property and contractual rights were found to be particularly significant determinants of growth. The historical evidence reviewed in this chapter analysing the divergent performance of the Asian Empires and Western Europe indicates that the emergence of political systems which enable a control of arbitrary power, and permit the establishment of the rule of law, is a fundamental underlying factor, and a necessary condition, for property and contractual rights to be protected. Starting from a similar economic base in about 1000 A.D., the Asian Empires, and in particular China, showed technical and mercantile progress up until the 14th or 15th centuries. However, after this they stagnated because monarchs continued to rule in an arbitrary manner and the state remained despotic, predatory, and under the control of parasitic elites. Western Europe, on the other hand, got off to a firm start in the 11th century with merchant capitalist elites dominating the city states in Northern Italy, the Low Countries, and the Baltic, where political and legal institutions were created which guaranteed property rights and the enforceability of contracts. Once nation states had been established in Europe, the early modern period was dominated by a clash of interests between the emergent wealth-holders and monarchs, who quite naturally believed that they had a right to continue ruling in an absolutist and arbitrary manner. This conflict was first resolved in the 17th century in England and in the Dutch Republic, though it took much longer to work itself out in continental Europe. However, throughout Western Europe the emergent mercantile and propertied classes eventually gained dominance and were able to introduce and firmly establish a rule of law state, with self-enforcing economic and political institutions that eliminated the arbitrary power of monarchs, protected property rights, and provided a firm basis for the development of markets. This formed the institutional basis for modern economic growth.

The West European model of institutional change described above has three fundamental characteristics. First, the process by which the new structures and systems were established was gradual and evolutionary, with advances, retreats, and incremental changes occurring over a long period of time. Second, the main drivers of change were endogenous forces, with exogenous factors having a limited impact on the character or pace of institutional change. The new economic and political institutions that emerged were the consequence of a process of collective bargaining that occurred between the dominant or controlling elite and the emergent forces within those societies. Strong group interests generated ideas and ideologies around which individuals could organize themselves, overcome the free-rider problem, and confront the concentrated interest of the ruler or state. Thus communes, guilds, associations, and city councils played a central role in facilitating the bargaining with rulers, extracting concessions, and placing constraints on their arbitrary rule. No such process can be observed in the Asian empires. Third, the historical evidence on the relationship between institutions and economic development does not provide any support for the view that economic growth by itself can cause favourable new institutions to come into being Chang (2011). In Western Europe, as in Britain, both at the micro- and macro-levels, significant institutional innovations and development preceded the acceleration of economic growth. This relationship is confirmed by the experience of the Eastern Empires, where the initial mercantilist impetus could not gather pace precisely because such institutional changes did not occur.

The pace of change in Western Europe, and the institutional trajectory, depended on the relative bargaining strength of the protagonists, and this was a function of a range of technological, social and economic variables. This is a vast topic which is beyond the scope of this book, with theories ranging from those which focus on material factors such as natural endowments, to those which emphasize the centrality of innovation and technology, and others which focus on religion, beliefs and culture as the primary determinants of the eventual character of a society's institutions and the manner in which institutional change occurs. The more limited focus of our analysis has been to understand the nature of the new institutions which emerged, rather than elaborating on these grand socio-economic forces or their relative importance in influencing the character of the institutions that emerged. What is important, however, from the point of view of this book, is that in the West European context, irrespective of whether it was material or technological factors, or beliefs, ideas, ideologies and mental models that motivated the main actors in the process of institutional change, all these elements were integral and endogenous to the culture and history of these societies. This gives us a specific model of institutional transition, which we can now use to compare with and assess the more recent experience of Asia and Africa. In doing so it may be possible to identify whether certain factors, rather than others, have had a greater influence on institutional development in the non-Western world.

7. Discontinuous institutional change

The economic history of the non-Western world shows that outside Japan sustained economic growth over a long period of time, as occurred in Europe and its offshoots such as the United States, Canada and Australia, is a very recent phenomenon. Based on the theoretical, empirical and historical evidence presented in earlier chapters, we argue that this indicates that in these regions there was no historical development of the institutions that underpin modern economic growth. The necessary institutions did not emerge incrementally or spontaneously, in response to endogenous forces, as occurred in Europe. Nevertheless some successful institutions seem to have occurred in Asia and Africa. It is therefore of relevance to this book to consider some case studies and attempt to understand the manner in which these transitions occurred and whether the forces that underlay this change conformed to the West European model, as discussed in Chapter 6, or not.

To explain the non-emergence of beneficent institutions in the developing world, we shall use the conceptual framework elaborated on by North, Wallis and Weingast (2009) to explain institutional development in general. They argue that contrary to the traditionally held view about primitive man, recent anthropological literature indicates that primitive societies were extremely violent (Keeley 1996, Otterbien 1989). Keeley (1996: 16) gives examples of the Yanomamo tribe of Venezuela and Brazil, who were constantly embroiled in warfare, and whose men displayed a great propensity to perpetrate violence against everyone. Similarly, the Kung San or Bushmen of the Kalahari, who are portrayed as a very peaceful society, in fact had a homicide rate between 1920 and 1950 which was 20 to 80 times greater than that of the major industrialized nations. Although the two World Wars of the 20th century are portrayed by many as indicating the propensity towards violence amongst so-called civilized nations, Keeley indicates that there is simply no proof that warfare in small-scale societies was less frequent or bloody than that amongst modern states.

Based on this proposition, North et al. argue that first and foremost this human violence needs to be contained for any society to develop a social order. Historically, the end of the Ice Age, about 10,000 years ago, is seen as the point of transition from primitive to post-primitive society. During this period it is suggested that the state began to emerge in some form or the other as the primary mechanism for controlling violence amongst individuals and groups. In a primitive setting, such a mechanism of governance or state would obviously fall under the control of the most powerful individuals or dominant elites in that society. Left to themselves such elites, based on their control over the instruments of violence, would inevitably assert themselves and establish a rent-seeking natural state. The main function of such a rent-seeking state would be to prevent disorder and enhance social stability by creating a set of self-enforcing agreements amongst the elites themselves. North et al. argue that the natural state has been the dominant social order since the end of the Ice Age. It is a stable social order in the sense that the economic, political, military and religious systems are organically related to each other. And given the persistence of institutions, fundamental changes in one system cannot occur without fundamental changes in the others. However, given that the natural state is based on rent-seeking and a balance of violence amongst the rulers, it can also be seen to have an inherent fragility. This balance must inevitably break down from time to time, leading to wars within and between states. Such a condition is obviously not favourable to the protection of property rights and the expansion of private markets.

To progress beyond the natural state and achieve a more stable social order, as we noted in Chapter 3, the mainstream new institutional economics literature argues that an evolutionary process must be gone through led by dominant elites. Based on the West European experience this process is seen as happening incrementally – at the margin – and one that gradually extends the access of the majority to the organizations of control in a society (North 1981, 1990). However, as we argued in the previous chapter, this model does not fit with the historical experience of the non-Western world. Here, the necessary endogenous forces either did not exist or were not strong enough to control predatory behaviour by the elites and bring about the establishment of a new economic and social order based on consensus and the application of a set of self-enforcing rules. Even North et al. (2009: 70) would now agree there is nothing automatic about a transition from a natural state to what they call an 'open access order', where the use of violence has either been reduced or eliminated as a means of political and economic competition. This suggests that the West European model of institutional change that we discussed in Chapter 6 has limited applicability to the situation in developing countries. The question therefore still remains as to how a society can establish the institutions required to control violence, eliminate fragility, and allow sustainable economic development to occur. As neoclassical theory does not raise these issues it is of no help to us in providing any answers to these puzzles.

At a theoretical level, however, modern information theory has applied itself to a consideration of some of these issues. The proponents of these ideas, such as Stiglitz (1989), Hoff (2000), and Hoff and Stiglitz (2001), argue that the presence of information problems, transaction costs and distributional considerations affects the nature of contracts, incentive structures, and therefore outcomes. These factors are seen as being fundamentally dependent on the existing institutional frameworks, historical legacy, and the distribution of wealth in a particular society. Even with similar endowments, therefore, different historical initial conditions and cultural beliefs will influence agent expectations such that multiple equilibria and low-level equilibrium traps will result. Furthermore, where path dependent processes and self-reinforcing mechanisms are at work, vested interests will ensure that sub-optimal situations continue to persist even if alternative Pareto superior equilibria are known to exist. As an example of this model, Bardhan (2001) discusses the impact of an unequal distribution of wealth and asymmetries in bargaining power on outcomes. He argues that vested interests will resist changes to their pre-existing rent extraction machinery because of the uncertain prospect of a share in a potentially larger pie in the future. Thus while all parties may gain from a change in institutional structures, there is no guarantee that such a Pareto superior position will be achieved. On the contrary, the most likely outcome is that the presence of collective action problems will cause the persistence of dysfunctional or sub-optimal institutions. Modern information theory therefore supports the view that there is no guarantee that local evolutionary processes, which as we have seen are determined by the internal characteristics of a country, will generate the institutions required for sustainable economic growth. Thus, in the presence of low-level equilibrium traps, the only way to achieve institutional change and move to a higher-level equilibrium is for an exogenous event or intervention to occur.

INSTITUTIONAL TRANSITIONS

Since the grand socio-economic forces that formed the basis for the endogenous development of West European – institutions such as emergent social classes, innovation and technology, or religion and culture – do not seem to have been a major beneficent influence in the developing world, how then can we account for the few successful institutional transitions that seem to have occurred in the last one hundred years or so? Perhaps, as modern information theory suggests, we should focus our attention on exogenous factors and exogenously inspired interventions. Let us therefore consider the nature of institutional change as it has occurred in the non-Western world during the late 19th or 20th century. A broad review of this issue suggests that change has primarily been of two types. The first has been where direct intervention by an external force, or the collapse of the main external support of a regime, has enabled progressive economic and political groups already present in a particular society to gain dominance. In such cases, while these groups may have been representative of important social classes, historically due to collective action or other problems, they did not have adequate capability to challenge the supremacy of the ruling political coalitions prior to the external intervention. In this category, for instance, we would find Japan, where at the end of the Second World War, the US and its allies swept aside the old dominant feudal coalition and put in its place an externally dominated administration that lasted for almost a decade. During this period fundamental institutional changes were brought about that permitted new social forces to gather strength. We could also include here much of what happened in Eastern Europe after the collapse of the Soviet Union. In Eastern Europe, progressive social forces that had been evolving prior to the communist take over were given renewed impetus, and were able to topple the weakened externally supported regimes after 1990.

The second model has been one where the main driver of change has been a radical or elite domestic group committed to modernization and socio-economic reform. Institutional transitions using such a process have occurred in several countries in the post-colonial Third World with differing degrees of success. Historically speaking, political institutions which could facilitate the more efficient functioning of markets were put in place in most developing countries as part of the decolonization process. In some countries this super-structure of new institutions endured and played a catalytic role in promoting the growth of larger social forces, whose interests in the long term underpinned the success of these new economic and political systems. India and Botswana could be considered successful examples of this model. In it primacy is given to the role of dominant elites in a manner similar to the mainstream literature (North et al. 2009). To understand the factors underlying successful institutional change in the non-Western world, therefore, three countries have been chosen from Asia and Africa for the purpose of undertaking more detailed case studies. These are Japan, India, and Botswana. The case studies are not exhaustive but illustrative, with the focus on key periods of change when the favourable institutional transitions seem to have occurred. In Chapter 6 we found that economic growth – both in the early medieval city states and later in the nation states of Europe was underpinned by political factors and certain types of political institutions which facilitated the control of arbitrary power and enabled trade and private markets to expand. Therefore, in our discussion on institutional development in the three case study countries, our primary focus will be on political institutions. However, the analysis will also consider the economic forces generated by changes in the political institutions, and the interaction between these two factors over time.

JAPAN

The analysis of Japanese history given below is derived from various sources, but primarily based on Lockwood (1968), Allen (1981), Gordon (2003), and the comparative history work of Barrington Moore Jr. (1967). Let us first consider Japan's economic performance since the early 19th century.

Table 7.1 shows us that prior to the 1870s, Japan's economic performance was much poorer than that of Western Europe and only marginally better than that of the rest of Asia. Subsequent to the Meiji Restoration of 1868, and up until the commencement of the First World War, Japan had a major acceleration in its growth rates. In spite of this initial growth spurt, however, per capita GDP levels, which were half that of Europe in the 1820s, were still around 40 per cent of the latter, even in 1950. High rates of growth in Japan are therefore a post-Second World War phenomenon, a consequence of which being, as the data indicate, that its per capita income level came to surpass that of Western Europe by 1998. From the table it is evident that Japan has had two periods of accelerated growth rates. The first was during the Meiji period, when the country broke out of its Asian mould of being a relatively static feudal economy. The second was the period after the Second World War and after the Occupation had ended. This enables us to put institutional change in Japan into a proper historical perspective, and provides concrete evidence of the impact caused by the major political and economic changes that occurred during the periods under consideration.

Table 7.1:   Per capita GDP – annual compound growth rates

	1820–70	1870–1913	1913–50	1950–73
Japan	0.19	1.48	0.89	8.05
Western Europe	0.95	1.32	0.76	4.08
Asia (excl. Japan)	–0.11	0.38	–0.02	2.92

Per capita GDP levels (1990 international dollars)

	1820	1870	1913	1950	1998
Japan	669	737	1387	1926	20413
Western Europe	1232	1974	3473	4594	17921
Asia (excl. Japan)	575	543	640	635	2936

Source: Maddison (2006: Tables 3-1a and 3-1b, p. 126)

A good point to start the story of modern institutional change in Japan is the Battle of Sekigahara in 1600. The victory of Tokugawa Ieyasu put an end to the period of warring barons and resulted in the establishment of the *Shogunate*. The Tokugawa system imposed a degree of centralized bureaucratic control over the country. Under the *Shogun* were the *daimyo*, or feudal lords, and below them were the *samurai* or warriors. The *daimyo* extracted rice levies from the peasants and from this paid their tribute to the *Shogun* and an annual stipend to the *samurai*. The leading political principle during the *Shogunate* was one of static feudalism, with primacy given to the maintenance of peace and order. Peace and expenditures by the feudal class encouraged the growth of commerce during this period. A merchant class began to emerge in the towns whose main functions were to purchase rice and other agricultural products from the *daimyo* and supply them with amenities. Over time the merchant class significantly improved its position and in some cases even obtained a stranglehold on sections of the nobility. To control their increasing economic power the aristocracy responded by using several weapons, such as forced loans, a refusal to pay debts, and outright confiscation. Several mechanisms of political control were also used to ensure that the commercial classes were enclosed within the feudal order. This included closing off the country and prohibiting foreign trade under the edicts of 1633–1641. In any event, since a large portion of the wealth that flowed to the merchants had originally been pumped out of the peasantry by the aristocracy, the former had little incentive to challenge the supremacy of the latter. These economic and political factors ensured that the merchant remained a dependent figure within Japanese society during the Tokugawa period.

The inability of the *Shogunate* to keep out the foreign incursions that began with Commodore Perry's appearance in 1854 was one of the main causes for the Meiji Restoration of 1868. The leaders of a section of the nobility, particularly those from the fiefs of Choshu and Satsuma – where feudal institutions and the *samurai* were strong – defeated the more backward looking feudal elements with the purpose of creating a modern centralized state that would keep out all foreigners. The Restoration was, therefore, a feudal revolution, with the Emperor now becoming the embodiment of national unity, beliefs and traditions. During the decade following the Restoration, sweeping reforms were forcibly carried out from above (Bardhan 1984), by a new clan of *samurai*-bureaucrats and what has been termed a 'progressive' feudal-commercial nobility around the throne. Lockwood (1968: 3) states that 'The speed with which Japan emerged from quasi-feudalism to become a modern state with a large sector of the economy organized along industrial, capitalistic lines is in striking contrast to the centuries of evolutionary growth characterizing the process in the West'. Emphasizing the nature of this period as a major discontinuity from the past, Allen (1981: 1) indicates that 'The new government quickly abolished the feudal institutions ... and set out on an ambitious course of modernization. The policy called for the introduction of Western systems of law, political administration, education, and communications ... and required an adaptation of the military, industrial and commercial organization according to Western models'.

By Imperial decree in 1871, all feudal domains were abolished and converted into prefectures or administrative units under the control of the central government. Through the Land Tax of 1873, the state put in place a mechanism for extracting revenues from the peasantry that could be re-directed towards modernization. The main impulse for economic growth during the early Meiji period came from the government. The state led the process of industrialization. The government established a new fiscal system, set up banks, and built railways, shipyards and factories to produce, amongst other things, iron, steel and textiles. The new industrialists and financiers were largely from the ranks of the *samurai* and prosperous landlord classes, rather than from the old mercantile classes. Between 1870 and 1885 the government spent about 20 per cent of the national budget on promoting industry. However, most of the state-owned enterprises turned out to be loss-making. Consequently, after 1880 mass privatizations were undertaken through which most of these assets were sold to well-connected private entrepreneurs for a fraction of their cost. This process in due course resulted in the formation of business conglomerates or *zaibatsu*. *Daimyo* and other aristocratic families became dominant members of the emerging financial oligarchy. By 1880 it is estimated that 44 per cent of the stock in national banks belonged to the new peers. The new feudal-capitalist oligarchy also extended their dominance over the old merchant classes of the Tokugawa period, who as a consequence remained a subordinate class. The industrialization that occurred during this period was therefore very much in the feudal-military tradition of the country. The *zaibatsu* themselves were structured in a feudal manner and shared the political views of the ruling elite. The Meiji period thus created the framework for large-scale enterprises and the future industrial growth of the country.

In the agricultural sector, the latter half of the Tokugawa period saw substantial improvements in agricultural techniques. These resulted in improved productivity, higher agricultural production, and greater marketable surpluses. Markets, and the use of money, spread into the rural areas. These economic advances and the shortage of labour led to the demise of traditional farming. Large holdings being cultivated by dependent small-holders were replaced by family farms and landlord-tenant farming, with an increased use of wage labour. Many of the new landlords emerged out of the richer peasantry rather then being part of the old feudal aristocracy. The landlord-tenant system of land tenure that developed during this period remained stable up to the Second World War. Thus, while in 1903, 44.5 per cent of arable land was cultivated by tenants, in 1938 this percentage was almost the same at 46.5 per cent. Landlords did not become a rural capitalist class because increased productivity and the pressure of population drove up rents and the new rentiers managed to squeeze out greater and greater surpluses out of the peasantry. There was therefore no need for a change to occur in rural economic relations. It is estimated that landlords extracted three fifths to two thirds of production as rents. To maintain its dominance in the rural areas this parasitic class needed repression by the state to keep the peasantry in check. It therefore allied itself to the commercial-feudal oligarchy behind the Emperor to keep the populace under control.

The economic outline presented above provides us with a framework to understand the political changes that occurred during the period. Dominant elites during the Meiji period kept political change under control. Although a new constitution with a *Diet* or parliament was created in 1889, the right to vote was given to a very limited electorate and only men of substantial property were eligible to become members of the assembly. Out of a population of 50 million, about 460,000 men received electoral rights. The *Diet* had few powers and governments stayed in power only if they had the confidence of the nobility, bureaucrats, and the military. General Yamagata, an influential soldier, dominated national politics from the later Meiji period until his death in 1922. Elites propagated the view that obedience to the state and the emperor was the highest secular obligation of an individual. In spite of a veneer of constitutional government, therefore, this period was characterized by bureaucrats and generals ruling the country in the name of the emperor. On the economic front, from the First World War onwards there was a major spurt in industrial growth and an expansion of Japanese capitalism. However, this expansion occurred mainly under the direction of the *zaibatsu*. They of course mainly controlled large industry. But by using their market power, advancing funds, and providing technical advice, they also established control over a large segment of the small enterprise sector.

The industrial revolution that started during the Meiji period slowly transformed Japanese society. By 1936 factory employment was almost 2.9 million and one in three Japanese lived in a city of 30,000 or more (Lockwood 1968: 73). These new endogenously emergent forces began to challenge the old authoritarian order. Mass movements and urban riots during the early part of the 20th century brought about some political changes and ushered in what has been termed the period of 'imperial democracy'. In 1925 adult male suffrage was introduced and the first elections were held in 1928. The land-owning interests who had controlled the *Diet* up until then suffered some declines and there was an increase in the power of the commercial classes. However, elected politicians – and the cabinets formed by them – continued to play a limited role in government. The military, the bureaucracy, and men of substance, continued to wield political power throughout the period. Even the limited democratic structures established during this period did not last long. The early 1930s saw several assassinations and attempted coups by the radical right, and by 1940 the country had reverted to open authoritarian rule. What is evident from this narrative is that unlike Western Europe, the emergent endogenous forces did not have sufficient strength to bring about an economic, political and institutional transformation of society. As Lockwood (1968: 658) states, 'Once again it was demonstrated that sustained economic progress is never a sufficient condition of democratizing political power'.

During the inter-war period the *zaibatsu* developed into huge agglomerations that were involved in trading, industrial and financial activities and had a close association with the military oligarchy and civil bureaucracy. Fascist rule consisted of an alliance between the *zaibatsu*-led commercial-industrial elite, the military, and the land-owners in the agricultural sector. The military were of course the mainstay of the regime. Between 1920 and 1927 it is estimated that almost 30 per cent of those entering the cadet corps were the sons of landlords, rich farmers, and the urban petty bourgeoisie. This group believed in patriotism and frenetic Emperor worship. In sum, therefore, at the beginning of the Second World War Japan was an incipient capitalist society with a growing middle and working class. However, both economically and politically it continued to be dominated by a quasi-feudal militaristic elite that encouraged conformity with belief systems dominated by Confucian concepts of loyalty, obedience and piety. The industrial and capitalist development that took place occurred under the leadership and auspices of this group, rather than through a democratic bourgeois revolution as happened in Britain, Europe, and the United States.

In the discussion above, we have outlined in some detail the fundamental nature of Japanese society as it existed at the end of the Second World War to show how different this was from the economic and political system as it exists today. Modern Japan can therefore be seen as a product of two short periods of radical institutional change – the first led by a small nationalistic feudal group with progressive ideas that brought about reform from above during the Meiji period, and the second at the end of the Second World War, brought about by an occupying external force. During the second period, as part of the post-war solution, the Allies imposed a new political and economic system on the country, with this new framework being based on western structures and values. In the seven years after 1945 the Allies rewrote laws, restructured the economic and political system, and sought to influence culture and beliefs. In 1946 a new constitution was promulgated which guaranteed freedom of speech, the press, and assembly. Compulsory education up to the ninth grade was introduced and the public universities were opened to all. Democracy was to be the cornerstone of this new Japan. Land was expropriated from the feudal class and distributed to tenants. The ownership of *zaibatsu* was taken away from the families that controlled them and restructured as public companies. As a consequence of these measures significant impetus was given to the previously subordinated classes and Japan soon witnessed the growth of a substantial middle class, both in the urban and rural areas. Over the past 50 years, the exogenously inspired political and economic structures created in the immediate post-war period have in the main endured and strengthened. As a result of the new egalitarian culture traditional values and beliefs were undermined, a fact noted by many Japanese authors of the protest school. Of course in some ways institutional structures have been modified to integrate more traditional Japanese ways of thinking and precepts of behaviour. However, the profound changes in Japan's economic and political systems, its culture and values, as compared with the pre-war period, are evident and need no further elaboration.

INDIA

The analysis below has been drawn from many sources, but is primarily based on Spear (1978), Brown (1985), Bardhan (1984), and Maddison (2006). Let us first consider India's economic performance since the heyday of the Mughal Empire in the 17th century.

The data below show that per capita GDP levels in India during the late Middle Ages were very similar to those in other parts of Asia. In the next four to five hundred years however, up until the early part of the 20th century, income levels stagnated. As discussed in Chapter 6, there is very little evidence to support the view that India had a relatively rich or dynamic economy prior

Table 7.2:   India – per capita GDP levels (1990 international dollars)

1600	1700	1820	1857	1901	1947	1960	1970	1980	1998
550	550	533	520	608	618	753	868	938	1746

Source: Maddison (2006), Tables 2-30, p. 114 and A3-h: 203

Per capita GDP: annual compound growth rates

1820–70	1870–1913	1913–50	1950–73	1973–98
0.00	0.54	–0.22	1.40	2.91

Source: Maddison (2006, Tables A3-d: p. 216)

to the advent of colonialism in the early 18th century. Maddison (2006), based on his careful review of the available data sources, states that income levels probably declined from around 1700 to 1850, initially because of the collapse of the Mughal Empire, and subsequently due to colonial exploitation. The per capita GDP figures do show that there was some positive growth between 1870 and the beginning of the First World War. However, the subsequent period shows negative growth. Stable and sustained growth rates are therefore a purely post-independence phenomenon, with a significant acceleration in economic performance only occurring after the economic reform and market-based liberalization programme began in the early 1980s. This progression of events suggests that, from the point of view of sustained economic growth, the only relevant economic and political developments that need to be studied are those of post-independence India, particularly the economic reform measures that commenced around 1980 and gathered apace in the 1990s. However, since many of these institutional changes have their roots in the past it is useful to commence our investigation at an earlier starting point.

The nature of Mughal rule has already been discussed in Chapter 6. It was essentially an oriental despotism in which a small ruling elite extracted huge surpluses from the peasantry to maintain the structures of a feudal system, while leaving the latter in complete destitution. The system of justice was arbitrary and not protective of property rights. Confiscation of the properties of nobles and rich merchants by the emperor, particularly at the time of death, rendered the accumulation of wealth a hazard. By the middle of the 18th century, Mughal hegemony had been weakened and India had decayed into a system of petty feudal kingdoms that were often at war with each other. Fundamental changes in the economic and political institutions therefore have been a phenomenon that began only with the advent of British rule. After the Battle of Plassey in 1757 British hegemony in India operated under the auspices of the East India Company. The Company's activities were characterized by unequal trade and plunder. The import of cheap textiles from Britain – a product of the Industrial Revolution – resulted in the destruction of the native textile handicrafts, causing further immiserization in the rural areas. From the point of view of economic change the most important development during this period was the introduction of private property in land. Through what is called the Permanent Settlements, starting in 1793, the British gave property rights to landlords and the peasantry. Land became a marketable commodity with the legal system largely protecting property rights. However, this institutional change did not encourage the growth of capitalist agriculture. On the contrary, a parasitic landlordism developed with indebtedness causing much of the land to pass into the hands of the richer peasantry and moneylenders. Thus over time tenant farming and sharecropping became the dominant forms of agricultural production. The National Sample Survey (1958)

conducted soon after Independence showed that India had a huge rural prole-
tariat. Half of rural households owned less than one acre, with about a fifth
owning no land at all.

India became a crown colony after the Mutiny of 1857. British rule,
however, continued to depend on an alliance with the native princes and the
landlords in the countryside. The colonial state and the land-owning classes
soaked up the agricultural surpluses generated by the peasantry. In spite of
this heavy exploitation, the second half of the 19th century did see the emergence of a new industrial-commercial entrepreneurial class and an educated
professional class. By 1892–1893 there were about 150 cotton and jute mills
employing almost 200,000 workers. Thus by the 1880s India could be said to
have had a small but distinct modern middle class. The expansion and growing strength of this educated middle classes was something that was recognized by the colonial rulers themselves, as a statement by Lord Minto, one of
the Viceroys of that time, testifies to (Brown 1985: 141). This new bourgeoisie was opposed to British economic and political domination and its
views finally found expression in the establishment of the Congress Party in
1885.

The Congress supported the new business classes and opposed the old aristocratic interests. Gandhian ideology promoted the idea of purchasing local
goods and supported the fundamental notion of private property. The extent of
Indian industrialization during the pre-independence period was, however, not
an indication of the degree to which an indigenous capitalist class had developed. This was because until Independence, a significant proportion of industry was either owned or controlled by Europeans. At the turn of the century,
for instance, Europeans owned all the jute mills in Bengal and 622 out of a
total of 652 tea plantations. Although there was an increase in Indian ownership during the inter-war period, many of the new industries continued to be
run by, and remained under the control of, British business houses called
Managing Agents. Subsequent to Gandhi's taking over leadership of the
Congress, the social base of the independence movement was widened beyond
the middle classes to include wider sections of the peasantry and other classes
in rural India. In spite of this, however, throughout the pre-independence
period the party remained dominated by the educated middle classes and
reflected their interests and aspirations. This was evident from the composition
of the delegates that attended its annual congresses. Between 1892 and 1909,
for instance, an analysis of the social and occupational origins of its delegates
shows that about 25 per cent were from the landed gentry, 10 to 15 per cent
from the commercial classes, and the balance of 60 to 65 per cent from professional groups such as lawyers, journalists, teachers, etc. (Brown 1985: 180).
This middle class dominance had an important influence in the manner in
which political institutions developed in pre-independence India.

At the turn of the century there were about 30,000 graduates in India out of a population of 220 million. This intelligentsia was heavily influenced by ideas imbibed from the literature of their rulers and so those concerning equality, civil liberties and constitutional self-government became an integral part of their nationalistic thinking. However, the political objectives of the new intelligentsia were not revolutionary. Rather, they were defined in terms of obtaining a greater participation in, and control of, the structures of governance in India. The Liberal victory in Britain in 1906 gave impetus to these aspirations of an increasingly assertive educated class. The colonial government implemented changes whereby more Indians were brought into closer association with the government and administration. Through the Indian Councils Act of 1909, a limited property franchise was introduced. Both the Imperial Legislative Council and the Provincial Councils were then expanded to include a certain proportion of directly elected seats. The intensification of the independence movement during the early part of the 20th century, and the advent of the First World War, resulted in more significant reforms in 1919. Under the Montagu-Chelmsford reforms, a new Legislative Assembly was created with 140 seats, of which 106 were elected. The official majorities in both the Viceroy's Council and the Provincial Councils were abolished. The limited franchise of 1909 was increased to include a nationwide property qualification, as well as special qualifications such as a university degree. The newly constituted Provincial Councils had an electorate of 5 million, and that of the Legislative Council about 1 million. Taken together this meant that about 2.8 million of the population had been enfranchised. This was a very small percentage of the total population. However, there is little doubt that these reforms meant that a move had been made from bureaucratic control to more representative forms of government, as well as from a limited to a mass electorate.

The inter-war period saw a further internal integration of the Indian economy, an expansion of industry, the further growth of an educated middle class, and a strengthening of the freedom movement. All this culminated in the Government of India Act of 1935. This was a point of no return in terms of constitutional development. Dominion status was accepted as the goal, federalism the framework, and parliamentary institutions as the accepted form of government. The powers of the Provincial Assemblies and Provincial Ministries were expanded to encompass all areas of government and the electorate significantly increased. The franchise was still property based, but its scope was enlarged to include about 30 million voters, or about one sixth of the adult population. In the provinces the influence went largely into Indian hands. The importance of the 1935 Act can be seen from the fact that significant elements of the post-independence constitution were drawn from it. At a political level, the institutional transformation of the structures of governance in India took place largely as a consequence of the Acts of 1919 and 1935. These essentially transplanted modified forms of Western political institutions into Indian society. Since the Indian elite had in effect internalized these institutions through an evolutionary process over the previous 75 years, they accepted them as appropriate mechanisms for the satisfaction of the needs and aspirations of an Asian society although they were based on ideas that were alien to indigenous structures, beliefs and ideologies.

At Independence in 1947, therefore, India was characterized by a semi-feudal agricultural sector controlled by parasitic landlordism, a limited modern industrial sector, and a small but politically dominant bourgeoisie. The bourgeoisie included entrepreneurial groups but primarily consisted of the educated professional classes. Over time, a superstructure of democratic and representative institutions had been created, but their role and influence at this point were limited. In terms of the populace at large, the social structure and cultural attitudes continued to be dominated by the hierarchical requirements of the caste system, and traditional beliefs conditioned by karma or the inevitability of one's fate, and consequent passivity. Nevertheless a Constitution had been put in place that was based on a separation of powers, the independence of the judiciary, and the protection of property rights. Consistent with the class alliances within the independence movement, and based on their stated ideology, one of the first steps the new government took was to abolish the remnants of feudalism in agriculture. Although in many areas landlords evicted their tenants so they could hold on to the land, the abolition of the *zamindari* system by and large eliminated the parasitic intermediary class of rent-receiving landlords. The rural areas now came to be dominated by rich peasants and petty landlords, who over the next few decades undertook the capitalist transformation agriculture, particularly after the Green Revolution of the 1970s.

In the industrial sector, since the entrepreneurial classes themselves were small and did not have adequate resources to undertake the industrialization of the country – consistent with the Fabian socialist ideology of the ruling Congress party led by Jawaharlal Nehru – the state itself stepped in to play a major role in this area. This led to a state-directed, command economy type of approach to economic policy in general and industrialization in particular. While this resulted in a major expansion of the industrial sector, since much of it was state-owned, it also resulted in a substantial increase in the bureaucratic control of the economy. Between 1956–1957 and 1965–1966, manufacturing industry expanded at a rate of 6.9 per cent per annum. This decelerated to about 5 per cent per annum in the subsequent 1966–1967 to 1981 period. In spite of its socialist orientation though, state policy favoured the dominant classes in the Indian economy. These were the industrial bourgeoisie, the rich farmers and the middle classes, including educated professionals and the bureaucracy (Bardhan 1984). Consequently, over time these policies encouraged the growth and expansion of a rural capitalist class, propertied business and commercial classes, and an urban middle class (Nayar 1989: 330–350). These forces gathered critical strength and momentum in the late 1970s and early 1980s, causing government policy to gradually shift way from its Nehruvian statist mould to one which was more pro-middle class, pro-business and pro-capitalist.

The new-found strength of the propertied and middle classes can be witnessed in the political fortunes of the Congress Party and its leader Indira Gandhi during the 1970s and early 1980s. Indira Gandhi won the 1971 General Elections based on a populist-socialist agenda that included the nationalization of banks, strengthened anti-monopoly laws, new taxes on the rich, ceilings on the ownership of urban land, and new rural land ceilings. These policies, and the continued emphasis on the public sector as the commanding heights of the economy, however, only served to depress the already low per capita GDP growth rates that had been experienced between 1950 and 1970, with the result that these fell below 1 per cent during the whole decade of the 1970s. The populist policies resulted in a stagnant economy with a rising tide of discontent in the country, leading Indira Gandhi to declare a State of Emergency in 1975, suspend the Constitution and rule by decree. When elections were finally called in 1977, the Congress Party suffered a crushing defeat. The opposition alliance that came to power in 1977 reversed some of the authoritarian excesses of the earlier period. However, due to internal discord, this collapsed and Indira Gandhi came back into power in 1980. This time around the policies of the government were quite different from the populist-socialist agenda of the 1970s. This was not a change of heart in the leadership of the Congress Party, but a recognition of the power of the emergent classes in Indian society both within its structures and amongst its elected representatives. The new government downplayed redistributive concerns, prioritized economic growth, and sought alliances with the private sector. The significance of economic planning, and the role of the Planning Commission, was downgraded. Several high level committees were set up to consider reforms to the economic administration, trade policy, and the fiscal system. Pro-business reforms were also started, including new tax concessions to encourage business investment and a dilution of the Monopolies Act to permit big business to expand.

Table 7.3 gives the real per capita GDP growth rates for the Indian economy since 1950.

As can be seen, the initial acceleration in growth rates commenced around 1980. This was a consequence of the reversal of the anti-growth policies of the 1970s and the introduction of more pro-growth and pro-private sector-oriented policies, starting in 1980. Private sector investment responded immediately to

Table 7.3:   India – per capita GDP growth rates since 1950

1950–1980:	1.3%
1965–1979:	0.7%
1980–1990:	3.8%
1990–2000:	4.1%
2000–2010:	5.5%
2011 (est):	7.0%

Sources: IMF (various); Planning Commission, Government of India

the new more favourable business environment. Thus while gross capital formation by the private corporate sector averaged 2.3 per cent of GDP during the 1975–1980 period, it doubled to 4.5 per cent of GDP between 1980–1985 (Kohli 2006). Subsequent governments reinforced the new policy orientation, with major and radical market-based reforms and a liberalization of the economy being undertaken post-1991. The consequences of this new policy framework are evident from Table 7.3. Over the past 30 years the adoption of a market-oriented system, based on the protection of property and contractual rights, has brought about a major expansion of the Indian economy. Growth rates accelerated significantly after 1990, resulting in a doubling of per capita incomes over the following 20 years. In recent times India has achieved sustained and high levels of growth which today rank amongst the highest in the world.

One of the major impacts of economic liberalization has been to change the structure of the private industrial sector. While industry as a whole still continues to be dominated by state-owned enterprises in terms of assets and sales, there has been a major change in the organized private sector. Table 7.4 is

Table 7.4:   Number and assets of private firms 1988–2005

A. Number of firms:	1988/90	%	2003/05	%
Firms (inc. those incorporated before 1985)	7551	70	5685	40
Firms (inc. those incorporated after 1985)	3031	30	8864	60
Total private registered firms	10582		14549	
B. Asset value (Rupees crores in constant prices):	**1988/90**	**%**	**2003/05**	**%**
Firms (inc. those incorporated before 1985)	73,013	10	269,427	52
Firms (inc. those incorporated after 1985)	3,079	90	244,100	48
Total asset value	76,092		513,527	

extracted from a study by Alfaro and Chari (2009) which covers data for all registered firms in India for the period 1988–2005. The firms covered in the study account for 70 per cent of industrial output and the data include only private firms.

The data show that liberalization, post-1991, made a huge difference to the ability of new firms to enter the market. Whereas incumbent firms (that is, those registered before 1985) accounted for 70 per cent of total firms in the private corporate sector in 1988–1990, it was the new firms registered after 1985 that were the majority by 2003–2005, accounting for 60 per cent of the total. Likewise, while incumbents accounted for 90 per cent of the total assets of the private corporate sector in 1988–1989, confirming that pre-liberalization the private industrial sector was dominated by a few big business houses, this changed radically by 2003–2005. By the latter year new firms accounted for almost 50 per cent of the total asset value of the organized private sector. The broadening of industrial capitalism in India after the advent of liberalization is evident from this. This conclusion is further supported by the fact that by 2010, the small-scale industrial sector – which now accounts for 95 per cent of all the units in the industrial sector – was contributing almost 40 per cent of the total value added of the industrial sector (Ministry of Micro, Small and Medium Enterprises, Government of India 2011).

In the discussion above we noted that the new ruling elite in India after the withdrawal of the British were the professional and educated middle classes, supported by a small indigenous commercial class and sections of the peasantry. In terms of class or group interests there was no reason why this elite should not have moved the Indian political system in a more authoritarian direction after Independence, as happened in most other countries in the developing world after the Second World War. The petty bourgeoisie have, after all, been avid supporters of fascism and authoritarian regimes in many countries. The fact that Indian democracy survived this early period needs some explanation, since no dominant social forces existed at that time whose interests corresponded with the maintenance of a democratic political system or an economic system based on the protection of property and contractual rights. For this we have to turn to the insights on institutional change outlined in Chapter 3. In this we had stated that ideas and ideologies, particularly those that inspire a ruling elite, are a fundamental force in bringing about favourable institutional transitions. India's case provides a good historical example of exactly such a process. The political elite that emerged out of India's freedom struggle were deeply influenced by democratic values, and as we noted above, many of the key demands of the independence movement were in fact to bring into existence representative institutions. Jawaharlal Nehru, the first Prime Minister of India, was for instance a man of high intellectual standing with a deep commitment to western liberal and Fabian socialist values. What distinguished India from other developing countries that had gained independence in the post-war era was therefore the ideological commitment of the political leadership to democratic values and systems. Furthermore, such ideas were to a large extent already ingrained in their thinking and habitual processes from the lengthy experience that they had gained from working with partial democratic structures during the 50 or 60 years of the freedom struggle.

However, it is also evident that such a system – which is not grounded in the interests of the broad majority of the people – is fragile. This fragility was vividly brought out in 1975, when Indira Gandhi, the Prime Minister at that time, suspended the Constitution and declared a state of emergency to avoid prosecution by the courts for corrupt electoral practices. She was supported in her actions to abrogate the democratic processes by a pliant and subservient parliament. In spite of this aberration, however, over the past 60 years the adoption of a political system based on representative institutions and a separation of powers, the protection of property rights and the promotion of a capitalist market economy has resulted in the emergence of strong social forces whose interests now underpin the existence of these very systems. Contrary to the views of some analysts (Bardhan 1984, Kohli 2006), India is not dominated by a narrow heterogeneous ruling alliance, which permits a democratic state to function because it is a convenient mechanism for conflict management and sharing the spoils of the system. In the rural areas a huge agricultural capitalist class has developed as a consequence of the government's promotional policies, in particular since the Green Revolution of the 1970s; in the industrial sector, as we have discussed above, a broad-based industrial capitalist class operating both in the organized and informal sector has emerged; and by some estimates there is now a middle class of some 300 million people. This vast group eschews values, in spite of indigenous variations, that are not very different from their western counterparts. Consequently, democratic and market-based values and institutions have strengthened over time and become an integral part of Indian society. The economic system and institutional structures are now reflections of well-established endogenous forces rather than being implants kept in place by a small intelligentsia inspired by western ideas. Over time, the new institutions themselves have also had a fundamental impact on traditional values and belief systems. Today, competition and advancement are the slogans of new India rather than passivity and inevitability. Democratic values are deeply ingrained in the minds of the people, with high voter turn outs, and aggressively fought elections.

Some of the key developments in the Indian polity over the past 20 years or so, which support this view, are outlined below. The analysis is primarily based on the work of Rudolph and Rudolph (2001, 2002).

- The system has enfranchised the lower castes who constitute the majority of the populace. They now have powerful political parties that specifically claim to represent them, and the 'status growth' of these castes has increased the support and legitimacy of the system.
- Political parties with a base in only one of India's federal states have increased their share of the vote to almost a third. These parties are an expression of the rise of regional interests, and suggest that there has been a considerable expansion of the propertied and middle classes at the regional level.
- A lack of effectiveness and corruption have led to a general disillusionment with politicians and consequently brought about a decline in the status and power of the Executive and legislatures where this group plays a primary role.
- The rising influence of the middle classes, who care about the reliability and security of the system – characteristics which can only come from good governance and the rule of law – has led to increasing support for other institutions that act as enforcers of the rules that safeguard the legitimacy of the democratic system, in particular the Supreme Court and High Courts, the President, and the Election Commission.
- The empowerment of these new centres of power within the polity has led to increased judicial activism to protect the framework of lawfulness and to limit malfeasance; increased use of the discretionary power of the President to hold the Executive in check; and an increased role for the Election Commission to ensure that political parties follow the rules required for free and fair elections. Polls confirm that the increased activism of these institutions has wide public support.
- There has been a massive upsurge in non-governmental organizations (NGOs) and social movements since the early 1980s. By some estimates there are up to 100,000 NGOs at work in India today.
- Matters of good governance have become a common concern for the public at large. The recent hunger strike (August 2011) by one individual – Anna Hazare, a social activist – on the content of anti-corruption legislation, effectively brought the central government to its knees because of the wide public support that the protest stirred up on this issue.

These developments suggest that the political system in India is not a convenient mechanism for conflict management between narrow ruling groups and has instead transitioned to become a broad-based democratic system with checks and balances that continue to evolve with socio-economic change and as such increasingly reflects the aspirations and values of the people.

BOTSWANA

When Botswana gained independence in 1966 it was one of the poorest countries in Africa. It had no paved roads, a handful of university graduates, and nearly half of its active male population worked outside the country. Since then, while the rest of Africa stagnated, Botswana has achieved one of the highest growth rates of per capita income in the world and made significant progress in improving its human and social development indicators. Diamonds, which now account for about 40 per cent of GDP, have of course made a significant contribution to this achievement. However, unlike in other parts of Africa, they have not been a resource curse encouraging rent-seeking and predatory activities on the part of the ruling elite. Botswana has not suffered from the neo-patrimonialism that has been a characteristic of most African states and has undermined economic performance throughout the continent. There is a general consensus that the county's success can be traced to good institutions and good governance. Since independence there have been freely contested elections. The government has also followed good economic policies aimed at protecting private property and limiting predation. Of the six widely used indicators of governance (Kaufmann and Kray 2002), Botswana has the highest scores in Africa for government effectiveness, regulatory quality and the control of corruption. In some of these categories Botswana scores better than France and Japan.

The institutions of a liberal democratic state were put in place by the British colonial masters around the time of independence. It is generally agreed that human agency in the form of Seretse Khama, first President of Botswana, his deputy Quett Masire, and their group, was responsible for the consolidation of democratic structures, the establishment of an effective and relatively uncorrupt bureaucracy, the rule of law, and the pursuance of good economic policies in the country. Some recent studies, however, have downplayed the role of this domestic elite and suggested that the favourable economic and political outcomes are a consequence of certain inherent factors in Tswana society (Acemoglu, Johnson and Robinson 2001; Robinson and Neil Parsons 2006). Let us therefore consider which model better explains institutional development in Botswana. Two major factors have been mentioned in these studies as the underlying reasons for Botswana's particular trajectory of institutional change. First, it is argued that the Tswana developed a state in pre-colonial times, with institutions that limited the power of chiefs and ruling elites. The main focus here is the *kgotla* or popular assembly, which was used to discuss and decide upon any major issue raised by the chief that was of concern to the community. Second, emphasis is given to the fact that the political elites in control of the state at the time of independence were heavily invested in the country's most important economic activity – ranching. It is suggested that this gave them a strong incentive to promote the security of private property and limit predation.

We shall argue here that none of these factors were peculiar to Tswana society, and in fact taken in conjunction with other socio-economic variables, indicate that Botswana was ripe for the kind of neo-patrimonialism and predation seen in other post-independence African societies. Historically Botswana consists of eight inter-related Tswana chiefdoms. Considering African political systems, Fortes and Evans-Pritchard ([1940]1970: 6) state that unlike many of the stateless tribal societies on the continent, the Tswana states fall into that category of societies which had the formal political and administrative structures normally associated with government. Schapera (1940), analysing the political organization of the Ngwato – the largest of the Tswana tribes – elaborates on this issue. The Ngwato had centralized authority, administrative machinery, and judicial institutions. Within these structures there were sharp divisions of rank, status and wealth corresponding to the distribution of power and authority. The chief was the central figure around whom tribal life revolved: 'He is at once its ruler and judge, maker and guardian of its law, and director of its economic life' (Schapera 1940: 64). Although all significant matters of tribal concern were dealt with before the assembly of adult men in the *kgotla*, and it was not unknown for the assembly to overrule the wishes of tribal leaders, the decisions made were generally the same as those arrived at previously by the chief and his personal advisors (1940: 72). Opposition, if any, was bound to be cautious, for fear of reprisals. For instance Kgama III, the great chief of the Ngwato (1837–1923), was known to brook no opposition. For the most part, the *kgotla* was a vehicle to mobilize public support for decisions already made by the community's political elite (Molutsi and Holm 1990). In addition the *kgotla* was not inclusive in that it excluded women, younger adult males and most minority groups from its deliberations (Schapera 1955). In sum, therefore, the indigenous polity was highly authoritarian and had little semblance of democracy. The country's social class structure was rigidly hierarchical and various authorities have indicated that it was probably one of the most inequalitarian in Africa (Holm 1988).

Comparing Botswana with other traditional African societies, it further needs to be noted that there was nothing exceptional about the Tswana *kgotla*. Most pre-colonial African societies, particularly cattle-owning ones, had similar consultative and decision-making structures. These included the *oluhia* of the Bantu, and the tribal assemblies of the Masaai, Nuer and Dinka of Eastern Africa. Neighbouring regions such as Basutoland (subsequently Lesotho) had similar structures as well, but these did not promote a democratic polity. In Lesotho for instance, soon after independence, the Basutoland National Party led by Chief Lebua Jonathan mounted a coup after losing in the elections. The difference between Botswana and the rest of Africa, however, was that in the

former the Botswana Democratic Party (BDP) under Seretse Khama reinforced and amplified the tradition of the *kgotla* so that over time it became an
integral part of the country's democratic institutions (Holm 1988). Thus
around the time of independence the practice of 'freedom squares' was started.
Under this system any political party or group of political activists had the
right to call a freedom square, with very few limits on the freedom of speech.
In practice what this meant was that a political activist, candidate in an election, or anyone who wanted to express a view could use any park or open
space as a 'speaker's corner' to espouse their views. The freedom square has
endured and strengthened over the years and has also become one of the main
forums for political debate in the country. Our analysis therefore indicates that
it is not the inherent nature of the *kgotla*, but the manner in which the ruling
elites in Botswana used this traditional institution to enhance the democratic
polity, which needs to be emphasized.

Let us now consider the role of indigenous cattle ranchers, or what has been
termed the 'beefocracy', in influencing Botswana's favourable institutional
outcomes. Historically the chiefs dominated the tribal economy, by allocating
land, and until the end of the 19th century, by controlling or owning all the
cattle. As a consequence, upon independence in 1966 large cattle ranchers
were a small group led by Seretse Khama, consisting mainly of the traditional
aristocracy and socio-political elite. This economic reality was reflected in a
survey undertaken in 1974, eight years after independence, which showed that
Botswana was not only a very poor country, but also had very high inequalities in income and in the ownership of assets (i.e. mainly cattle). This level of
inequality was comparable with some of the most unequal countries in Latin
America. As Acemoglu et al. (2001) themselves admit, such an environment
where a very small fraction of the population holds all the economic and political power is not the most ideal for the general security of property rights. The
institution of property, for its preservation, requires that effective property
rights and ownership be spread over a large segment of the population.

Engermann and Sokoloff (1997) consider this issue within the context of
the differential growth performance of Latin America and the United States. In
the 1700s there was virtual parity in the GDP per capita of these two regions.
They argue that the differential performance of the two regions since then can
be explained by inequalities in the ownership of land and other resources.
These inequalities influenced the character of the institutions that developed in
the two regions, which in turn affected the economic outcomes. In Latin
America the economy was based on plantations – *latifundia* – and other forms
of large-scale commercial agriculture and livestock production. Most of these
assets were in the hands of people of European descent, leading to a concen-
tration of wealth and extreme inequality. Furthermore, control of the state by
such elites led to laws and legislation that were designed to protect their

economic interests and privileges and inhibit the spread of commercial activities to the general population. This resulted in the establishment of authoritarian, rent-seeking regimes. In the United States, on the other hand, the economy centred around family farms and independent proprietors, leading to a more equal distribution of wealth. This greater equality of economic circumstances encouraged increased participation by the general population in commercial activities, and eventually, more democratic political institutions. Taking per capita incomes as the dependent variables and a range of institutional variable as independent estimators, Engermann and Sokoloff undertake an econometric analysis which confirms their historical hypothesis. It shows that the divergent paths of the two regions since the early 19th century can be explained by reference to the superiority of institutions in the United States, namely more political rights and greater democracy, less rent-seeking, more security of property, etc.

From the above, it is evident that Botswana's favourable institutional performance cannot be ascribed to the presence of a small 'beefocracy'. In fact, in Botswana the problem of inequalities was further compounded by the situation at independence whereby the state had practically no resources and between 1966 and 1971 was financially dependent on Britain to cover the costs of administration and development. Therefore when the diamond revenues came on stream in 1971, the fundamental socio-economic realities meant there was a small but powerful elite, there were gross inequalities of income and wealth, the population at large were illiterate with a handful of school and university graduates, and the state was poor. In the circumstances there were no incentives for the ruling elite to limit rent-seeking and put in place a system that protected property rights. On the contrary, these factors suggest that the country was ripe for the establishment of a neo-patrimonial state once the indigenous elites had taken over the reins of government. Based on this evidence, therefore, it is difficult not to ascribe the good institutions, and the good economic and political governance observed, to a conscious choice made by the political elites led by Seretse Khama. Rather, Botswana's experience – like India's under Jawaharlal Nehru – is a powerful example of the key role played by ideas, ideology and human agency in influencing the institutional trajectory of a country and catalysing the eventual emergence of larger social forces in whose interests the survival and strengthening of the new institutions so created would be.

DISCONTINUOUS CHANGE

The case studies discussed above indicate that institutional transitions in the non-Western world have characteristics that are different from the West

European model. First, they reveal how the actions of key individuals or small highly motivated domestic groups – or in one case even a powerful external force – can influence the institutional trajectory of a country, with major changes occurring in an historically abrupt rather than an evolutionary manner. Even in India, where institutional change at the political level seems to have occurred more gradually, most of the structures and systems were in fact put in place between 1919 and 1935. A conscious intervention by human agency is therefore a fundamental force in institutional change. Second, they show that new institutions can be successfully introduced by an elite group, inspired by ideas and values that are exogenous to the system and not necessarily in consonance with the traditional interest structures or the prevailing cultural attitudes and beliefs. At the same time, however, the historical events in the case study countries also indicate that, at least initially, the rules of the game for the new set of economic and political institutions created in this manner are by no means self-enforcing and therefore there is no guarantee that a successful institutional transition will occur. Hodgson (2006: 7), arguing in the old institutionalist tradition (Veblen [1899]1949), states that for such institutions to be successfully established and become the rules of a society, they have to be enforced to the point that the avoidance or performance of the required behaviour becomes customary or acquires a normative status.

Given the lack of a strong domestic base for the new institutions in the countries we have discussed above, the elites that introduced or inherited these systems and structures could quite easily have put their countries onto different institutional paths, and there would have been little or no resistance from other social groups to such a move. As it happens, this is exactly what occurred in most of the post-independence developing world. Here ruling elites used their anti-colonial and nationalist credentials to keep the population in check, while causing rent-seeking and predatory institutions of direct benefit to themselves to develop. The major difference between our case study countries where successful institutional transitions seem to have occurred, and the large number of other countries in the developing world where institutional decay has been observed, is that the ruling groups in the former were committed to ideas and ideologies which were by and large democratic and capitalist and to the preservation and functioning of the systems put in place based on these ideologies. This resulted in a process of 'reconstitutive downward causation' (Hodgson 2006: 7) whereby the new institutions led to regularities of behaviour and concordant habits based upon congruent purposes and beliefs amongst significant sections of the populations, who initially may not have necessarily shared these beliefs and values. As a consequence over time, the new institutional frameworks facilitated the emergence of larger social forces in whose direct interests lay the preservation of these very institutions. Our case studies therefore provide substance for one of the main propositions derived from the new institutional economics literature – that ideas and ideology, in particular those held by a ruling elite, matter, and are thus a fundamental force in institutional change.

The post-independence economic history of India provides an excellent example of this process. The economic and political institutions put in place, and the economic policy followed by the new state since the early 1950s – in spite of a plethora of bureaucratic controls – by and large promoted the development of a capitalist economy. This resulted in the growth of a strong agricultural and industrial capitalist class, and a powerful educated and professional middle class, which eventually asserted its interests and brought about a market-oriented liberalization of the Indian economy, initially in the early 1980s and then more forcefully after 1991. Likewise, in terms of political institutions, there exists today a much broader political consensus, and much greater support from wide social classes, for India's democratic system, than there was even 25 to 30 years ago. A challenge to the system, as occurred in the mid 1970s, is extremely unlikely, with no significant political group that may even venture to question the legitimacy of existing institutions. Similar historical processes can be observed in our other case study countries as well, where currently there are powerful social forces that accept the rules of the game, resulting in the economic and political institutions gaining self-enforcing characteristics. In sum, therefore, the experience of Japan, India and Botswana gives substance to Montesquieu's observation that at the birth of new polities, leaders will mould institutions, whereas afterwards institutions will mould leaders (Putnam 1992: 26).

8. Southern Sudan: a case study in discontinuous institutional change[1]

In the preceding chapters we reviewed: the empirical and historical evidence on the factors underlying modern economic growth in the West; the more recent good economic performance in certain developing countries; and some of the favourable institutional transitions that have occurred in the non-western world. The empirical evidence considered in Chapter 5 showed that institutions are the deep determinants of growth and development. The vast majority of econometric studies reviewed also show that variables of economic and political governance, such as the security of property rights, the rule of law, the quality of the bureaucracy, and the absence of corruption, which reflect the nature of institutions in a society, explain most of the observed cross-country differences in the growth of per capita income in the developing world. The historical evidence considered in Chapter 6 illustrated that the necessary favourable political and economic frameworks in Europe emerged through a gradual evolutionary process that took several hundred years and was the consequence of an interaction and clash between forces largely endogenous to those societies. In the eastern medieval civilizations, on the other hand, no such institutional change occurred. The economic and political systems continued to be dominated by predatory feudal despotisms. Consequently, there were no constraints on arbitrary power, which as we saw in Chapter 6, is a fundamental pre-requisite for the development of a modern state and the protection of property and contractual rights. In recent times, however, some favourable institutional transitions have occurred in the non-western world. The evidence from the case studies considered in Chapter 7 suggests that such transitions have not been the consequence of deep historical forces that evolved endogenously in these societies. Rather, the transitions

---

[1]   The analysis in this chapter is based on primary data collected from field work and an active participation in Southern Sudan's institutional development programme over the period 2004–2009. In early 2004, the present author was one of the key personnel on the USAID team which undertook high-level consultations with the Sudan People's Liberation Movement/Army (SPLM/A) in order to design a comprehensive institutional and governance-related programme. Subsequently, he led a major component of this programme, the focus of which was to establish the key ministries and other apex organizations in the Executive of the new Government of Southern Sudan (GOSS).

were brought about through the conscious intervention of human agency, either in the form of a small but progressive local elite, or by an external force, or a combination of the two.

The evidence presented in Chapters 5, 6 and 7 on economic performance and institutional change conforms to the 'visible hand' and 'made order' perspective of this study. This hypothesis emphasizes the key role of human agency and a conscious human intervention in introducing and establishing the political and economic frameworks required for sustainable economic growth and development to occur. It therefore provides a model which has potential applicability to development policy and practice in certain circumstances. These circumstances are the presence of a local ruling elite who are inspired by democratic and capitalist ideas, and in conditions where such an elite may not be strong enough to engineer the necessary institutional change, support from an exogenous force or forces inspired by similar ideas and ideologies. Against this view, it could be argued that this was more or less the situation that existed at the time of decolonization and the emergence of newly independent countries in the developing world. At the time of their independence, most developing countries were bequeathed a strong set of formal democratic political institutions and a market economy characterized by different degrees of backwardness. However, over time as these institutions did not conform to the interests of the new ruling elites there was institutional decay and the establishment of rent-seeking predatory states, particularly in Sub-Saharan Africa. Our case studies of Botswana and India contradict this point of view. They show that where the new ruling elites were inspired by progressive ideas and ideologies, institutional decay did not occur. Rather, efforts were made to strengthen the formal institutions inherited at the time of independence and over time the capitalist developmental policies that were put in place resulted in the emergence of economic and social forces, such as an educated middle class and strong indigenous business groups, whose interests underpinned the continuance and reinforcement of these very institutions and systems.

The most recent institutional transitions, whether successful or with outcomes that are still uncertain, have occurred in the context of war or civil war. A partial list would include the Democratic Republic of Congo (DRC), Liberia, Sierra Leone, Southern Sudan and Libya, in Africa; Afghanistan and Iraq, in Asia; and Yugoslavia, in Europe. All these cases have involved differing degrees of external or 'exogenous' involvement. Of these, Yugoslavia probably represents the most successful case of institutional change, where the former communist state has now been replaced by a number of democratic market-based republics, all of whom are likely to become members of the European Union in due course. In the early period of transition, in particular the creation of democratic republics in Slovenia and Croatia, the domestic forces within these societies played the dominant and leading role. However, the emergence of the later republics required significant intervention by the international community, including an armed campaign by NATO.

In Afghanistan and Iraq, the prime movers of institutional change have been invading external forces. In both countries, and particularly in Iraq, the United States and its allies have introduced formal democratic structures and systems to varying degrees, but the extent to which these institutions have been accepted or absorbed into these societies is by no means clear. The African examples mentioned above present a mixed picture as well. In the DRC, for instance, the international community – led by the United Nations – put in considerable human and financial efforts to introduce some formal democratic institutions and conduct a 'one-off' major election to select the new government. Subsequent reports of repression against opposition groups and increasing levels of corruption suggest that these external efforts might have facilitated the end of the civil war in that country, but have also set the stage for the emergence of a typical rent-seeking and predatory African state. On the other hand, in Liberia, Sierra Leone and Southern Sudan, the new post-conflict ruling elite groups, with considerable support from the international community, seem to be more committed to bringing about favourable institutional transitions. Evidence to this effect can be found in the fact that both Liberia and Sierra Leone have Polity scores that are greater than three (the level associated with the presence of democratic institutions), and over the past ten years both countries have shown significant improvements in macroeconomic management as well as their overall governance and corruption scores.

To give substance to our 'made order' hypothesis in the African context, in this chapter we shall undertake a detailed analysis of institutional change in Southern Sudan, which recently became Africa's newest country. This region of Sudan provides an appropriate case study, because it is an isolated area of central Africa where the social order until very recently was primarily maintained through tribal structures and informal traditional institutions (Evans-Pritchard 1941). Independence in 1956 did not contribute much to this region in terms of formal governance structures. Instead the civil war between the central government and southern rebels – which commenced around the time of independence and continued for almost 50 years – destroyed the few formal structures that had been inherited from colonial times. The period between the 1950s and the present day therefore offers us a situation wherein it is possible to assess whether institutional change occurs in response to evolutionary endogenous forces and socio-economic circumstances prevailing over a long period of time, or whether it requires the conscious and forceful intervention of human agency. The fact of conflict does not change this assessment. Historically, after all, war and conflict have played a major catalytic role in bringing about the emergence of new institutions. As it happens, and as discussed in greater detail below, during the period of the civil war much of the socio-economic fabric of the region was destroyed; the traditional tribal institutions decayed or remained static at best; and no formal institutions to speak of or viable mechanisms of governance emerged. Nevertheless, the ruling group that emerged through the civil war in the southern region had progressive political and economic ideas and was particularly open to assistance and support from the international community to build a democratic capitalist society. This context gave external forces a window of opportunity to undertake a serious economic and political engagement with the domestic elite with a view to bringing about fundamental institutional change.

Brinkerhoff and Brinkerhoff (2002), summarizing the concepts and practice of international assistance underlying the current worldwide governance reform movement, state that these have converged into a common model with economic, administrative and political dimensions. The economic and administrative dimensions include developing a market-supporting regulatory framework; maintaining the rule of law and enforcement of property rights; promoting private sector investment; ensuring sound macroeconomic policy management; establishing an efficient bureaucracy and public administration system; encouraging decentralization; and enhancing service delivery. The political dimension of the model focuses on democratic governance mechanisms, including electoral systems for the selection of leaders, improved oversight of the executive, political accountability, and the devolution of power. In terms of the governments or agencies that have taken a leading role in providing international assistance in the areas mentioned above, Brinkerhoff and Brinkerhoff (2002) indicate that the World Bank and IMF have played a primary role in economic and market governance reforms; the World Bank and agencies of the United Nations have concentrated on improving public administration systems, service delivery, and decentralization; and bilateral organizations, such as the United States Agency for International Development (USAID) and Britain's Department for International Development (DFID), have been the main actors in promoting democratic governance, including electoral systems, civil society and legislative strengthening, judicial reform and anti-corruption. Considering democratic governance in particular, Carothers (1999) states that the US government's programmes have been the most systematic effort to build state institutions, procedures and legal frameworks from scratch; revise constitutions; strengthen the rule of law; support the legislature and promote free and fair elections; and strengthen civil society and an independent media.

Thus USAID's Democracy and Governance programme has been in operation for almost 20 years, accounting for between 10 and 15 per cent of its total budget in recent years. Given this track record therefore, and its experience in the area – in terms of being the external force to assist Southern Sudan's emergent leadership in building new institutions of democratic governance, accountability and a market-based society – USAID clearly had a comparative advantage. This factor was reinforced by the unusual political situation in Southern Sudan, which was that although many of the leading western nations had been involved in the peace process leading to the end of the civil war and the signing of Comprehensive Peace Agreement (CPA) in 2005, because of issues relating to the sovereignty of Sudan as a whole, most of these countries were hesitant to engage separately with the liberation movement in the southern region or facilitate the creation of new governance structures and institutions. The US government, on the other hand, did not have any such hesitations because the central government based in Khartoum was seen as a sponsor of terrorism, having hosted Osama bin Laden at one stage, and consequently support for the Southern Sudan People's Liberation Movement (SPLM) had been part of US foreign policy for some time.

As a consequence of this policy stance, the US government fielded a Democracy and Governance team to visit Southern Sudan in mid 2004. The objective of the exercise was to engage the leadership of the SPLM in consultations that would result in the design of a programme of wide-ranging and deep institutional interventions, which – while being consistent with the provisions of the CPA – would result in the establishment of effective and accountable structures of governance in the region. The team's view was that Southern Sudan was at a crossroads. An historical window of opportunity existed to build a new Southern Sudan based on principles of democratic governance and a market-based economy. However, if this opportunity were not grasped, there was a strong likelihood that the region would fall into the usual African pattern of authoritarian government, with mismanagement and poor governance. Worse still, there was the possibility that the area would go through a process, as had occurred in neighbouring Somalia, where the lack of a legitimate governance framework would lead to the spread of warlordism and the accompanying socio-political disintegration. The proposals put before the SPLM leadership, therefore, while taking account of the region's specific socio-historical characteristics, were based on the idea that open and inclusive systems of economic and political governance should be put in place, arbitrary rule needed to be controlled through the establishment of a political system based on a constitutional separation of powers, and a new structure of government must be created that would deliver services to the people in the short run and promote a free market-oriented economic system in the long run. In order to analyse the nature and impact of this 'made order' programme, we shall first outline the socio-economic context in southern Sudan, including the historical background to the conflict.

TRADITIONAL SOCIETY

Southern Sudan consists of the three provinces of Sudan that were defined as the Southern Region during the colonial period, prior to independence in 1956. The region has a population of about 12 million, with an African-Christian-Animist majority, as against the northern provinces of Sudan, which are primarily Arab and Muslim. Although the south has several distinct tribal groups, the two major tribes are the Dinka and the Nuer, who ethnically form part of the River Lake Nilotic peoples of East Africa. To have a proper under-standing of the underlying institutional setting of this pastoralist society, it is first necessary to consider its tribal political organization. The discussion presented below is based on research that E.E. Evans-Pritchard undertook on the Nuer in the 1930s (Evans-Pritchard 1941) and other work by Fortes and Evans-Pritchard ([1940]1970). However, various ethnographic sources have also been consulted – such as Radcliffe-Brown and Forde (1970) and Lienhardt (1958) – and on this basis it has been found that Evans-Pritchard's analysis is equally applicable to the Dinka, who are in effect the tribal 'cousins' of the Nuer.

Fortes and Evans-Pritchard ([1940]1970), in their study of eight primitive African societies, concluded that the Nuer were part of that group of soci-eties which lacked centralized authority, administrative machinery, and a constituted set of judicial institutions, in which there were sharp divisions of rank, status, or wealth. The Nuer, and other African tribes similar to them, therefore formed a group which could be classified as stateless societies. In the absence of an over-arching hierarchical political authority the social structure was based on kinship, with linkages between clans being provided through a system of segmentary lineage. This lineage structure provided the framework of the political system and governed relations between indepen-dent clans who controlled their own territorial segments. The function of chiefs in this system, whether they had ritualistic authority like the leopard skin chief (or fishing spear chiefs in the case of the Dinka) or had been given official status as part of government structures, was to play a mediating role along with elders or influential members of aristocratic clans, in resolving disputes, based on established conventions. The constitution of Nilotic tribes was therefore highly individualistic and libertarian, with an absence of bureaucracy, or any form of centralized government, in their political struc-tures. This was best termed as a system of 'ordered anarchy' (Fortes and Evans-Pritchard [1940]1970: 296). This individualism was reinforced by the manner in which economic assets, particularly land, were held. Since such assets were held communally by the clan with common usage being permit-ted for all, these furthered a sense of equality amongst all members of a community.

In spite of the severe dislocations during the civil war, the social and political structures described above have persisted in more or less their original forms until the modern day. These structures therefore provide the underlying setting and context in which subsequent changes to the institutional framework of Southern Sudan need to be viewed.

INSTITUTIONS DURING THE CIVIL WAR

The civil war between the north and the south commenced around the time of independence in 1956 and continued intermittently for a period of 50 years until the Comprehensive Peace Agreement (CPA) was signed in January 2005. Over two million people, mainly from the south, died during the conflict. The fundamental division between the north and the south was well recognized in colonial times. One of the principal elements of the British Native Administration policy was to administer the south as a separate entity from the north, with measures such as the Closed Districts Ordinance, in place to prevent the spread of Islam and Arab influence in the south. Discontent in the south with the manner in which the independence process was evolving – and in particular increased fears of northern domination and colonization – led to the Torit Mutiny in 1955. Soldiers of the Southern Equatoria Corps killed their northern officers and fled into the bush. The rebellion emerged as the *Anyanya* (snake venom) secessionist movement in the early 1960s. Unable to suppress the movement, the Khartoum regime under General Numeiri negotiated with the southern political leaders, resulting in the Addis Ababa Agreement of 1972. Under that agreement, the three southern provinces were brought into a new self-governing Southern Sudanese Region, with a Regional Assembly of 60 members and a High Executive Council. The Regional Assembly was empowered to elect or remove the President of the High Executive Council, subject to confirmation by the President of the Republic. The first elections for the Assembly were held in 1973. The Regional Government was to have control over health, education, mineral and natural resources, and the police.

The absence of any investment from the central government, in-fighting within the southern political leadership, and the continuation of a low-level guerrilla war by elements of the Anyanya who refused to accept the Addis Ababa agreement, resulted in an ineffective administration in the south during the decade following the establishment of the Southern Regional government. By the early 1980s, the Addis Ababa agreement had itself begun to look shaky as a result of Numeiri's wavering commitment to its provisions, and in particular, his efforts to abolish the Southern Regional government and re-divide the south. In mid 1983, dissatisfaction with Numeiri's policies resulted in major mutinies and the desertion of soldiers from several garrisons across the south.

These forces soon unified with remnants of the earlier secessionist movement and formed the Sudan People's Liberation Movement/Army (SPLM/SPLA) under the leadership of Colonel John Garang. A new phase of the civil war had begun, one which only ended twenty-two years later with the signing of the CPA in 2005.

During the course of the civil war the SPLM/A gained control over most of the rural areas. The SPLA divided the south into a number of areas or zones, which were put under military/civil administrators and commanders. At a local level the tribal structures, particularly the role of the chiefs in settling conflicts based on customary law, was reinforced. After the first National Convention in 1994 the SPLM began a limited process of separating military and civilian structures. The Civil Administration of New Sudan (CANS) was set up to administer a new hierarchy of rural civil administration. Within this framework a number of secretariats were established in areas such as finance, health, education, legal affairs and local government. However, these secretariats remained rudimentary and with limited personnel up until the end of the war. Given the fluid nature of the conflict, military structures continued to dominate the movement throughout the period. In terms of a formal legal framework, the SPLM did adopt a small number of civil and criminal laws in the last days of the civil war. These were either borrowed from the north, or based on earlier colonial laws. In any event, in the absence of an established judicial structure, they had very little applicability in practice.

The northern government, on the other hand, continued to control Juba, the capital of the south, and a few other major towns. After the abolition of the Southern Regional government in 1983, the south was re-divided into a number of smaller provinces under the control of a Coordinating Council. Provincial administrations, based on the old colonial bureaucratic model – with ministries staffed by under secretaries, deputy secretaries, clerks and messengers – were established in all the provinces. Since the northern government did not have physical control over the provinces, the purpose was primarily political rather than to provide a proper civil administration. As a consequence the provincial administrative structures were housed in the few military garrison towns under the control of the north and did little other than exist. The laws and legal structures governing these provincial administrations were those of the north (i.e. based on the *Shari'a*).

At the beginning of 2005, therefore, the institutional and governance frameworks in Southern Sudan were fragmented and fragile. The civil administration was divided between rudimentary structures in the SPLM-controlled areas and an unknown number of relatively low-skilled personnel in the northern controlled garrison towns. The limited social services being provided to the population were being delivered through international NGOs and funded by donor organizations. There was no Constitution. The legal framework consisted of a small number of laws that had been approved by the SPLM Leadership Council. The SPLM itself was the only legitimate political force, with almost all the other political groupings operating as armed militias. These militias tended to have control over their own areas and sub-territories. Although there was a formal distinction between the SPLM and the SPLA, in practice it was the senior commanders of the guerrilla army who controlled the movement's Leadership Council. Finally, after all these years of civil war, there were no civil society organizations, information dissemination systems, or media coverage, to speak of.

THE COMPREHENSIVE PEACE AGREEMENT

The CPA (Government of Southern Sudan 2005) was the product of negotiations between the two main protagonists in the civil war: the government in Khartoum led by the National Congress Party (NCP) and the rebels in the south led by the SPLM. The negotiations, which commenced around 2002, were mediated by the Inter-Governmental Authority on Development (IGAD), a grouping which included the UN, AU, and interested developed and developing nations. The Power Sharing Protocol (IGAD, Kenya 2004) of the CPA contains the most wide-ranging effort to provide Southern Sudan with a formal institutional framework in its history. Since the structures contained in the protocol have had an important influence on the direction of institutional development in the south, it is necessary to fully describe and analyse its content.

Under the CPA, Southern Sudan was to establish its own autonomous government – the Government of Southern Sudan (GOSS) – using a model of asymmetric federalism, with the possibility of secession through a referendum, after a six-year interim period. Southern Sudan was to have its own constitution and legislative assembly, as were the ten southern states in the region. The Power Sharing Protocol defined the exclusive competencies of the three major levels of government. The national government in Khartoum had exclusive control over defence, foreign affairs, immigration, customs, currency and monetary policy. The Government of Southern Sudan could maintain a security apparatus and military in accordance with the provisions of the CPA; implement taxes and raise revenues to finance its own budget; establish a GOSS civil service; and undertake the planning and coordination of social services in the southern region. The ten state governments in the south could establish their own civil services; oversee local government structures; provide social services; and undertake local taxation to raise revenues for local expenditures.

One of the consequences of having fought a brutal dictatorial regime, and having had the strong support of western democratic countries during the latter part of the liberation struggle, was that the leadership of the SPLM had made their commitment to the creation of a democratic society based on the protection of human rights and the rule of law well known. This commitment was reflected in the Power Sharing Protocol, which stated that its underlying principles were good governance, transparency, the rule of law and democracy. Thus it was agreed that human rights should be protected in accordance with international conventions and treaties and that there should be the right to liberty; the right to fair trial; protection against arbitrary arrest or detention; freedom of expression, thought and religion; and the right to peaceful assembly. Furthermore, there should be fair electoral laws, the free establishment of political parties, and elections at all levels of government, with the first general elections being held three years after the signing of the CPA. Finally, a decentralized system of government was to be established with a significant devolution of powers to the states. From the content of the protocols contained in the CPA, as described above, it is evident that the leadership of the southern rebel movement were strongly influenced by progressive ideas and ideologies, which as the case studies in Chapter 7 show is a necessary condition for any successful institutional transition to occur.

DEMOCRACY AND GOVERNANCE (DG) PROGRAMME

In the analysis that follows, we shall consider how the provisions of the CPA, and external interventions, mainly under the auspices of the US government's Democracy and Governance Programme, but also including other programmes that were started subsequently by other organizations such as the United Nations, World Bank and DFID, have affected the institutional trajectory of Southern Sudan since 2005. In the north, the regime continues to be dominated by a military dictatorship which is intent on maintaining a genocidal campaign in Darfur. Consequently, the provisions of the CPA have had little impact. However, in the southern region, as we noted earlier, the willingness and interest of the military/political elite to create a more open society have created a different set of circumstances. In developing the DG programme, two key characteristics of Southern Sudan's traditional political structure – the libertarian and individualistic culture of the people, and the fact that the region was effectively starting with a *tabula rasa* of formal institutions – were kept in mind. Both factors encouraged the democracy and governance team to translate the provisions of the CPA into bold proposals for democratic governance. The specific elements of the programme were to be:

- to provide some facilitation for the preparation of a democratic constitution and a legal framework that would enshrine a separation of powers and guarantee civil liberties;

- to give wide-ranging support for the establishment of responsive central institutions in the Executive, along with transparent and accountable systems for economic and political governance;
- to help the SPLM in transforming itself from a rebel movement to a democratic political party;
- to assist in designing and funding a programme that would increase access to public information and facilitate the growth of an independent media sector.

Given the intensive political engagement that such actions would involve, wide-ranging and detailed discussions were held with the SPLM leadership at the highest level to ensure there was a full consensus between the domestic and external forces on the content and approach to be taken. It was agreed that since most institutional structures and decision-making systems had to be built from scratch the question of sequencing was not relevant and a simultaneous approach to implementing activities on all fronts should be undertaken. The major interventions undertaken by USAID's DG programme and other donors, and any observable influence that these may have had on important variables of economic and political governance between the period 2005 to 2009, will be considered below. The discussion will assess whether the new institutional frameworks, systems and other activities have had any impact on controlling arbitrary power and introducing checks and balances into the political system; encouraging federalism and a devolution of authority; improving the rule of law and the security of property and contractual rights; improving economic governance and macroeconomic management and controlling corruption; and changing the culture in government to become one which is more oriented towards the requirements of a modern nation state that delivers services to its people.

THE CONSTITUTION

Although Southern Sudan became independent in July 2011, it is still governed by an Interim Constitution. Adopted in 2005 (Government of Southern Sudan 2005a), this is primarily based on the principles and provisions contained in the Power Sharing Protocol (2004) of the CPA. Thus the clauses relating to the protection of human rights and civil liberties, the establishment of political parties, free and fair elections, and judicial independence are drawn from there. Since the representation of different political parties in the new South Sudan Assembly had already been agreed to as part of the CPA, the existence of a multi-party system was a foregone conclusion. The establishment of a decentralized system of government, with a significant devolution of powers, was also part of this agreement. However, on a range of other issues – such as the protection of property rights, the separation of powers between the executive and other branches of government, the limitations on the powers of the President and his terms of office, the oversight powers of the legislature, the relative powers of the federal versus state governments, and the extent of judicial independence – the content of the constitutional provisions still had to be agreed upon and it was by no means evident what the final conclusion would be. The drafting committee for the Constitution had members from varied backgrounds with differing views. It had human rights lawyers from the South Sudan Law Society, tribal leaders who believed that to accommodate Southern Sudan's diversity of tribal groupings the provincial governments should be given considerable autonomy, and political leaders from the SPLM, who being more concerned about security and control issues argued for less federalism and a greater centralization of powers.

Within this complex arena the DG programme, and the support given it under the auspices of the United Nations, played a crucial catalytic role in bringing about consensus in the drafting committee of the Constitution. Members of this committee, along with other senior leaders from various political parties, were exposed to resource materials and various draft consti-tutions that reflected alternative possibilities and international best practice. Expert opinion was also provided which emphasized that a democratic consti-tution was necessary to repair the dislocation and disintegration caused by the long-running civil war and encourage the emergence of an inclusive and participatory society. The eventual draft Constitution that emerged from this process can only be termed as exemplary for a war-torn society with no tradi-tion of democratic governance. The draft had a number of standard elements found in other countries such as a Bill of Rights, the limitation of the Presidential term to two terms, and a separation of powers between the exec-utive, legislature, and judiciary. It also clearly specified the right to own prop-erty as a fundamental right, and that no expropriation could occur save through the due process of the law, and then in return for fair compensation. However, it also went well beyond the CPA in a number of respects. Judicial indepen-dence was strengthened by the requirement of a two-thirds majority in the Legislature for the removal of justices of the Supreme Court. Further – unlike in many other countries where the judiciary are under the financial control of a parent ministry in the executive – the draft Constitution proposed that the judiciary would maintain the right to prepare budgets and manage their finan-cial affairs.

The proposed draft also reinforced the vision of a federal system of govern-ment, as contained in the CPA. The states within the federal system were to have their own constitutions and legislative bodies, with a considerable devo-lution of administrative powers. These included the appointment and control of state civil services, oversight of all local government institutions within the state, the management and provision of all social services, and the ability to raise local taxes to finance the state budget. That the draft Constitution was contentious, and probably seen as being too 'democratic' or promoting too much 'federalism' by some key members of the political leadership, is shown by the fact that for many months after its preparation it was neither debated nor placed before the Leadership Council of the SPLM. The draft only came into the public domain after the death of Dr John Garang, the Chairman of the SPLM/A, in August 2005, and it was adopted by the SPLM and the Legislative Assembly soon after.

At a formal level, the Constitution of a country is the most important institution governing the manner in which its political and economic systems function. In Southern Sudan's case, the Constitution guarantees a separation of powers between the executive, the legislature, and the judiciary. Formally, therefore, there is a dispersion of political power. Although it is hard to predict how this Constitution will influence the long-term evolution of the other institutions of governance in the country, given the commitment of the political leadership to its provisions, one can expect that it should have a major impact on their functioning. In the discussion below we shall consider the manner in which some of the institutional structures governed by the Constitution – such as the federal system, the legislature, and the legal system – are performing. This preliminary evidence is suggestive that these institutions are in fact working to control the arbitrary exercise of power and introducing checks and balances into the system in a manner which is likely to result in a more participatory and democratic form of governance emerging over time.

THE LEGISLATURE

In consonance with the principle of a separation of powers, the Interim Constitution gives the South Sudan Legislative Assembly (SSLA) a strong role in the structure of governance. The Assembly's significant functions include approving the laws of the land and enacting other enabling legislation; approving the plans, programmes, policies and budget of the GOSS; overseeing the performance of the Executive and summoning Ministers as required: and having the power to impeach the President in certain circumstances. Apart from these normal oversight functions, the Constitution gives the SSLA some innovative powers. First, it has the role of regulating the terms and conditions of service of the judiciary. This is an important function, one that is intended to strengthen the position of the judiciary *vis-à-vis* the Executive, thereby increasing the dispersion of political power between the various arms of government. Second, to strengthen the concept of multi-partyism and increase the respect of the party in power for the political opposition, the Constitution gives the Leader of the Opposition in the SSLA a high constitutional status. This position has been included in the official hierarchy of the State and ranked fourth in terms of precedence after the President, Vice-President and Speaker. As can be seen from these provisions, the powers of the Legislature go well beyond what may have been envisaged in the CPA.

After the formation of GOSS in July 2005, and with the elections not to occur before 2010, the first members of the SSLA were chosen through a process which involved public input. Gatherings attended by the general public, tribal elders, and activists from political parties and civic groups, were held in each of the 200 Assembly constituencies to select the candidates. As envisaged in the CPA, 70 per cent of the members were from the SPLM, with the balance being southerners representing other political parties such as the National Congress Party (NCP), the Union of Sudan African Parties (USAP1 and USAP2), the South Sudan Defence Force (SSDF), etc. With such a domi-nance of the ruling SPLM in the legislative assembly, there was considerable danger that it would play a minimal oversight function over the Executive. This possibility was compounded by the fact that when the SSLA was first convened in 2006, almost none of its members had any legislative experience or were clear about the constitutional role of the Assembly. In the circum-stances, the DG programme played a significant role in putting in place an intensive programme of training for the new legislators. This consisted of a detailed consideration of the Constitution, training in legislative and oversight functions, and support for the Speaker in setting up a number of committees in the legislature. These included a Legal Committee to review draft laws and other legislation and a Finance Committee to oversee the government's economic policies, programmes and annual budget.

As a consequence of these interventions, the SSLA has begun to play an increasingly active legislative and oversight role. In spite of the SPLM's domi-nance in the legislature, Ministers have been repeatedly summoned to explain many of their actions. Since 2006, the Budget proposals of the Ministry of Finance have been closely reviewed and each year a number of amendments are made to the proposed pattern of expenditure. The Legal Committee and other SSLA members have played a particularly active role in scrutinizing the key laws in the new legal framework being prepared by the Executive. In a number of cases the laws were returned to the Ministry of Legal Affairs because members felt that the provisions were not adequately explained or justified, or were incompatible with the principles contained in the Constitution. As a result of the 2010 general elections, the overwhelming pres-ence of the SPLM in the SSLA has increased. About 90 per cent of the legis-lators are now from the ruling party. However, given that the basic structures of executive oversight have been put in place, and will be further strengthened in the future, it can be expected that the SSLA will play an increasingly significant role in Southern Sudan's system of governance over time.

THE LEGAL FRAMEWORK

Until the establishment of the new government in mid 2005, Southern Sudan had a legal framework that had been derived from the northern regime in Khartoum. Many laws had their origins in colonial times. As a consequence, the few laws that were in place were repressive and not protective of civil liberties, human rights or property rights. Given the new Constitution, a major exercise was started under the DG programme to work with the Ministry of Legal Affairs to revise all the laws and come up with a framework that was consistent with the new democratic dispensation. A total of about 40 key laws were revised or drafted from scratch between 2006 and 2008. Some of the significant laws that have been enacted so far include the Penal Code, the Criminal Procedures Code, the Civil Procedures Code, the Law on Evidence, the Judiciary Act, and a Human Rights Act to enable a new independent commission to be set up. In terms of the economic enabling environment, a Companies Act, a Private Arbitration Act and an Investment Act have been passed. Through these new laws, many of the repressive elements of the pre-2005 laws – such as restrictions on the freedom of assembly, the broad definition of what was considered subversive, the easy ability of the state to expropriate private property, etc. – have in the main been eliminated and a legal framework for the development of a market-based system of democratic governance has been put in place. Along with the provisions in the Constitution this framework has strengthened private property rights and the ability of the courts to enforce contractual agreements made within the provisions of the law. One indicator that the new laws are encouraging private economic activity is that formal private contracting has become a common phenomenon in the business community, both between private agents and between the private sector and the government.

FEDERALISM

As noted earlier, under the CPA and the Interim Constitution of Southern Sudan, a federal system – with constitutional protections and exclusive competencies for the states – has been put in place. The purpose here has been to bring about a genuine devolution of power and prevent any dominance either by the central government or the current regional government in Juba. Thus the ten southern states have their own Constitutions, elected assemblies, and state executives headed by a Governor. Under the Interim Constitution state governments can establish their own civil services, provide social services, and undertake local taxation. During 2008–2009 all the state governments in the south and the state legislative assemblies were constituted. As a consequence of the 2010 general election the SPLM has come to dominate the state legislatures as well. However, in several states there is a significant presence of legislators who stood as independent candidates or are from other political parties. It is particularly significant that many of the elections for state governorships – which are based on direct elections – were hard fought. Out of the ten governors, nine were elected from the SPLM. However, in three of the latter contests, the SPLM candidates were opposed by very strong independents. In Eastern Equatoria the SPLM candidate had to beat the immediate past governor; in Upper Nile the SPLM candidate was opposed by a former minister in the regional government; and, in Unity State, the ruling party candidate had to fight off a strong challenge from the wife of the incumbent Vice-President of South Sudan.

Since most of the federal structures have been put in place very recently, it is too early to assess how federalism will work out in practice. Nevertheless there are some recent developments which suggest that a more devolved federalist system may develop in Southern Sudan. These include:

- the formation of the State Governor's Forum to coordinate activities amongst the states and consider common policy positions *vis-a-vis* the federal government, indicating that the forces favouring a decentralization of political authority are beginning to assert themselves;
- the refusal of Bahr-el-Jebel State to hand over the territory of Juba to central control so that it could become a centrally administered capital, suggesting that even in these early days, the federal government has a limited ability to brow-beat state governments.

THE EXECUTIVE

The executive is the most powerful institution of a state. Consequently, its behaviour and performance are central to the achievement of favourable levels of economic and political governance. In Chapter 6 we considered why the state needs to credibly commit to curtailing its own powers so that productive economic activity is encouraged. In the discussion below, therefore, we shall consider the extent to which new structures and systems introduced in key areas under the DG programme, and by other external agencies, have introduced checks and balances to control arbitrary power within the executive, and whether these systems have contributed to more consensual systems of decision-making, controlling corruption and improving macroeconomic management.

As noted earlier, at the end of the civil war the administrative structures existing in Southern Sudan consisted of the rudimentary secretariats of the SPLM and the old non-functional provincial administrations of the northern regime. The latter consisted mainly of a large number of teaching, junior technical, administrative, unskilled and other similar personnel. In spite of these large numbers, no coherent structure of government or civil service existed at the Southern Sudan federal level to permit proper decision-making and effective governance. Thus in late 2005 the DG team began the implementation of a major programme to build the required structures and new decision-making systems for the new executive. At a later stage other external agencies such as the United Nations and the World Bank also came on board with this programme. In view of the vast task of creating new structures, in most cases from scratch, it was decided to focus on the few central institutions that could have a major influence on government performance. The organizations chosen were the Ministries of Finance, Public Service, Legal Affairs, and Information, and the Bank of Southern Sudan. In addition, the centre of government – the Offices of the President, Vice-President, and the Council of Ministers – were targeted for assistance in developing coherent inter-related organizational structures, mandates and operational systems. The confines and the purpose of this book do not permit a detailed discussion of all the institutional development activities undertaken under the auspices of the DG programme, or by other donors. Therefore, the discussion below only focuses on the contribution made by certain new structures and systems introduced in key areas of government to improved executive decision-making and policy formulation.

High Level Decision-making Structures

In an historical context, we have discussed at length the importance for economic progress of systems that control arbitrary rule at the highest political level and enable the state to provide a credible commitment to limit its own power. More recently, the key role played by checks and balances and the mechanisms for collective decision-making at the apex level of government, as factors underlying the stellar economic performance of both India and China, has been emphasized by Keefer (World Bank 2007) and Montinola, Qian and Weingast (1996). In Southern Sudan's case the introduction and establishment of such systems of decision-making were made all the more difficult by the culture of military-style authority and leadership. Thus it is well known that in the few years prior to the signing of the CPA, few meetings of the National Liberation Council or Leadership Council were held. Most decisions were taken by Dr John Garang, the supreme military leader, and a small group of inner advisors. This style of unilateral decision-making led to considerable dissatisfaction amongst SPLM leaders, finally leading to the Yei incident in late 2004. In this incident, General Salva Kiir – now President of Southern Sudan, but then the number two leader in the SPLM hierarchy – and a number of other senior political leaders and military commanders refused to have any further dealings with John Garang because of his autocratic style of decision-making. The differences amongst the leaders were subsequently resolved. However, this event emphasized that with the onset of peace new non-military methods of decision-making based on consultation and consensus, and structures and systems which formalized and supported such processes, were necessary to control arbitrary behaviour and improve political governance.

By late 2005, most of the ministerial and other senior appointments of the GOSS had been completed. Given the new government's explicit objective to bring together the various fractious tribal, militia, and other political elements under one Southern Sudanese umbrella, the DG programme was tasked by the leadership to develop the necessary structures and systems which would promote consultation, cohesiveness and collective decision-making at the apex level of government. Therefore in spite of having a Presidential system of government in an African context advice was given to the government that a more Cabinet-style decision-making system, with a greater role being given to the Council of Ministers (COM) in discussing and deciding on all major issues, should be adopted. Subsequent to the acceptance of this core concept by the leadership, an institutional development programme was started in 2005 to strengthen the Ministry of Cabinet Affairs so that it could function effectively as the secretariat to the Council of Ministers. Under this, a regular timetable for meetings with appropriate protocols for decision-making, a proper set of procedures with formats for the receipt, review, prioritization and discussion of proposals, and requirements for follow-up and reporting, were introduced. In early 2006, all these systems and procedures were formalized through a *Council of Ministers' Handbook* (Government of Southern Sudan 2006). These procedures have been adhered to and improved upon by the Cabinet Office since 2006.

The collective decision-making systems put in place at the apex of government have so far minimized unilateral decisions being taken by the President using temporary ordinances or residual powers. The Council of Ministers meets regularly on a pre-assigned day of the week and decides on all major issues concerning the government. To enhance efficiency, a number of Cabinet sub-committees or clusters have been set up to consider policy and administrative issues relating to different sectors of the government. As a major gesture to embedding the concept of cohesiveness and collective decision-making amongst the political leadership, in mid 2007 the President (who is from the dominant Dinka tribe) transferred many of the mandates and responsibilities of his position to the Vice-President (who is from the Nuer tribe). All these developments have contributed to more stable, consensual, and better informed economic and political decisions being taken over the past few years, and have also prevented the new state from developing into an overbearing entity with a powerful Presidency.

Economic Policy

Although the GOSS has not released any formal document concerning its economic policy stance, from the public statements of political leaders at regularly held private investment conferences, and discussions with visiting international investors, the commitment of the government to a market economy based on private ownership is evident. The recently passed Investment Act 2009 has reinforced this commitment, with provisions designed to promote and safeguard both domestic and foreign investment. Southern Sudan is a relatively easy place to do business. There are few regulatory requirements and under the new Companies Act it is possible to register a company in a few days. There are also no exchange controls. At the fiscal level, under the new Revenue Act 2009, the tax system has been kept simple, with both income and corporate taxes being levied at low rates which compare favourably with other African countries. The local level taxation of goods is a more problematic area, with taxes being levied by multiple levels of government. This has caused a cascading of indirect taxes in a manner that could potentially become a prohibitive barrier to the flow of goods across the country. In spite of such problems, however, the economic policy framework is liberal and the regulatory system simple. This has resulted in a flood of private investment entering the country, particularly from East Africa and from the Southern Sudanese diaspora living in western countries. Prior to Independence in July 2011, several key industries such as banking, insurance and the oil sector were under the regulatory control of the central government in Khartoum. This resulted in restrictive entry requirements or opaqueness in the policy environment and consequently little development took place. The new government has now commenced elaborating and putting in place a policy and regulatory environment in these areas, with assistance from the international community. It is expected that the new policies will be based on international best practice and will facilitate the development of Southern Sudan's rich oil reserves.

Corruption

The empirical evidence reviewed in Chapter 5 showed the strong impact that the extent of corruption in a country will have on its economic performance.

As observed earlier, the manner in which a government deals with corruption can also be taken as a proxy of the quality of its economic governance. With this in view the DG programme, and other donors such as the World Bank, undertook an intensive dialogue with the political leadership soon after the formation of GOSS in 2005 so that the new government would give a high priority to this issue. As a fundamental initial step efforts were centered on the creation of a well-defined Ministry of Finance and Planning, with mechanisms for the preparation of annual budgets based on policy priorities and financial management systems to control expenditure allocations and account for disbursements to line ministries and agencies. In 2006 transparent and government-wide procurement procedures and regulations were adopted and soon after an Anti-Corruption Commission, empowered under its own Act, was established. These systems and the commitment of the political leadership to control corruption have resulted in the campaign to fight corruption developing a very high profile in Southern Sudan. Towards the end of 2006, for example, four senior civil servants were dismissed for following improper procurement procedures and other alleged corrupt activities. Subsequent to this a Presidential Commission was appointed to review all contracts signed by the government since its formation in mid 2005. In early 2007 the Minister of Finance was removed from office because of serious allegations of corruption. More recently, as part of a Cabinet reshuffle undertaken in mid 2007, the powerful Minister of Roads and Transport was moved to a non-ministerial advisory position, and the portfolio of the Ministry of Housing was taken away from the Vice-President, due to complaints about improprieties in contracting and irregularities in procurement procedures.

In spite of these serious efforts to control corruption, however, traditional modes of thinking originating in the tribal cultures of the political leadership continue to undermine the implementation of modern methods of financial management and procurement. In particular, since the formation of the GOSS in 2005, the phenomenon of irregular and un-controlled procurement by almost all ministries has become increasingly endemic. Since the SPLM remained a cohesive and disciplined political force during the 50 long years of civil war, this pervasive fiscal indiscipline soon after the formation of a government needs some explanation. It is argued here that since most of the GOSS leaders have their roots in a tribal society wherein key economic assets such as land are held and used jointly by the community (Evans-Pritchard 1941, Fortes and Evans-Pritchard [1940]1970) and thus their attitude and behaviour towards the oil revenues of the new government are probably best modelled as a common pool problem. As in the case of the classic 'commons', this has led to rivalries in consumption, but also non-excludability, and consequently over-use. Thus in the case of oil revenues, the manifestation of this common pool problem is to be found in individual government ministries and agencies competing with each other to sign up agreements and contracts for infrastructure development, the delivery of goods, and the provision of services, leading to endemic over-expenditure and the irrelevance of budgetary allocations or ceilings.

This unrestrained behaviour to use what is considered a common resource resulted in 2009 in the most severe financial crisis since the government came into existence in 2005. By early 2009 various government agencies had signed contracts for the procurement of various goods, including local grain for the strategic food reserve worth almost two billion US dollars – an amount greater than the total government budget for the year. This crisis, however, also opened the way for a deeper engagement between the government and external agencies to consider ways and means of addressing a range of financial and economic management issues, including irregular procurement practices, which if left unchecked could easily cause corruption to become entrenched. As a consequence of this dialogue, in July 2009 the government signed what has been termed the Juba Compact with its donor and development partners. Under this Compact, in return for substantial flows of external assistance, the government agreed to undertake several measures, which included:

- fast-tracking the adoption and implementation of laws relating to public financial management, audit and procurement;
- temporarily freezing all new contracts, including those already signed for the procurement of food reserves, and putting in place an effective contract management system;
- limiting budgetary expenditures to the approved Appropriations Act for 2009;
- developing a growth strategy that would focus on private sector-led development and poverty reduction.

It is expected that these measures will contribute to placing restraints on traditional ways of decision-making and create the necessary institutional environment that will permit modern methods of financial, contract and procurement management to be practised, corruption to be controlled, and the economic governance environment in Southern Sudan to be improved.

INSTITUTIONAL DEVELOPMENT 2005–2009: SOME OBSERVATIONS

The discussion above shows that Southern Sudan's experience with institutional change has so far been mixed. However, five years is a very short period in the history of a country. It is therefore too early to predict whether the new institutional frameworks created will generate forces over time that will ensure these very institutions will become self-enforcing. One of the most important developments in this respect is the return of a large number of people from the Southern Sudanese diaspora that had settled in the West during the long years of civil war. It is estimated that the Southern Sudanese diaspora living abroad number several million. The return of an educated diaspora into government, professional activities, and particularly the business sector, is likely to play an important role in facilitating the growth of an incipient middle class in Southern Sudan, with its attendant interest in reinforcing the security of property rights and the rule of law. While this chapter has focused on the positive elements of institutional development since 2005 there are of course any number of negative factors which in the foreseeable future could bring about an institutional decline and deterioration in the governance environment. Prominent amongst these are:

- a re-commencement of the conflict due to unresolved issues between the north and the south, such as the demarcation of the border, the control of the oil fields in the bordering areas, use of the oil pipeline to the Red Sea, etc.;
- the re-emergence of militarism and authoritarian tendencies in the SPLM – in spite of the many new checks and balances, federalism, a separation of powers and external influences, none of these are self-enforcing at present and the SPLM remains the predominant force in Southern Sudan;
- entrenched irregular financial and procurement practices, causing rent-seeking and corruption to become endemic in government.

Nevertheless, in line with the 'made order' perspective of this study, and the thesis of institutional discontinuities discussed in Chapter 7, the period under review has been long enough for there to be a significant break from the past and for the developments during this period to be an important influence on the future trajectory of institutions and governance. Political structures and decision-making systems have been put in place with inherent tendencies to encourage a dispersion of power, control the exercise of arbitrary power, and thereby facilitate the protection of property and contractual rights. In this sense the period has witnessed a fundamental change in formal institutions and rules and the preliminary evidence available suggests that these changes are beginning to influence informal practices and modes of thinking as well. Furthermore, all these changes have been introduced through externally supported interventions that have worked closely with the domestic political elite and the process is still ongoing.

South Sudan gained its Independence in July 2011. Consequently, there is no longer any direct interference from the northern regime in its political processes. The new institutions established therefore now have the possibility of interacting with other endogenous forces in a manner which should enable them to evolve and become a more integral part of that society. Although the democratic and federalist systems put in place could be said to be in consonance with the individualistic and libertarian spirit of the Nilotic peoples, the structures of government that have been established since 2005 have radically moved away from the traditional stateless society or 'ordered anarchy' of the region. In fact many of the problems faced by GOSS – such as the resistance to the use of centralized and well controlled expenditure and procurement mechanisms, and common pool problems in the use of government oil revenues – are a reflection of the conflict between the traditional structures or informal institutions of Southern Sudanese society, where loyalties and modes of thinking were primarily attuned towards one's own local community or tribal group and the requirements of a modern nation state. However, as the narrative above indicates, the new institutional structures are beginning to influence old habits and ways of thinking and are also encouraging the emergence of forms of behaviour that are more consistent with the spirit of the new formal systems being put in place. This is consistent with the process of institutional change observed in Japan, India and Botswana and discussed in Chapter 7. Southern Sudan's experience therefore gives further substance to the view that new institutions can lead to a behavioural change by bringing about congruent purposes and beliefs amongst people who initially may not have shared those same beliefs or values (Hodgson 2006).

9. Markets and institutions

We are now in a position to compare the insights that emerged from our assessment of the theoretical literature undertaken in Chapters 2 and 3 with the conclusions derived from the empirical evidence on human behaviour, and the empirical and historical evidence on economic growth and institutional change. Based on this material in this chapter we arrive at some generalizations which are then used to develop an empirically grounded theory of the performance of an economic system. In Chapter 10 we shall consider what our findings suggest for the process of institutional change.

First, at the behavioural level, the empirical evidence from cognitive psychology, genetics, and a vast literature on behavioural and experimental economics discussed in detail in Chapter 2, indicates that the neoclassical assumption that agents act in a rational self-interested manner is an unsafe hypothesis. Although self-interest is basic to human nature, this self-interest is by no means limited to the simple self-seeking maximization behaviour assumed by neoclassical economics. Self-interest in a broader biological, psychological and economic sense encompasses altruism, reciprocal altruism, opportunism and predation. Furthermore, since conflict of interest is a much more fundamental characteristic of observed human relations, this is more than likely to lead to a range of opportunistic and predatory types of behaviour, especially in circumstances where the economic system provides the opportunity or encouragement for such behaviour to exist. Since behaviour that goes beyond simple self-seeking wealth maximization is widespread and significant enough to affect decision-making by all agents, any model that tries to explain the functioning of an economic system must necessarily take such behavioural patterns into account.

This conclusion implies that one of the central assumptions of neoclassical economics – that actors can be modelled as a representative agent as has been characterized by *homo oeconomicus* in the literature – is not an empirically valid concept and needs to be abandoned. Wealth maximization in the context of a multiplicity of behavioural patterns will lead to a different set of consequences from that predicted by models that assume a harmony of interests or universal economic rationality. Apart from this fundamental empirical reality about human behaviour, the literature on evolutionary psychology reviewed earlier also indicates that the mind is not a general purpose tool designed to process information using a probabilistic rational calculus. Rather, it is a functionally specialized device designed to solve the natural adaptive problems that our hunter-gatherer ancestors had to face in their struggle for survival. Our neuro-physiological condition and computational capabilities are limited and this automatically limits the amount of information that can be processed and the manner in which this happens. As Simon (1957) has proposed, therefore, bounded or limited rationality is a more reasonable assumption to characterize our cognitive capabilities.

Thus by dropping the assumption of a rational self-interested representative agent, accepting a more empirically grounded range of motivational assumptions to explain human behaviour, and placing institutional variables at the centre of what determines actual behaviour in the market, the way can be opened to formulating a more realistic model of the functioning of an economic system and economic progress. As Coase (1984: 231) argues, our starting point should be to take 'man as he is'. Based on such an approach, as an initial step following on from evolutionary behavioural models, it is probably more appropriate to view human beings as predators and pirates, whose instincts for survival emerged out of the hunting Pleistocene, rather than as the rational self-seeking individuals who were part of the new bourgeoisie that emerged during the late Middle Ages in Europe. Such a view of human nature would be far more consistent with the anthropological evidence on primitive man, as compared to that suggested by the rationality model. We have already referred to the authoritative studies by Keeley (1996) and Otterbien (1989) which show that primitive societies were extremely violent and that conflicts and predation were common factors in pre-state societies such as tribes, bands and chiefdoms. Even the great ethnographer Bronislaw Malinowski, dismissing the commonly held view of the 'noble savage', observed in 1941 that anthropology had done more harm than good in confusing the issue by depicting human ancestry as living in a golden age of perpetual peace (Keeley 1996: 8).

This evidence suggests that predation is a much deeper reality in human history, while 'rational' behaviour is a more recent and perhaps more shallow phenomenon. As noted in Chapter 2, by predatory behaviour we mean using non-market means to encroach upon the entitlements and endowments of other people and appropriate benefits which would not have otherwise been available through the market mechanism. This contrasts with the behavioural assumptions of mainstream neoclassical theory, where an individual limits himself to using his own entitlements and endowments to acquire the fruits of his own labour peacefully through market exchange. We would argue that by using opportunism and predation as an underlying basis for understanding instinctual human behaviour a more useful explanatory hypothesis for institutional change and economic performance can be developed.

Second, our analysis has shown that the neoclassical institution-free vision of the functioning of an economic system has a weak theoretical, empirical and historical basis. As the institutional economics literature argues, all economic phenomena occur in an environment in which incomplete information and bounded rationality rule everywhere. Given the limits of our knowledge and computational abilities it is impossible to identify all future contingencies and consequently uncertainty becomes an inherent characteristic of human decision-making and a fundamental characteristic of the economic system. Elaborating on the concept of uncertainty, Keynes (1937: 213) indicated that the neoclassical system assumes that all the relevant factors are either known, or more or less certain, and where change is expected, such expectations are given 'in a definite and calculable form; and risks ... (are) supposed to be capable of an exact actuarial computation'. Further, 'the calculus of probability ... (is) supposed to be capable of reducing uncertainty to the same calculable status as that of certainty itself'. Refuting this view, Keynes argued that the future is in fact uncertain in the sense that there is no way of knowing what the price of copper or the rate of interest is likely to be twenty years hence. Thus he states, 'About these matters there is no scientific basis on which to form any calculable probability whatever. We simply do not know' (Keynes 1937: 214).

Since uncertainty is ubiquitous, it follows that all future contingencies can never be known. Neoclassical economics has therefore modified the unsatisfactory assumption of perfect foresight to the paradigm of rational expectations. Explaining this concept, Arrow (1986) states that rational expectations are a form of perfect foresight based on the theory of probability. To preserve economic rationality, the rational expectations paradigm holds that each individual forms expectations of the future based on a correct model of the entire economy and that all agents have this model. Given uncertainty, expectations take the form of probability distributions, with each agent's expectations being conditional on the information available to him. However, Alchian (1950) disagrees with the view that rational expectations can generate equilibrium solutions. He states that maximization is not possible under conditions of uncertainty. Rational decision-making under uncertainty involves identifying a distribution of potential outcomes for each action and choosing one that will generate the optimum distribution. However, there is no such thing as maximizing a distribution (Alchian 1950: 212). An optimum distribution cannot be assessed on maximizing criteria. Consequently, such as an assessment can only be a subjective process wherein risk and return will be balanced depending on the preference function of the decision-maker.

Arrow (1986: 210) admits that the logical consistency of rational expectations has been questioned since the existence of a forecast can alter behaviour such as to cause the forecast to be false or alternatively to make an otherwise false forecast true. Further, apart from the informational requirements of such decision-making, since future outcomes will depend on other individuals' predictions as well, to arrive at any unique equilibrium there needs to be common knowledge. Re-affirming this view, Minsky (1996) indicates that the power of rational expectations is derived from the specification that all agents have a common understanding or a common model of the environment that they operate within. This commonly understood environment or model is then logically equivalent to the unsatisfactory assumption of perfect foresight in neoclassical economics and enables the rational expectations paradigm to generate a unique equilibrium. Discounting this possibility, however, Minsky's view is that uncertainty eliminates the possibility of systematically extracting a consistent set of relations out of a situation. This is because the elements determining long-term expectations change so often that what happens in the economy at any date will be influenced by prior market conditions that will reflect actions determined by mental models that are very likely to differ from the model that now guides expectation formation and therefore actions. Agreeing with Keynes' (1921) *Treatise on Probability*, he states that 'uncertainty is a deep property of decentralized systems in which a myriad of independent agents make decisions whose impacts are aggregated into outcomes that emerge over a range of tomorrows' (Minsky 1996: 2).

In circumstances of such fundamental uncertainty, it is evident that some man-made devices are necessary to provide a framework and impose constraints on human interaction so that order and predictability are provided within which economic exchanges can occur. It is therefore incorrect to model a market as merely a disembodied structure within which agents will interact. Markets and the price mechanism cannot exist and nor can they function in a vacuum. Rather, as the old and new institutionalism states, to support its effective functioning a market-based system does require an institutional framework consisting of certain types of organizational structures, laws, regulations, values and customs. As Bates (1995) has argued, where there is imperfect information and costs for acquiring information, social processes to minimize costs such as contractual agreements that will be beneficial to both parties will emerge, and where fundamental uncertainty exists, governance structures, such the firm, will be created wherein long-term relationships can be established. Furthermore, since such structures are generalizable over time and place any analysis of the functioning of a market must necessarily take these into account. The powerful role of institutions is a direct consequence of their ability to determine the incentives and payoffs generated by a system. These payoffs and punishments, by influencing human action, bring about predictability in behaviour and reduce uncertainty. It thus follows from this, that where the institutional framework contains incentive structures which encourage productive activity, economic resources will be productively utilized and a society will develop. On the other hand, where dysfunctional institutions emerge endogenously or are consciously constructed, these will result in rent-seeking, opportunism, and predatory behaviour.

The theoretical view discussed above is supported by the empirical evidence. Thus the vast majority of recent cross-country and growth accounting studies considered in Chapter 5 indicate that institutions are central to economic performance and developmental outcomes. Variables of economic and political governance, which reflect the nature of institutions in a particular society, have been found to be the key determinants of economic performance. This conclusion is supported by the historical evidence concerning the emergence of modern economic growth in the city states of northern Italy and northern Europe and subsequently in England and the Netherlands. The regression and continued backwardness of the major eastern civilizations of the medieval world, namely China, India and Ottoman Turkey, can also be explained in terms of the non-emergence of the favourable institutions required to support development and growth. Thus in medieval Europe systems developed to check arbitrary rule and ensure that the state had a credible commitment to the protection of private property and contractual rights. This enabled mercantile and capitalist development to continue and gather apace. In the eastern civilizations of the same period, however, no such systems developed. Feudal despotism, arbitrary rule and predatory behaviour remained entrenched, preventing the economic growth and development of these societies.

Third, in Chapter 2 we discussed the causes of market failure highlighted in the welfare economics literature. These included indivisibilities in factors of production which can result in monopolies, the presence of production or consumption externalities, and the special case of public goods. In the context of economic development, production interdependencies or external economies in the production of goods can be particularly crucial in determining whether an industry has the potential to emerge as one having a comparative advantage or not. Stiglitz (1989) argues that there is, in fact, adequate evidence to show that there are fundamental differences between markets in developed and developing countries, with instances of market failure being common in the latter. Elaborating on this he identifies three areas of difference. First, the markets for knowledge and information are very imperfect in developing countries. These imperfections include difficulties in acquiring learning, limited knowledge spillovers, and the localization of learning. All these factors result in fragmented markets and low-level equilibrium traps that will then prevent the economy from being productively efficient. Second, it is known that non-market externalities affect the incentives, returns, and therefore the productive outcomes of a system. In developed countries, the resources and environment are such that externalities facilitate the production of commodities and skills required for progress. This is not the case in most developing countries. Stiglitz provides the example of entrepreneurship. Development requires that entrepreneurs take risks. But if the environment contributes to the failure of entrepreneurs, this will discourage others from undertaking such activities. Third, much of the production in developed countries takes place within large corporations, some of which can be the size of a small developing country. This scale of production enables firms to internalize many activities that may not be considered profitable otherwise. For instance, AT&T found it possible to spend large amounts on basic research that eventually led to the discovery of transistors and lasers.

The examples discussed by Stiglitz show that the coordination of economic activities is a much greater problem in developing countries and that there are significant areas where economic phenomena do not conform to the neoclassical vision of a market. For instance, industrialization may require large investments to be undertaken which have closely inter-related profitabilities. However, in conditions of imperfect knowledge, the market will not cause profit maximizing agents to actually make these investments. In these circumstances, government-assisted coordination in the interests of the dynamic efficiency of the economy will be called for. This is exactly the argument that underlies the concept of an interventionist capitalist developmental state, as has been practised by governments in the East Asian region. In Chapter 4 we reviewed the works of Amsden (2004), Wade (2004) and Chang (2002, 2004), analysing the economic strategies followed by Japan, Korea, Taiwan, and other late industrializing countries. These studies found that government policy not only acted to correct generic market failures, but also used a range of instruments to directly influence the allocation of resources by changing market incentives, and that this interventionist policy package was associated with sustained and high rates of growth. As Wade (2004) indicates, the Japanese were the first to recognize that an international competitive advantage could be deliberately engineered by a capitalist developmental state if it provided the critical coordination and policy support function through a committed economic bureaucracy.

From the discussion above, it is evident that markets cannot function as a mechanism for the efficient allocation of resources without the intervention of government. Of course it is possible for market failure to be corrected by private collective action, through the formation of non-market institutions such as the firm, or the use of informal norms such as ethical codes or trust to overcome coordination problems. However, such forms of private collective action cannot correct a macro-level or system-wide market failure. Consequently, the only real option is public collective action (i.e. intervention by the state). At a minimum, therefore, advanced developed markets require a legal/regulatory framework, which is enforced by the state to control opportunism and predation and provide an orderly and predictable framework for economic exchanges to occur in. In developing countries, in addition to this framework, more direct intervention is likely to be required to achieve the dynamic effi- ciencies which are part of the process of industrialization and the achievement of high rates of growth. From a theoretical point of view, therefore, it is gener- ally agreed that market failure can be corrected through the intervention of government. However, the historical experience of most developing countries in the 1960s and 1970s shows that in practice this government intervention itself is problematic. It can lead to severe 'government failure' that will have even greater negative consequences for growth and development. As Rodrik (1996) indicates, interventionist policies, which had been used widely in most developing countries since the 1950s, failed almost universally everywhere except in East Asia. So the question arises as to what the special characteris- tics of a state need to be for it to play a growth-oriented developmental role rather than a regressive or predatory one.

Before we discuss this issue, however, one final argument in favour of unfettered markets which has held sway in mainstream economics since the early 1970s needs to be considered.

EFFICIENT MARKETS HYPOTHESIS

If the core idea of the standard economic model – the rational expectations postulate – has validity, then it should at least prove to be a realistic theory that will explain and predict the functioning of ideal or near perfect markets. Yet against this, given the behavioural realities of how self-interest functions, the existence of opportunism and predation, the human characteristic of bounded rationality, and the presence of fundamental uncertainty, our theory predicts that there is no inherent reason for even well-developed markets to automati- cally function in an efficient or self-equilibrating manner. This issue can there- fore be best evaluated by considering the empirical evidence on the performance of what neoclassical theory accepts as being an almost perfect market. By definition an ideal market is one where prices provide accurate signals to decision-makers such that their actions will lead to equilibrium solu- tions and an efficient allocation of resources. Judged by this standard neoclas- sical economics, and its successors in the new classical school, hold that financial markets in developed market economies are very efficient. Based on this view the efficient markets hypothesis (EMH) asserts that, in equilibrium, financial prices will contain a summary of all the economically relevant public information that exists anywhere in the system (Fama 1970). Since within a rational expectations framework financial market prices or valuations should reflect the present value of expected cash flows, according to the efficient markets hypothesis the information sub-set available to investors is fully utilized by the market in forming the equilibrium expected returns and consequently current prices or valuations. One of the corollaries of this theory is the random walk hypothesis: this states that since by definition new information is unpredictable price changes in financial markets should follow a random walk and will not show any significant correlation from one day to the next or one period to the next.

Let us now consider the empirical evidence. In Fama (1970) we can find an initial assessment of whether the data on financial market behaviour in the US support the EMH or not. There are three types of studies that he reviews. First, there are the weak form tests which consider the independence of historical stock price or return sequences from one day or one week to the next. These tests show that while successive changes in prices or returns have positive serial correlations these are consistently close to zero. Fama concludes from this that while the positive dependence of prices from one period to the next violates a strict interpretation of the hypothesis the strength or degree of this correlation is not of sufficient importance to reject the EMH. Second, there are semi-strong tests which will assess whether prices fully reflect all the available information and will adjust to any new information-generating event such as stock splits or new issues. To test this, Fama, Fisher, Jensen and Roll (1969) considered 940 stock splits on the New York Stock Exchange between 1927 and 1959. They found that the information contained in stock splits concerning a firm's future dividend payments was, on average, fully reflected in the price of a split share at the time of the split. This evidence was supportive of the EMH. Third, there are the strong form tests which assess whether given investors or groups have monopolistic access to information relevant to price formation. Fama (1970) indicates that the studies show that while there may be some trading specialists or corporate insiders with private information, this does not affect market outcomes in general. Thus for instance we have the study by Jensen (1968). This evaluated the performance of 115 mutual funds over the period 1955–1964 and found that although fund managers were considered specialists, they were unable to pick securities that out-performed the norm (i.e. the S&P 500 index) over the study period. This indicated that all new information was quickly arbitraged by market players and that speculation eliminated any inefficiencies in market prices.

Over the years the EMH has become a mainstream orthodoxy in spite of empirical evidence to the contrary. Powerful critiques can be found in Shiller (1981, 2000), Summers (1986) and Akerlof and Shiller (2009). Shiller (1981) considered movements in the real S&P Composite Stock Price Index from 1871 to 1979, and compared these to their dividend present value (i.e. the present value for each year of real dividends paid subsequent to that year) on the shares making up the index. If the efficient markets hypothesis were correct and stock price movements are to be justified by the future dividends that companies pay out, then the volatility in stock prices can only be justified by a similar variability of dividends over long periods of time. In fact, Shiller found that the dividend present value moved in a very steady trend-like manner whereas the inflation-adjusted stock prices moved dramatically in both directions. For instance, during the bull market of the 1920s, between the low in 1920 and the high in 1929, the real S&P Composite Index increased by 415.4 per cent, whereas the dividend present value increased by only 16.4 per cent. Likewise, the real S&P index fell 80.6 per cent from its peak in 1929 to 1932, whereas the dividend present value declined only 3.1 per cent. Considering the entire 1871–1979 period, Shiller concluded that 'if stock prices are supposed to be an optimal predictor of the dividend present value, then they should not jump around erratically when the true fundamental value is growing along a smooth trend' (2000: 188) and that the observed movement of stock prices appeared to be too volatile to be in accord with the efficient markets theory. In Shiller (2000) the data-set relating real stock prices to the present value of dividends was extended up to 2000. These data show an even more remarkable disconnect between these two variables, with stock prices sky rocketing after 1992 relative to dividends, beyond anything observed before.

The recent credit crunch and financial crisis that commenced with problems in the US sub-prime mortgage market has further questioned the neoclassical view of efficient self-equilibrating markets. This crisis has shown that capital markets have endogenously generated financial instability (Minsky 1977) and the notion fuelled by the efficient markets theory that financial markets work perfectly and can regulate themselves is grossly wrong. Based on the experience of the recent sub-prime crisis, and data on speculative bubbles and market disequilibrium since the Great Depression, Akerlof and Shiller (2009) assert that there are significant deviations in the manner in which an economy actually works from those predicted by the rational expectations model and efficient market theories. Following Keynes (1936, 1937), they argue that people are not always rational in the pursuit of their economic interests, but that much of economic activity is governed by animal spirits and that these are the main reason why the economy fluctuates as it does. Criticizing orthodox theory, Keynes had stated that faced with uncertainty people will adopt certain rules of judgement that will result in human behaviour being subject to 'vague panic fears and equally vague and unreasoned hopes', and people will have a vision of the future that is 'subject to sudden and violent changes' (Keynes 1937: 215).

Akerlof and Shiller (2009: ix) indicate that the behavioural factors emphasized by Keynes make capitalism inherently unstable and left to their own devices capitalist economies will pursue excess, resulting in manias, panics and speculative bubbles. Using the behavioural economics literature and other empirical findings, Akerlof and Shiller elaborate on five aspects of the content of Keynesian animal spirits which they indicate will influence the nature of economic activity at any time. These aspects are the importance of confidence or trust; the fact that fairness is just as key as other motivations in making economic decisions; fluctuations in a personal commitment to the principles of good behaviour and the absence of predatory activity; the influence of money illusion on wages and prices; and the extent to which stories or perceptions will affect markets and the real economy. Based on these aspects of animal spirits, they argue that if one classifies the motives underlying market behaviour into four categories (i.e. rational, irrational, economic and non-economic) then neoclassical economics only explains that part of behaviour which is rational and economic – which of course, as we have seen already, does not necessarily constitute the major part of human decision-making.

Using the Keynesian model of the economy, Summers (1986) further considers the validity of the efficient markets theory and the statistical models used by its supporters to confirm their hypothesis. First, he argues that statistical failure to reject a hypothesis is not equivalent to its acceptance. Using parameters based on observed variances in stock market returns, he shows that in a theoretical sample of 600 monthly observations (i.e. monthly stock market returns covering 50 years) with a standard deviation of 30 per cent – which implies that market valuations will frequently differ from rational expectations of the present value of future cash flows by more than 30 per cent – the statistical tests do not permit a rejection of the null hypothesis of a zero serial correlation of returns (i.e. that markets are efficient). Summers then estimates that based on the values, variances, standard deviations, etc. of the observed data, in order to have a 50 per cent chance of rejecting the null hypothesis it would be necessary to have monthly data for over five thousand years. Second, he argues that to test whether the EMH is true or false, the data need to be evaluated against an alternative hypothesis. The alternative formulation that he postulates is that market valuations will differ from the rational expectation of the present value of future cash flows by a multiplicative factor. This multiplicative factor could be due to animal spirits or excess volatility due to an overconfidence in or over-reaction to new information. Given these two models, when stock prices respond to new information, since such a reaction can be expected in both cases, Summers states that it will be impossible to discern whether the data support the EMH or the animal spirits hypothesis. In either case prices will respond to the new information and no predictable excess returns can be earned once the new information has been released. Thus he concludes that market valuations can differ substantially and persistently from the rational expectation that valuations should reflect the present value of cash flows, without leaving any statistically discernible traces in the pattern of returns.

Our discussion indicates that markets in reality – both ideal or near perfect financial markets in the developed world, and more embryonic or imperfect ones in developing countries – do not function or adjust in the manner predicted by neoclassical general equilibrium theory. For the theoretical reasons summarized above, markets more often than not are subjected to systematic discrepancies, dramatic disequilibrium, and low-level equilibria. This has been borne out by the history of manias and bubbles in financial markets and more recently again by the events of the 2008–2010 financial crisis and world recession. In sum, therefore, the neoclassical model and its derivations such as the efficient markets hypothesis are not of much value either from an explanatory or policy perspective. Economic theory needs to look elsewhere to find answers to the problems of growth and development.

THE VISIBLE HAND AGAIN

In this section, we shall construct a simple alternative conceptual framework based on the inductive generalizations that emerge out of this study. The framework is applicable to a well-developed market economy in which agents will interact under conditions of uncertainty and be motivated by the broader conception of self-interest discussed in Chapter 2. It does not cover the different set of conditions faced by developing countries, where large-scale market failure is likely to require more forceful policy intervention by the government to resolve the coordination problem and bring about structural change and economic growth. This is discussed later in the chapter.

Figure 9.1 attempts to summarize the relationship between markets, transaction costs, the possibilities of opportunism and/or predation, and the need for an institutional framework with an appropriate level of laws and regulations that will be necessary to permit markets to function in a stable manner. This diagram is not a formal model, but an attempt to integrate all the elements of the system into a simple structure so that the inter-relationships between the variables can be easily seen. The view of the functioning of a market-based economic system embedded within it conforms to the mainstream new institutional economics vision of North (1981, 1990, 2009), that all economic phenomena are embedded in an environment where incomplete information, bounded rationality and opportunism rule everywhere, and consequently all economic transactions will entail costs. It also bases itself on some of the fundamental concepts and views of older institutionalists such as Veblen ([1899]1949), Commons (1934) and Polanyi (1944). Veblen and Commons placed a conflict of interests at the centre of economic relations between agents, thereby opening the way for self-interest to function in an opportunistic or predatory manner. As Polanyi argued that for self-regulating markets to operate effectively, an appropriate framework consisting of certain organizational structures, regulations, customs, laws, and an appropriate economic role of the state, would be necessary. These institutions would provide the underlying framework that would permit the laws of the market to function freely.

The behavioural or microeconomic foundations of this approach are evident from our earlier discussion. Thus where the institutional framework restrains or prevents opportunistic or predatory behaviour our model indicates that individual agents will function as simple self-seeking actors, and other things being equal, the market can be expected to function in the manner predicted by neoclassical economics. However, this is only a limiting case. Where opportunism or predation are possible, an individual who has scope for such activities will continue to engage in these up until the point where the additional cost of encroaching on the entitlements or endowments of others is greater than the potential benefits that can be generated out of such behaviour. In terms of the impact on the allocation of resources therefore:

- opportunism results in higher transaction costs in the economy, thus diverting resources away from goods and services which can be used to satisfy needs;
- predation results in resources being allocated to the mechanisms through which predatory behaviour can be executed. The costs of running these mechanisms can broadly be included in the concept of transaction costs, and constitute an unproductive use of resources;
- both opportunism and predation will result in a lack of trust and greater uncertainty, lowering the incentive to produce and trade, thereby disrupting economic activity and preventing a market from functioning efficiently.

Since the type of behaviour discussed above affects the allocation of resources, it will result in sub-optimal solutions. The model specified below enables us to see this crucial link at the microeconomic level between institutions and economic performance once self-interest is redefined to include opportunism or predation. In game theoretic terms, the existence of opportunism and predation leads to non-cooperative games between agents, and as Arrow (1994) indicates, it is difficult to define a competitive equilibrium as the outcome of a non-cooperative game. Consequently, unless there is some framework of rules which can control non-simple self-seeking behaviour such that market exchanges become a cooperative game, there will be a built-in tendency in the system towards fluctuation and disequilibrium. In spite of such behavioural foundations, however, the model outlined below is not based on methodological individualism. Rather, it accepts the view discussed earlier that the macro economy cannot be reduced to certain micro-foundations

(Hoover 2001) and that complex systems cannot be understood from an analysis of the components of the system alone (Colander 2008). Therefore the aggregate behaviour of the system cannot be deduced from the characteristics of a 'representative' of the population.

Starting in the top left-hand quadrant, the vertical axis represents the proportion of transaction costs to the total income of a country. The graph indicates that as markets become more pervasive or complex in an economy, the transaction costs of the functioning of the system increase. The underlying logic of this relationship is that a market is by definition a place where transactions occur. In simple markets dominated by arm's-length exchanges, the costs of transacting will obviously be very low. However, the more complex a market becomes, the less easy and more costly it will be to obtain the complete information that is necessary to make a well-informed choice, and given bounded rationality, the more difficult and costly it will be to process the available information. Therefore, in an advanced economy involving deep and complex markets with a huge volume of transactions, this implies high transaction costs. In the US for instance, 45 per cent of the national income is devoted to transacting (Wallis and North 1986). However, at some high level of complexity, the transaction costs per unit of income are likely to level off. The top right-hand quadrant shows the relationship between the presence of transaction costs and the possibilities of opportunism available to economic agents operating in the market. Since transaction costs arise from uncertainty and imperfect information, a higher quantum of transaction costs is indicative of the greater scope for opportunism and the possibilities for some agents to gain from such behaviour. The relationship between transaction costs and opportunism, however, also depends on the complexity and effectiveness of the institutional framework in place designed to control this opportunism. A stronger institutional framework will result in vector shifts to the left because a given level of transaction costs will be associated with a lower level of potential opportunism. With a weaker institutional framework the vector will move to the right.

The lower right-hand quadrant indicates the relationship between the potential opportunism in an economy and the complexity and effectiveness of the institutional framework required to control this opportunism. This is a negative relationship because the higher the level of potential opportunism – both that which is easily identifiable and that which may remain hidden within the complexities of the system – the greater is the extent and sophistication of the institutional framework of formal rules, regulations and governance structures, and their enforcement, required to prevent, limit or discourage such types of behaviour. Informal rules which promote trust and cooperation would, of course, lower the extent of the formal rules required. But in today's complex markets where only a small proportion of transaction are conducted at arm's

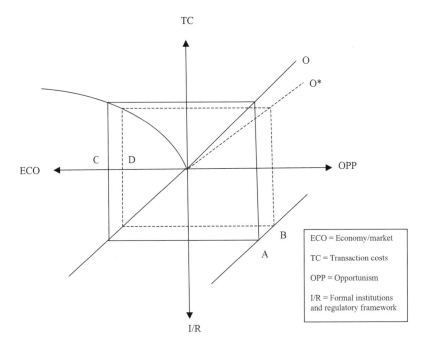

Figure 9.1   Institutions and market performance

length, even with high standards of moral values or trust, smooth transacting will require a significant presence of formal laws, rules and regulations to ensure that the right governance structures and incentive systems are in place. Without such a framework, economic exchanges between agents will be subjected to a high degree of unpredictability because the vector of prices in the market will be a product of distorted information and unequal exchanges. From the point of view of the individual economic agent, this will result in the gains from production and trade becoming highly uncertain, thereby lowering that agent's incentive to undertake productive activities and bringing about lower levels of overall economic activity. Following on from this, the lower left-hand quadrant indicates that to permit markets of a given level of complexity to function in a relatively self-regulating or stable manner, an appropriate level of formal rules, regulations, etc. needs to be put in place. These will provide the necessary institutional framework to control opportunism and predation and also supply a well-defined incentive framework to encourage productive behaviour.

As a test of the applicability of this model, we shall apply it to the recent sub-prime crisis in the US to evaluate whether it has any superior explanatory power compared to the mainstream model. Since the relevant facts pertaining to the sub-prime crisis are well known, they have not been included in the text and have instead been put in the Appendix. According to the efficient markets theory, based on the neoclassical model, financial markets – particularly in the US – are accepted to be the closest approximation to a perfectly competitive model that can be found anywhere. Such markets should therefore have had inherent self-regulating and self-equilibrating properties. However, as we well know, this was not the case. The framework outlined above, on the other hand, which is based on the observed human tendency towards opportunistic behaviour – whether motivated by a desire for immediate gratification or otherwise – bounded rationality, and incomplete information, and emphasizes the relationship between institutional or governance structures and incentives, seems however to provide a better basis by which to understand the genesis, mechanics and evolution of the recent market failure. Using this framework we can predict what is likely to happen if there is an imbalance between the size and complexity of an economy and the necessary level of laws and regulations required to sustain this system in a stable manner. This result is shown in the lower right-hand quadrant of the diagram. For the economy represented in Figure 9.1, and its given level of potential opportunism, the minimum institutional/regulatory framework required is that shown by point A in the bottom right-hand quadrant. However, if the formal institutional/regulatory frameworks are weak, as indicated by point B, this will lead to a downward shift in the opportunism vector from O to O* because for any given level of transaction costs the potential opportunism will be greater. This will lead to a proliferation of opportunistic and/or predatory agent behaviour which results in systemic risk, a disequilibrating cycle of events and possible market failure, causing the economy to contract from point C to point D.

PERVERSE INCENTIVES

To elaborate further on the model above, we shall consider two inter-related insights of Hayek's (1937, 1945, 1960). The first concerns the relationship between governance structures and incentives as they have developed historically within a capitalist economy; the second relates to the nature of the knowledge available within the economic system. Hayek (1960) argued that there was an inseparable link between personal responsibility and the capitalist order. Thus he stated that 'liberty not only means that the individual has both the opportunity and the burden of choice, it also means that he must bear the consequences of his action and will receive praise or blame for them' (1960: 71). Based on this view, Van Eeghen (1997) holds that the modern corporation, by violating the principle of personal responsibility, stimulates irresponsible behaviour. In other words, the manner in which the limited liability joint-stock corporation has evolved in recent times has resulted in incentive structures developing within such organizations that contribute to excessive risk taking by their managements. Incorporation, by removing the jurisdiction over a firm's assets from its owners, gives management a significant degree of autonomous power within a firm. Corporate managers have control over a firm's assets, while at the same time being free from the full responsibility of ownership (i.e. the liabilities that ownership automatically entails). In the absence of private accountability this leads to irresponsible behaviour.

In terms of the institutionalist model, the division between ownership and management creates the principal-agent problem – moral hazard – and the potential for opportunism. Moral hazard is a situation in which the agent, in this case the management of a corporation, is better informed, and whose true level of effort is unobservable by the principal, in this case the shareholders. Moral hazard opens the door to opportunistic behaviour and as Williamson (1975: 26) points out the hazards of opportunism are significant in any hierarchy like a large corporation because of sunk costs, information impactedness, the high costs of distinguishing between faulty and meritorious behaviour, and the small numbers bargaining problem. Furthermore, such opportunism in large organizations is particularly dangerous to the equilibrating process in the market because it can lie hidden within the hierarchy for a long time, and its costs can multiply and accumulate before it eventually emerges to affect market behaviour and market performance.

One of the major symptoms of the principal-agent problem and opportunism created by the division between ownership and management is that over time this has resulted in a system whereby the senior managers, including board members, of public companies have become more or less free to fix their own remuneration with little or no oversight from the real owners – the shareholders. This is particularly so in financial companies where in recent times the culture has become one in which the annual bonus for senior management has come to be much more important than their regular pay package. Since these bonuses depend on immediate turnover and profits there is a strong incentive for management to take excessive risks, because if the bet succeeds it is more likely to increase quarterly and annual profits and therefore their bonuses. Furthermore, since the share prices of public companies have shown themselves to be highly responsive to quarterly and annual profit statements, increasing such short-run profitability has become a central concern of managements in large corporations. In such circumstances, focusing on some nebulous concept of long-term viability and profitability would clearly not be the primary objective of management decision-making. These perverse incentives have been compounded by the fact that senior management are offered generous retirement pensions, and exit packages/golden parachutes in case of early termination, as part of their contracts at their time of appointment. Thus the long-term well-being of these individuals is protected irrespective of what happens to the firm or its shareholders. Consequently, the incentive of a senior manager is to maximize what he can extract from the present employer, without worrying too much about what the long-term effects might be on the viability of the organization. The huge bonuses received during the recent financial crisis by managers of Wall Street firms that subsequently went bankrupt support the view that corporate managers, particularly in the financial sector, are motivated by perverse incentives and opportunism.

In the banking sector, the moral hazard and potential opportunism created by the structure of the modern corporation represent an even more serious problem. This is because the banking system is based on the use of fractional reserves to create money and this has an inherent fragility. The assets which banks hold against their deposit liabilities consist to a large degree of illiquid non-marketable loans and advances. Inherent risk is created by the fact there is a maturity mismatch between these illiquid assets and highly liquid deposit liabilities and only a small amount of cash reserves will be held against the deposit liabilities. The only way to reduce this risk is to have a lender of last resort in the form of a central bank that provides systemic risk protection. However, this guarantee from the central bank encourages excessive leverage and risk taking because moral hazard is created since the banking system is considered too important to the economy to be allowed to fail and the expectation is that bailouts using public funds – such as the Savings & Loans bailout of the late 1980s and the more recent rescues of Wall Street banks and firms – will occur. Van Eeghen (2008: 65) argues that the fractional reserve system with guaranteed accommodation from a central bank results in institutionalized irresponsibility in the financial and banking systems. To contain the resultant irresponsible behaviour a maze of formal regulations is put in place. However, the problem remains because rules and regulations always have loopholes and can be circumvented, whereas the root of the problem, which is the fact that personal responsibility has been compromised, remains unaddressed.

In the financial and mortgage industries, apart from the systemic causes discussed above that contribute to moral hazard and opportunism, there are other specific factors which underlie the existence of a disequilibrating or perverse self-interest based on incentives. First, there is the small numbers bargaining problem. The problem is of particular significance in the US financial industry because of the Wall Street culture that has existed for the past decade or so. In this culture, anyone reaching the higher levels of one of the major banks or investment management firms was given iconic status as a financial guru. This created a restricted market in senior financial managers, thus generating rents and enabling such individuals to demand remuneration packages that were well beyond what might be considered reasonable, given the levels of expertise and effort required in more competitive circumstances. As it happens, events later showed that many of these so-called financial wizards were in fact incompetent and excessive risk takers who were driven by greed, with the high performance of their firms actually having been driven by excessive leverage and dubious financial innovations which eventually drove these firms to bankruptcy (see Appendix for more details). In 2006, for instance, Wall Street executives earned record compensation levels which included almost twenty-four billion US dollars in cash bonuses (Coval et al. 2009). By early 2008, however, three of the five largest Wall Street investment banks had gone bankrupt and most of their senior financial managers had lost their jobs. Recent revelations that the US financial authorities are investigating senior executives at Lehman Brothers – one of the investment banks that collapsed – for misleading investors and committing financial fraud, are consistent with this point of view.

Second, in the case of the US mortgage market, the specific nature of the 'originate and distribute' system as it emerged and functioned until very recently resulted in perverse incentives developing for all the actors participating in this market. The 'originate and distribute' system is based on mortgage brokers, mortgage banks, investment bankers and the credit rating agencies' earning fee income. Consequently, all the actors had a strong incentive to maximize their fee income by increasing the mortgage loan flow and the securitized products based on these flows, rather than to conduct business in a prudentially sound manner that would involve a proper assessment of the borrower's credit risk. Thus at all levels the presence of perverse incentives created the circumstances for opportunism, and given bounded rationality and short time horizons, it was inevitable that this would result in the development and expansion of an unsustainable sub-prime mortgage market, along with the issuance of hundreds of billions dollars worth of sub-prime based derivatives of dubious value.

INFORMATION IMPERFECTIONS

The second insight of Hayek's (1937, 1945) which is of relevance to our model is that knowledge in an economic system is inherently localized and decentralized and therefore the information available to any agent is necessarily incomplete. As Hayek argued, the economic data required for the allocation of resources are not a given. These do not and cannot exist in any person's mind. Rather, each individual will have knowledge about a particular resource and particular opportunities and it is the free market adjustment process that will enable all actors to use this information to generate the necessary data for decisions to be coordinated. In essence Hayek's argument is that although the information held by an individual is inherently limited, the price mechanism provides the necessary coordination through an adaptive process for such limited information to become the complete information necessary for efficient solutions to emerge at an aggregate market level. In this way, through the operation of the price mechanism, the central assumption of the neoclassical model of complete information is fulfilled. While such an observation may be valid for simple markets handled by a Walrasian auctioneer, the question that needs to be answered is whether the price – as a key economic statistic or variable – contains all the necessary information to ensure the coordination of actors and the achievement of efficient allocative solutions in today's complex markets.

At a theoretical level there are two issues that need to be considered here. First, while accepting Hayek's view of decentralized knowledge, in the context of uncertainty and bounded rationality there is no reason why this should lead to adaptive solutions. On the contrary, in circumstances of uncertainty, dispersed and incomplete information can lead to asymmetric and imperfect information amongst economic agents. Market prices will then not reflect the true opportunity costs and open the way for unequal bargaining and sub-optimal solutions. Second, because of the structure of the modern corporation which consists of layer upon layer of hierarchy, resulting in information impactedness and the principal-agent problem (Williamson 1975), much information that would be of relevance to the functioning of a market inevitably remains hidden within large companies and outside the ambit of the market. Such hidden information reduces the intrinsic ability of prices to reflect the true value of the goods and services being produced or traded by these companies and the price mechanism's ability to facilitate a market-clearing adaptive process.

The empirical evidence suggests that our theoretical conjectures do have some validity. In the context of financial markets, the weakness of prices to act as a key statistic to facilitate efficient allocative solutions has become increasingly obvious as a result of the recent sub-prime related financial crisis. This is shown by the following four examples.

First, in the case of financial products, the market price is supposed to reflect the risk-adjusted discounted value of future cash flows, with the expectation that the security prices generated by the generally used statistical models will follow a normal distribution. In such a distribution, the likelihood of an observation occurring many standard deviations beyond a 95 per cent confidence interval is infinitesimal. Pricing and risk assessment models will therefore ignore such possibilities. However, such wide price fluctuations are precisely what have been observed during financial bubbles such as the collapse of the LTCM hedge fund in 1987 and the Asian financial crisis. More recently, in August 2007, when two large Goldman Sachs hedge funds collapsed, price moves of up to 25 standard deviations away from the expected normal distribution were observed several days running (Crotty 2009). Such unexpected and large impact random events have been termed the 'black swan' problem in financial economics (Taleb 2007). These examples indicate that the pricing of any financial product in what are considered to be 'normal' market conditions depends on the assumptions made in the underlying model. Such prices are therefore likely to be just as much a reflection of subjective assessments as being indicators of relevant objective factors in a market. In 2007 for instance, Fitch, the rating agency, was using a model which assumed a home price appreciation in the low single digits. As accepted by its own analysts, this model would completely break down, and the ratings of mortgage-backed securities generated would be completely different, if an extended period with house price depreciation of even 2 per cent per annum occurred (Coval et al. 2009).

Second, the pricing of risk has become a much more difficult issue in recent years with the development of the derivatives market. This problem is symptomatic of the current trend towards new and structured financial products, and not limited to the financial innovation in the mortgage market. Of course derivatives based on the sub-prime mortgage market epitomized this increasing complexity and opaqueness of products. Thus, for instance, sub-prime-based collateralized debt obligations (CDOs), which were already complex tranched mortgage-backed products, were further tranched into instruments called CDO squared products. Roubini (2008) states that as such products were marked to model rather than marked to market, it was doubtful if anyone could really price them correctly. Consequently, when uncertainty increased in this market, unprecedented fluctuations in prices occurred. For example, in February 2009, many triple A-rated CDOs composed of mezzanine (as against senior) tranches lost 95 per cent of their value.

Third, Crotty (2009) reports that 80 per cent of the 680 trillion US dollars worth of traded derivatives are sold over the counter in private deals negotiated between investment banks and customers. Since such private deals do not constitute a transparent competitive market, it is not evident to what extent such prices can be considered 'efficient' from the point of view of resource allocation.

Fourth, given the complexity of financial markets and financial products, the human characteristic of bounded rationality – in particular our computational limitations – is likely to become a serious constraint on the ability of market players to undertake the necessary risk/return or price calculations necessary for any maximization process to be meaningful. The availability of computing power does not change this situation, since all computer programmes need certain assumptions to be built into them, and such assumptions require the necessary human cognitive capabilities to understand all the relevant parameters of the market being considered. Take the example of mortgage-backed securities. Coval, Jurek and Stafford (2009) show that the high credit ratings given to senior tranches of CDOs was based on two incorrect assessments by the rating agencies. First, it was based on the confidence that they could estimate the default risks associated with the underlying securities with a considerable degree of precision, and second, that they could assess the degree to which likely defaults in this pool of securities would be correlated. As it happens their assessments, based on historical data and their understanding of the functioning of the housing market, were both wrong.

As a consequence of the factors discussed above, the profit/income maximization behaviour of key actors in the banking, financial, and mortgage industries, induced by perverse incentives and imperfect information, resulted in a sub-prime mortgage market worth hundreds of billion dollars developing. The systemic risk generated by this behaviour was compounded by banks and financial institutions creating even greater liquidity based on leveraging this mortgage lending to bring into existence a huge market consisting of new financial instruments and debt obligations. The consequences on financial markets and the world economy in general of the unravelling of the US sub-prime and related derivatives market are well known and need no further discussion here. What is important to note though is that once the ripple effects started affecting one market after another there was no self-regulating or self-equilibrating reaction. On the contrary, substantial and coordinated interventions by governments on a world-wide basis were required to prevent total market failure. Consistent with the model summarized in Figure 9.1, the sub-prime crisis and subsequent credit crunch have shown that since the existing formal regulatory structures and governance mechanisms at the time were inadequate to control opportunism and support the smooth functioning of existing markets, most financial markets in the developed world either shrank or collapsed, resulting in a precipitous decline in economic activity.

In sum, therefore, our analysis indicates that markets do not function in the manner proposed by neoclassical theory. At a fundamental level the recent events show that there is a considerable difference between the impact of maximizing behaviour in simple demand and supply-driven markets of the type that inspired classical and neoclassical theory and that which occurs in the context of the complex integrated markets that exist today. In simple markets maximization behaviour, through the quick adaptive process that Hayek emphasized, can impact on demand and supply and result in a self-equilibrating and self-regulating system. However, this is not the case any more in the modern economy. First, the governance structures that exist within modern capitalism, particularly in the financial sector, have changed the nature of incentives faced by key actors in the system. These structures result in moral hazard and perverse incentives, leading to opportunistic behaviour amongst market participants. Second, the economy contains a lot of hidden information. In particular, the hierarchical structure of the large corporation automatically creates such hidden information, and since such corporations account for a substantial portion of the output generated in an advanced economy, this means that key economic information remains unavailable to market actors.

Finally, even where all the public information is in the price, that price may itself be the product of models based on subjective assessments. This is particularly so for most financial instruments, where the price is an estimate of the risk-adjusted return. Unfortunately, in spite of this intrinsic reality, until the recent financial crisis, modern metric-based risk management models, which use mathematical formulae to calculate the value of financial derivatives, claimed a degree of accuracy that gave investment managers a false sense of objectivity. Thus the Black-Scholes and other models based on default probabilities were widely used on Wall Street and elsewhere, although they had been criticized as being dangerous by many financial analysts and mathematicians (*Economist*: Special Report on Financial Risk, 11 February 2010). As it happens, contrary to what was assumed in these models, the recent history of financial markets has shown that events do not follow a statistical normal distribution – 'black swans' and extreme fluctuations occur with greater frequency than expected. Consequently, such probabilistic models based on historical data have proven to be wrong time and again, showing that risk evaluation is an inherently subjective activity.

A direct consequence of the factors discussed above is that modern markets are subject to a great deal of uncertainty and incomplete information is the inevitable situation faced by all market actors. These information imperfections, particularly in financial markets, imply that the market-generated price may not be a sufficient statistic to guide adaptive behaviour towards efficient solutions. And since the financial sector accounts for such a dominant part of a modern economy – in 2006 in the US this sector generated about 40 per cent of corporate profits, and the value of financial assets was over ten times the value of GDP – mispricing or uncertainty about the true value of its products will clearly have a disequilibrating impact on the performance of the economy. Thus, as emphasized by Keynes (1936, 1937), Minsky (1977) and Akerlof and Shiller (2009), capitalism left to its own devices is inherently unstable and naturally subject to volatility. Therefore to eliminate or at least minimize this tendency towards instability a 'visible hand' of appropriate institutional frameworks – both formal and informal – and governance structures that will generate the right kind of incentives is required. Such institutions and structures can play the role of:

- reducing the opaqueness of markets and promoting greater transparency so that fuller information is available to market participants such that more realistic assessments of risk and return can be made;
- reducing uncertainty by creating a more rule-bound and predictable framework for economic transactions;
- controlling opportunism and predation and providing a framework which generates incentives that will encourage all actors to behave in a benign simple self-seeking manner which will contribute to efficient solutions being achieved.

Any model that attempts to explain the functioning of the modern economic system must necessarily accept these insights. Unfortunately, the neoclassical model and efficient market theories based on this model misguided policy decision-makers about the true nature of markets and persuaded them that deregulated markets and uncontrolled capitalism would lead to the most efficient solutions. This resulted in a paradigm shift away from the regulatory frameworks developed subsequent to the Great Depression of the 1930s, culminating in the free market ideologies of the Thatcher-Reagan era. In the US, for instance, financial deregulation accelerated after the 1980s, finally resulting in the repeal of the Glass-Steagall Act of 1933 and the passing of the Financial Modernization Act in 1999. Through the latter Act, the legal division between commercial and investment banking that had been in place since the 1930s was abolished and unregulated financial innovation was given free rein. The extent to which academics and policy-makers were misguided by the mainstream neoclassical model is shown by the testimony of Alan Greenspan before the Congressional Committee on Oversight and Government Reform in 2008 (www.nytimes.com/2008/10/24/business/economy/24panel.htm). Greenspan was Chairman of the US Federal Reserve Board from1987 to 2006. He was also a staunch free-market ideologist and one of the most important and influential financial regulators during that period. In his remarks he admitted that he had put too much faith in the self-correcting power of free markets and had also failed to anticipate the self-destructive power of wanton mortgage lending. Referring to the conventional economic wisdom that unfettered financial markets would spread risk widely, he noted, 'This modern risk management paradigm held sway for decades. The whole intellectual edifice however, collapsed in the summer of last year' (*New York Times*, 23 October 2008).

THE STATE AND THE MARKETS

In this chapter we have argued that the effective functioning of the market mechanism as an instrument of coordination – both to promote stable economic growth, as well as to fulfil the dynamic needs of economic development – requires the intervention of government in one form or another. A developed market economy at a minimum requires an adequate framework of laws, rules and regulations to provide order and predictability. In contrast to this, a developing country with weak and fragmented markets requires deeper intervention by the state to overcome information imperfections and coordination problems. This latter situation, where an economy is characterized by widespread market failure, can also be analysed using the transaction cost-based four quadrant framework presented earlier. In Figure 9.2 we compare two economies X and Y with similar per capita incomes and economic structures, but economy Y has a greater extent of market failure than economy X. Greater market failure implies that the coordination problem is more severe and thus there will be a higher level of transaction costs per unit of output and greater potential for rent-seeking and predatory behaviour. Economy X will be able to correct the market failure with a lower level of government intervention, as shown by the low state intervention and regulation vector AB in the bottom right-hand quadrant. However this degree of intervention is inadequate for economy Y. To compensate for the greater information imperfections and

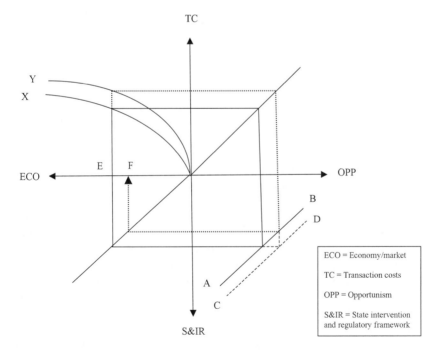

Figure 9.2   Institutions and opportunism/predation

coordination problems a deeper level of government intervention is required, as represented by the high state intervention and regulation vector CD. In Figure 9.2 the quantitative and qualitative difference in the extent of government intervention required to correct the greater degree of market failure is represented by an outward shift of this vector rather than marginal movements along it. Without this more complex framework of interventions economic performance in Y will either remain static or show declines, shrinking to a point such as F in the top left-hand quadrant.

An important assumption which is implicit in the model above is that the state is an independent and benign actor that will act in an optimum manner to correct market failure and fulfil the requirements of economic efficiency. However, since the fundamental nature of the state is that it is an organization which has a monopoly over the use of violence, there is no reason why this coercive power may not be used for the benefit of the few who are in control of the machinery of the state. For Marxists this is not a problematic view since the state is seen as an instrument of repression to protect the interests of the ruling classes. As we discussed in Chapter 3, for new institutionalists as well the state is seen as having the potential of being used as an instrument of predation whereby ruling elites will extract monopoly rents and distribute these amongst the dominant coalition (North 1981, 2009). Thus, for instance, North and Weingast (1989) and Levi (1988) refer to the rulers of France and Spain in the 17th century who acted in a predatory manner, extracting as much revenue as they could from the population and creating property rights structures and economic institutions that were not conducive to economic efficiency. Such predatory behaviour is, of course, not just an historical phenomenon, but as we discussed in Chapter 2, also a common occurrence in the developing world. In Asia, Africa and Latin America there have been any number of kleptocratic dictators and neo-patrimonial regimes that have used the machinery of the state to systematically plunder their own countries for the benefit of small ruling elites.

This problem of state power and the nature of the state has been succinctly phrased by Weingast (1995: 1) who points out that a state 'strong enough to protect property rights and enforce contracts is also strong enough to confiscate the wealth of its citizens'. The central question therefore is how to get the state to credibly commit to limiting its own power and to adopt a set of policies that will preserve markets and promote economic efficiency. A large literature now agrees that the state's ability to make commitments which are credible depends on the nature of the political institutions that constitute that state (Moe 1990, 1991; North and Weingast 1989; Persson and Tabellini 2000; Weingast 1995). Barzel (2002), for instance, argues that the best way to achieve a self-enforcing arrangement that limits the power of the state is to have a rule of law state, where the power of the state is itself divided through a separation of powers. Such a separation will result in mechanisms within the state that will act as checks and balances for each other. Democracy is one such system which has a separation of powers. However, as the survey of empirical evidence on the relationship between democracy and economic growth in Chapter 5 showed, there is a weak association between these two variables and achieving high rates of growth does not necessarily require a democratic state.

While democracy may not be a necessary condition for good economic performance, nevertheless a set of political institutions that will result in the control of arbitrary power and the establishment of a rule of law state does seem to be a fundamental requirement for the state to be able to credibly commit to the protection of property rights and the preservation of markets. Thus North and Weingast (1989) show that in feudal 17th century Britain, after the Glorious Revolution of 1688, the emergent capitalist classes were able to introduce new political institutions which controlled arbitrary power and enabled the state to make a credible commitment to the protection of property rights. Similarly, in communist China, Montinola, Qian and Weingast (1996) discuss the changes in economic and political institutions after 1980 which brought about a credible commitment of the state to the system of what they call 'market preserving federalism'. They argue that as a consequence of political decentralization, fiscal autonomy, the market-oriented ideology of the Communist Party, and the opening up of the economy, the discretionary authority of the national government was significantly limited and competition amongst sub-national governments was encouraged. This brought about a balance of power, and a credible commitment to the system from whoever might be in power, without elections and a formal separation of powers as is the case in the West.

In conclusion, therefore, the discussion above indicates that while government has a legitimate role in preserving markets and facilitating economic growth, 'government failure' is a significant danger because the state can act, and has commonly acted, on behalf of narrow elites (including the state bureaucracy itself) rather than in the interests of overall economic efficiency. Greater state intervention increases the possibilities of rent-seeking and predation. Therefore, for increased government intervention to have a positive impact on efficiency, it will need to be done in the context of better institutions of economic and political governance. Otherwise, the increased state intervention is very likely to result in higher opportunistic and predatory behaviour, particularly by the agents of the state, as has been widely observed in the countries of the developing world that have followed such interventionist policies. To minimize the danger of government failure our analysis suggests that a number of conditions are necessary.

- First, while the evidence indicates that political pluralism may not be necessary, the political institutions of the state must be such that there is a dispersion of political power among its different structures so that a system of check and balances emerges.
- Second, a rule of law state must be established which protects property and contractual rights.
- Third, while free markets have failed, the dominant state has also failed. On the other hand, the experience of the East Asian economies, India and China after 1980, and more recently the advanced countries after the sub-prime related financial crisis, indicates that economic performance is best advanced by a market economy with regulation and/or intervention by the state in a manner which is designed to enhance the functioning of markets.

As discussed in Chapters 2 and 3, all these conditions can be reinforced by progressive ideas and ideologies as well as the informal rules or social capital in a society. Social capital in particular can play a significant role in influencing agent behaviour to commit to a common vision or ideology of how society should be organized and function. Where such social capital or nationally 'inherited ethical habit' (Fukuyama 1995: 34) is strong, as seems to have been the case in the East Asian economies, opportunism or predation motivated by private self-interest is likely to be constrained by a vision of the common social good. This is probably one of the main reasons why the state bureaucracies in the East Asian countries managed to function in a relatively uncorrupt manner and vigorously promoted the industrialization of their economies in the 1970s and 1980s, whereas such interventionist strategies failed in the rest of the developing world.

10. Mechanisms of institutional transition

Our final task is to apply the 'visible hand' or 'made order' perspective of this study, and the generalizations arrived at through the theoretically informed inductive approach, to the process of institutional change. The purpose is to attempt the construction of a theory of institutional change which provides a more coherent explanation for the observed transitions that have occurred in the past hundred years or so, particularly in the developing world. Such a framework is necessary, because the presence of low-level equilibrium traps and dysfunctional institutions which encourage rent-seeking and predatory behaviour in large parts of the developing world, challenges the classical notion (Hayek 1973, Smith [1776]1904) that the necessary beneficent order will emerge spontaneously, or evolve naturally through some adaptive process, to facilitate productive economic activity. In Chapter 6 we found that the favourable institutions underlying modern economic growth in Western Europe emerged in a manner that could be interpreted as being spontaneous and evolutionary. However, this has not been the case in the non-Western world. As the case studies of Japan, India and Botswana showed, in the context of the non-Western world, societies do not seem to have the necessary endogenous forces to bring about the emergence of institutions that encourage good economic and political governance in a gradual, incremental, evolutionary manner. It has generally been the case in these societies that elite behaviour has tended to be dominated by predation rather than rational self-seeking. In these circumstances unless the forces in society that support favourable change can overcome the collective action problem, or the ruling elites themselves are inspired by progressive ideas, beneficent social and institutional change will not occur.

This view implies that irrespective of whether it is through the collective action of interested groups or the leadership of an elite, ideas and ideologies will become the central force underlying institutional innovation, with institutional change only occurring when there is the explicit intervention of human agency. In our case studies this human agency was found to be the activities of a small and enlightened domestic elite; an individual leader of great prestige; or in certain circumstances, even an external agency. Such an intervention is necessary to break the low-level institutional trap that a country is stuck in, and through a process characterized by discontinuities and historically abrupt changes, can bring about the establishment of superior institutions. As Hodgson (2006) argues, institutional change of this kind can become self-enforcing over time through a process of reconstitutive downward causation, as the case studies of Japan, India and Botswana have shown, if the new institutions bring about behavioural change and generate the necessary social forces required to ensure the efficient functioning of the newly created institutions themselves. The detailed account of deep institutional interventions undertaken in Southern Sudan by an external force in cooperation with local elites since 2005 further suggests that this is a useful and potentially successful model for development policy and practice, particularly in post-conflict or fragile states.

INSTITUTIONS, RATIONALITY AND PREDATION

Based on this 'made order' perspective, a model of institutional change can be developed. We would argue that such a theory will provide a more coherent explanation for the observed transitions that have occurred in the past hundred years or so, particularly in the developing world. A starting point for such a hypothesis would be the behavioural model discussed in Chapter 2 that emerges out of modern genetics and cognitive psychology. In the context of society, this model of man leads to the Hobbesian view that given humanity's natural condition of war against each other, or in other words a conflict of interest, it is only by a common agreement to recognize certain restraints or covenants of behaviour that the natural state of violence can be transcended and a cooperative social order established. Developing on this theme we have North's (1981, 1990, 2009) insights that institutions are the formal and informal rules of the game and their enforcement characteristics which human beings have devised to govern interaction amongst themselves. Anthropology shows us that the initial formation of such rules is based on customs and other informal norms. Subsequently these informal rules accumulate as the social capital of that society depending upon the culture, beliefs, and history of that country or region. By social capital we mean the informal norms, obligations and expectations that have evolved from prior social interaction and determine trust and other forms of cooperative behaviour in a society. Such capital inheres in the structure of relations between actors, enhances the information and coordination of markets, reduces transaction costs, and eventually contributes to the efficiency of productive processes (Coleman 2000). However, it is also in the nature of social capital that once it begins to accumulate and become more elaborate it will increasingly influence future modes of behaviour. The behavioural rules at a particular moment of time will therefore vary, depending on the interaction between the existing institutions – both formal and informal – in a society and the basic instincts for predation and survival that we have inherited from the past.

In a primitive society with no formal institutions and limited social capital, the basic instinct to survive would ensure that, beyond one's immediate family or group, behaviour would be primarily opportunistic or predatory. As a society develops agricultural communities and feudal institutions, survival and betterment would necessitate purely opportunistic behaviour to be overridden by new rules such as loyalty to one's tribe, clan, and eventually ruler. Finally, with the growth of capitalism and its formal institutions to regulate impersonal interaction and exchange, human beings would be encouraged to act in a more self-interested yet benign manner. The creation of a more well-defined set of opportunities available within an established institutional matrix would limit predation and encourage the development of value systems that, in principle, could approximate the paradigm of self-interested rationality found in neoclassical economic theory. Where a well-established institutional matrix exists, an actor could be expected to limit their choices to a basket of opportunities that would lie within his own budget and capabilities, rather than trying to take away the endowments of other individuals by choosing to rob, steal, plunder, or act in a predatory manner (Bardhan 2000). As predators and pirates we therefore respond to the incentives contained in the economic and political institutions we are confronted with and change our behaviour accordingly. This characterization of the role of institutions in conditioning beliefs and value systems does not in any way deny the validity of the historical arguments which show causation to be in the opposite direction. The comparative history literature has convincingly shown us the fundamental role played by religion, culture, homogeneity and historical legacy in determining the speed and depth of modern economic and political development. This only illustrates that the reverse effect of institutions on value systems is equally relevant, particularly in the context of institutional transitions in the non-western world.

If human nature is viewed along this continuum from predatory to rational self-seeking, in a socially undeveloped and institutionally backward society, a small group that has gained ascendancy due to historical, ethnic or religious factors will then be naturally motivated to utilize its political power to act in a predatory manner and use the resources of the state for the benefit of its limited constituency. Efforts to introduce more productive systems of economic and political governance in such circumstances will fail because the group will subvert these processes for its own benefit. However, with economic growth as the size of the elite group or groups increases in a particular society, there is a greater need for certain rules of interaction to emerge so that predatory activities do not result in conflict and mutual destruction. It could be argued that as the size of dominant economic groups increases, at some point diminishing returns to predation will set in. The accumulation of informal rules of interaction or social capital would then form the basis for formal institutional development. These informal rules include those that were emphasized by Smith ([1776]1904) a long time ago for the proper functioning of a market-based system, such as fair play, prudence and common understanding, as well as those highlighted by Arrow (1974) more recently, such as trust and honesty. Habitual behaviour based on such informal rules would ensure that as a society progresses, and the size of dominant groups become a larger and larger proportion of the population, economic agents will increasingly act in what is considered to be a rational self-interested manner, resulting in the social good. In the initial stages of institutional development it is particularly important to emphasize the role of informal rules of behaviour, because in the absence of self-enforcing systems ruling elites who have the power to make formal laws will not be constrained by such formal institutions.

In this model predation and piracy are constrained by institutional development in which are embedded both informal and formal rules of behaviour, which although perhaps contrary to our basic instincts are accepted as necessary for mutual benefit and will over the course of time become habitual to our thought and practice. This view enables us to understand why societies with large middle classes have more stable institutional structures, achieve a greater consensus on rules and systems for the enforcement of rules, display higher levels of per capita income, and achieve higher rates of economic growth, as compared to other societies (Easterly 2001). It is also consistent with the historical fact that in societies where a long period of evolutionary institutional development has resulted in mature economic and political institutions abrupt changes are generally not observed. The arguments presented above can be graphically expressed as follows (Chakravarti 2006: 91):

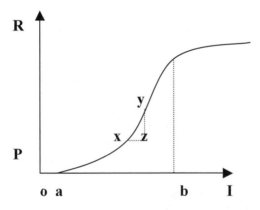

*Figure 10.1	Institutions and economic rationality*

Figure 10.1 above shows the relationship between the development of institutions and the progression from predatory to rational self-seeking behaviour. The X-axis shows institutional development, while the Y-axis shows increasing levels of economic rationality, in the standard neoclassical sense. Starting from a base level primitive society there would have to be some institutional creation up to point **a**, before any change in predatory activity could be expected. This would probably be in the form of an accumulation of informal rules of social behaviour. Subsequently, predatory and opportunistic behaviours are likely to respond slowly to institutional creation until a threshold of institutional development has been reached. This threshold level would be one where formal and informal rules have reached a point sufficient to underpin the emergence of incrementally more complex impersonal structures of exchange. Once a high level of economic rationality is reached, further institutional development is likely to have a limited impact on economic behaviour. However, as was argued in Chapter 9, since opportunism in one form or another will continue to exist, to permit the smooth functioning of more complex markets and economic systems more sophisticated institutional frameworks and governance structures will continue to be required. Thus there will always be a role for public collective action in the form of state intervention to provide an enabling legal and regulatory environment to facilitate the functioning of markets.

In this model, culture, beliefs, homogeneity and historical legacy have a central role to play in the interaction between institutions and behaviour. They determine:

- the intercept **oa** or the initial stock of social capital necessary to influence the primary move away from predatory behaviour;
- slope of the curve, which shows how strong the impact of institutional change will be on behaviour in particular society;
- the point **b**, where a long period of institutional development has permitted behavioural patterns to emerge which could, in principle, approximate the assumptions of the rational choice paradigm adequately for the neoclassical theory to offer an acceptable description of reality. It can be seen from the diagram, that the neoclassical paradigm is only a limiting case.

If we accept the plausibility of this hypothesis, it has significant implications for the way in which the process of development should be viewed and for the appropriate policy approaches that need to taken to promote sustainable economic growth. In Sub-Saharan Africa and countries of the former Soviet Union where institutional frameworks are weak and elite groups are small relative to the rest of the population, predatory action by the state will be the natural order of the day. Efforts to correct market failures that occur during the early periods of industrialization through increased state intervention are only likely to worsen economic outcomes, because the increased power of the state will be used for predatory purposes by the dominant groups that are in control of the state. On the other hand, in regions such as East Asia – where formal and informal rules of interaction have developed over long periods of time for the peaceful sharing of a society's wealth, and larger elite groups or middle classes have emerged – such predatory action is more likely to be constrained, and consequently there is more scope for successful government action to accelerate the process of development. There is clearly a threshold in each society where incentive structures develop to a point such that elite groups begin to find it more beneficial to modify their behaviour from being preda-tory to being more inclusive and socially productive. Consistent with the comparative history findings, this book agrees that the achievement of this threshold depends on the culture, beliefs, historical legacy, and the accumu-lated social capital in a society. However, although historically in Western Europe and North America the process of reaching this point has tended to be gradual and incremental, the more recent 20th century experience suggests that there could be discontinuities in the trajectory of institutional develop-ment, with abrupt movements occurring in either a favourable or unfavourable direction. A favourable move such as occurred in Botswana or Japan is shown in Figure 10.1 by a discontinuity which moves the society from point **x** to point **y**, moving along the dotted lines **xzy**. These discontinuities imply that there may be more non-deterministic and less path-dependent ways of achiev-ing higher levels of institutional development.

ENDOGENOUS *vs* EXOGENOUS FACTORS

In terms of the actual trajectory of institutional change, the historical experi-ence of Western Europe discussed earlier showed us that this depends on the outcome of bargaining between economic and political actors. The evidence indicated that since a ruler or dominant elite in control of a state represents a concentrated interest, the occurrence of institutional change depends on the presence of factors that will enable weaker forces to gain strength and confront the entrenched interests. In this context, the theoretical literature considered in Chapter 3 emphasized the role that ideas and ideologies play in providing a basis for overcoming the collective action problem and enabling weaker forces to organize themselves and undertake joint action against the concentrated force. While ideas and ideologies are of course important, this argument does not take into account the role played by the technology of violence in either facilitating or hindering the potentials or possibilities for successful collective action. In the early Middle Ages this technology was such that stone castles could not be easily breached. This gave scope to cities, communes and individual lords to function relatively autonomously from any central ruling power and resulted in a decentralized state of governance in Europe at that time. The introduction of gun powder and the cannon nullified this advantage and facilitated the formation of larger centralized feudal nation states.

Likewise, in modern times, the development of lethal weaponry makes it a virtual impossibility for unorganized masses to challenge those who are in control of the machinery of the state. So long as a regime in power is able and willing to use unrestrained lethal force, social unrest even on a large scale will have no impact. Recent events in Burma, Iran, Zimbabwe and Libya bear this out very clearly. This implies that while domestic solutions based on ideas and ideologies that have emerged from within a society may be the preferred mechanism to bring about institutional change, unless there are domestic forces powerful enough to challenge the entrenched interests such change is not likely to occur. As it happens, evidence on the continued presence of predatory regimes – and the persistence of institutional and poverty traps in large parts of the developing world – suggests that progressive domestic forces tend to be weak and incapable of bringing about endogenous change. In the circumstances, endogenous institutional change will only occur if the ruling elite is itself motivated by progressive ideas and ideologies. If this is not the case then change will not occur, unless it is supported or engineered by an external force.

Evidence which suggests that the endogenous view of social transition is incorrect can be found in other social disciplines as well. In anthropology, for instance, based on ethnological studies in East Africa, Thurnwald (1932) indicated that for simpler homogeneous societies to break out of their homeostatic condition and transition to more advanced forms, an exogenous force, in the nature of new cultural or other contacts such as warfare, will be required to initiate the process of change. Even in the sphere of economic policy it is commonly argued that at times interventions that originate from outside the market, such as an exogenous government intervention, may be the only way to eliminate a bad equilibrium in a private market and enable the economic system to function more efficiently. Based on the model outlined above, and the historical evidence we have considered, it could be argued that an international or 'exogenous' intervention may be the only way to move a country stuck in a low-level institutional trap onto a path of sustained efficiency enhancing institutional change. The increasing legitimacy of modern systems that guarantee economic and political freedoms, the globalization of values that emerge out of these systems, and the subordination of local culture and beliefs to certain commonly held human values reinforce the view that successful institutional change cannot be an agenda which is left to domestic groups operating within a nation state. Rather, a case could be made for the view that the elaboration of pre-designed institutional frameworks or templates which embody democratic and capitalist principles, and efforts to introduce them into the developing world, albeit with local variations in form, is a meaningful strategy to accelerate the process of economic development.

Rodrik (1999), elaborating on how the institutions of a market-based system can be acquired, states that there are two options that can be followed. First, institutional blueprints can be imported from successful economies, and second, if it believed that local conditions are very specific, then unique solutions based on local knowledge may be required. While Rodrik's distinction is valid, his juxtaposition is extreme, because while capitalism in the US may be different in certain respects from that in Japan or Europe, certain fundamental characteristics are common. These include the control of arbitrary power and the rule of law, security of property rights, effective legal systems to protect these rights, a reasonably efficient bureaucracy, the absence of corruption, political structures which permit the peaceful management of social conflict, etc. Local history, custom and culture undoubtedly influence the exact character of the institutions that are established or that emerge, however, to argue that countries have such a high degree of specificity that they require unique institutions goes against the empirical evidence presented earlier on the deep determinants of economic growth and development. The borrowing of market and non-market institutions which have proven to be historically successful is therefore a good starting point for any country. Institutional development in this scenario would then become a composite of local evolutionary tendencies, if any, and international models, supported by international action where necessary and possible, to accelerate the achievement of levels of economic and political governance which are more favourably disposed towards productive behaviour and productive activities. Such a process would be further aided and abetted by the present international political environment, which is increasingly hostile to elite groups acting in a predatory manner within the confines of their own borders.

DISCONTINUOUS CHANGE

The concept of discontinuous change presented here is very much in the Marxian tradition (Marx [1859]1958). However, it is an inversion of the Marxian system, in that we would argue it is the superstructure, (i.e. formal and informal institutions, the character of the state, etc.) that will determine the nature of the economic and political relationships between agents and whether they behave in a productive manner or not. More specifically, the model described above finds its inspiration in the works of Max Weber (1927, 1965,

1968). Weber's study of the variability of economic and political institutions across various societies convinced him that the institutional system of the modern Western world was not a 'natural' order that had evolved gradually, but that it was one which represented only one of several possible lines of social development. To him, ideas were fundamental and central in explaining historical processes. Thus he argued that the genesis of capitalism in the West was based on the historical ascendancy of the ideas of ascetic rationalism that formed the core of the Protestant ethic. This rationalism implied that custom and tradition had been devalued and everything was now judged according to a universalistic and generalized set of impersonal standards. As a consequence of this cultural evolution in the occident, two conditions had come to exist that underpinned the emergence of a modern capitalist economy. First, a mentality or set of attitudes to economic activity had come into being such that all actors oriented their decisions to the rational rather than traditional, weighing utilities and costs in a context of wide scope. Second, a political and legal order had emerged, which Weber called a rational-legal state, in which governance was based on an impartial universalistic legal system. Weber argued that these factors would result in social relationships, such as economic transactions between actors, where the effort was 'to attain control over opportunities and advantages which are also desired by others' (Weber 1968: 132) being conducted in a peaceful manner. While emphasizing the role of ideas on historical development, though, he made it clear that his aim was not 'to substitute for a one-sided materialistic an equally one-sided spiritualistic causal interpretation of culture and history' (1965: 183). Thus in a more complete analysis of social change 'it would also further be necessary to investigate how Protestant Asceticism was in turn influenced in its development and character by the totality of social conditions, especially economic' (1965: 183).

Returning to our model, this Weberian perception of the dynamic interaction between basic human instincts, ideas and institutions provides us with clues that are useful in explaining the different patterns of institutional change observed during the 20th century. While we have seen that 'rational' institutions can be introduced or imposed by an elite group, external force, or transitory event, it is evident that their successful absorption and development is a more complex issue. Our study indicates that a favourable progression of institutional discontinuities over time requires that social changes occur and social forces emerge whose presence will reinforce the functioning of these very institutions. The significance of the emergence of a middle class, with its interest in the security of property rights and the rule of law, has been widely emphasized (Easterly 2001). The role of education in promoting political development and rational modes of behaviour has also been highlighted by Lipset (1960). Glaeser et al. (2004) empirically tested Lipset's view and found that for a sample of 71 countries, over the period 1950–1980, schooling was a major causal factor explaining democratic institutions. Meanwhile Coleman (2000) and others have emphasized the catalytic role played by the initial stock of informal institutions or the reservoir of social capital available in a particular society.

Considering all these factors in the context of the case studies discussed above, the key common element that emerges is that the progressive elite groups, domestic or external, that brought about the initial institutional discontinuities, used their dominant position to ensure that the new frameworks and policies remained in place for a period of time that was long enough to facilitate the emergence of the new social forces and social attitudes that were necessary to underpin these very institutions. In India and Botswana, the domestic elite group supported progressive institutions and implemented policies favourable to the security of property rights, which gradually created a local middle class and a culture that supported a pluralistic society. In Japan, the external occupying force did much the same thing: demolishing the feudal system, allowing the growth of an indigenous middle class, and encouraging the development of an open society. Thus over time in these societies, as happened in Western Europe, the institutions became self-enforcing through the expansion of education, the development of a middle class, an increase in social capital, and associated changes in ideas, beliefs and behaviour.

Using this model, and the self-enforcing factors mentioned above, it is easy to understand the failure of institutional development in most of Sub-Saharan Africa. At the time of independence African countries did not have a middle class, they had low levels of education, and given the dominance of fragmented tribal structures, they had inadequate reserves of social capital to support the requirements of a modern developmental state. In comparison to the situation in our three case study countries, the elites in power were motivated by predatory tendencies which eventually resulted in the establishment of neo-patrimonial states. One significant difference between Sub-Saharan Africa and countries of the near and far east, is that the latter group – which includes Japan, India, and the countries of East Asia – is made up of old civilizations with reserves of social capital that have accumulated and deepened over many thousands of years. As Furubotn and Richter (2005: 25) note, the evolution of social capital takes considerable amounts of real resources and time to become effective. However, once certain socially enforced norms are in place and can influence inter-personal relations (e.g. trust or honesty) these will clearly form a good basis for the absorption and functioning of new and more complex institutions which will broadly conform to such values.

A caveat to the above argument could be that it has difficulty in explaining the institutional failure observed in the former Soviet Union, which shares much of the long history and culture of Europe. However, this seeming aberration in Russia can be explained by two factors. First, pre-communist Russia was in many ways a medieval society and one of the most backward of all European nations, with a ruling elite that was particularly small, authoritarian, and oppressive. Slavery was abolished only in the late 1800s. The country was almost completely agrarian and feudal until the Communists fast-tracked industrialization from the 1930s onwards. Therefore, in terms of social structure, it probably had a much greater similarity to many developing countries rather than to Europe. A second explanation – and one which is consistent with the idea of transitory events causing discontinuities in institutional development – is that 70 years (almost two generations) of communist rule based on predatory and opportunistic modes of governance debilitated the traditional conventions, norms and beliefs to such an extent that the social capital accumulated over centuries was effectively wiped out. A direct consequence of this institutional destruction was that the behaviour of elite groups, and the state, in the countries that belonged to the ex-Soviet Union reverted to its natural predatory form. This notion is supported by Taylor (1982) who argues that the coercive power of the state can destroy community norms and altruistic behaviour. Coleman (1990) also argues that the expansion of the bureaucratic organization of the state can lead to the atrophy of informal networks, thereby diminishing social capital.

In a broader intellectual context, the model of social and behavioural change elaborated on above is much more consistent with our present understanding of the evolution of life and the emergence of new species over geological time, rather than with the outdated mechanistic model borrowed by neoclassical economic theory from 18th century physics. Let us consider this issue. The traditional historical view of West European economic development, and one which is implicit in the institutional economics literature, is that society progresses in a gradual incremental manner. Underlying this view is the Darwinian theory of natural selection ([1859] 1996), which states that evolution works through a gradual process of mutation, recombination and selection, with new species arising from the slow and steady transformation of entire populations. Paleontological discoveries and the development of evolutionary thought (Eldredge 1985, Gould 1978) since the writings of Darwin, however, have suggested that this view does not entirely fit with the facts. It is now argued that evolutionary change through natural selection occurs at different levels in a population. Thus the process of natural selection affects not only genes or individual organisms, but also occurs at the level of the group or species (Sober 1984, Sober and Lewontin 1982, Wilson 1983, Wilson and Sober 1994). At the level of the gene it is accepted that this evolutionary change is a very slow and steady process, as postulated by Darwin. However, the emergence and extinction of groups or species rather than being gradual has been found to be episodic and discontinuous. Thus about 530 million years ago we have the Cambrian explosion, when organisms evolved beyond their individual cell structures and there was a great outburst of complex life forms (Butterfield 2007, Gould 1989). Subsequent to this there have been several major episodic extinctions. These include the Ordovician, 440 million years ago; the Devonian, 365 million years ago; the Permian, 250 million years ago; the Triassic, 210 million years ago; and the Cretaceous, 65 million years ago. During the Permian extinction, it is estimated that almost 95 per cent of all species vanished (Erwin 1993), while the Cretaceous extinction resulted in the disappearance of 70 per cent of species, including the dinosaurs.

Based on these new discoveries, modern palaeontologists (Eldredge 1985, Eldredge and Gould 1972, Gould 1978) arguing within a neo-Darwinian framework indicate that most species are in a state of homeostatic equilibrium. These homeostatic systems or steady states resist change by self-regulation. The history of the evolution and emergence of new species is therefore not one of an incremental, gradual and stately unfolding of change, but one of equilibria disturbed only rarely by rapid and episodic events, which will cause fundamental changes to the nature, diversity and type of life on the planet. This has been called the theory of 'punctuated equilibrium'. Thus, for instance, mammals as a species seem to have bided their time for millions of years until the dinosaurs perished in the Cretaceous extinction. They then burst forth in proliferation in the subsequent Tertiary period. This view of creation and destruction is much more consistent with the available fossil record which has shown itself to have significant breaks, with discontinuities being a commonly observed fact. Darwin himself was greatly concerned by the discontinuous nature of the fossil record. However, he explained this as being a consequence of several factors including the inherent fragility of living organisms and the specificity of the geological conditions required for the creation, preservation, and discovery of fossils. This, he argued, prevented a perfect fossil record from being available and therefore did not contradict his theory of evolution (Darwin [1859]1996: Chapter IX). Yet the presence of such major discontinuities, suggests that the emergence and dominance of certain species rather than others is characterized by episodic phenomena rather gradual transformation. Thus, for instance, we now have significant geological evidence to suggest that the KT event 65 million years ago, which brought about the Cretaceous extinction, was actually caused by a large asteroid or comet hitting the earth (Alvarez et al. 1980). Exogenous variables such as asteroids, volcanic activity and glaciation (or the reverse, for example the melting of what has been termed 'snowball earth' prior to the Cambrian explosion), which cause major changes in environmental, climatic or geological conditions, therefore seem to be the key factors that bring about the extinction of old species and the emergence of new ones.

Transferring this model from natural history into the realm of socio-economic change, we can find much to confirm the major propositions of our theory. First, although in the very long run society is in a continuous state of transition and transformation, during any given historical period it is likely to be in some sort of self-regulating equilibrium subject to path dependence. As modern information and institution theory have shown, this equilibrium will be determined by the history, balance of social forces, distribution of wealth, etc. in that society, and is more likely than not to be a low-level equilibrium trap, particularly in the case of developing countries. Second, to change this steady state, an exogenous intervention is required. We have argued that in the case of the non-western world this exogenous intervention has been in the form of human agency, either domestic or external. This exogenous intervention, by changing the social environment facing a society – or in other words its institutional framework – facilitates the emergence and dominance of certain types of groups and certain types of behaviour. While it is of course possible that such groups or behaviours may have been present in these societies in earlier periods as well, their existence would only have been in an embryonic form because of the dominance of predatory forces. This view of the role of human agency as being the essential factor in bringing about institutional change is similar to the geological view of the impact of the KT event at the end of the Cretaceous period on the evolution of life on our planet. This event brought about a fundamental change in the natural environment, causing the extinction of then dominant species such as the dinosaurs, and permitted the proliferation of other species, such as mammals – a process which eventually led to the emergence of man. To allow the progression and development of mammalian species, the dominant predators had to be destroyed through an exogenous event. This is quite similar to our argument about the necessity for more efficient economic and social institutions to be introduced and established by conscious human intervention, domestic or external, so that predation can be controlled, more rational levels of human behaviour encouraged, and higher levels of economic growth and development achieved.

Appendix

THE SUB-PRIME CRISIS: A BRIEF OVERVIEW

The sources for the information in this section include Kregel (2008), Coval et al. (2009), Brunnermeier (2009) and *The Economist* (October 2007 and May 2008). In the period after 2001, there was a huge increase in the liquidity of the western financial system. This was primarily caused by large US budget deficits combined with a large balance-of-payments deficit and high oil prices which led to foreigners holding substantial amounts of US dollar funds. These off-shore surpluses were invested in US financial markets. It is estimated that by 2007 there was a pool of almost 70 trillion US dollars invested in fixed income instruments alone. This increased liquidity occurred at a time when the Federal Reserve was trying to boost the US economy. Between May 2000 and December 2001, the Fed funds rate was reduced from 6.5 to 1.75 per cent. All these factors combined to generate a property boom in the USA. Within the property sector, competition amongst banking and non-banking financial institutions to increase lending, and the declared policy of the US administration to encourage home ownership, resulted in a decline in prudential lending standards, leading to an expansion of what has come to be known as the sub-prime mortgage market.

A sub-prime loan is a non-conforming mortgage loan in which the borrower is one who has a poor credit history, a lack of assets, and inadequate documentation of income. This results in the borrower being charged a higher interest rate on a mortgage. During 2001–2003, the share of sub-prime mortgages to total mortgage originations was less than 10 per cent. However, this had doubled to almost 20 per cent during the period 2004–2006. In 2005, 43 per cent of first-time borrowers made no down payment and were granted increasingly risky borrowing incentives and loan options. These included *ninja* loans – *no income, no job* or *assets* – and liar loans, in which the borrower could claim a given future income. The use of automated loan approvals further resulted in loans being made without proper review or documentation. In 2007, 40 per cent of sub-prime loans were from automated under-writing. Mortgage brokers of course profited from the home loan boom and the decline in credit standards. Since their income was derived from increased borrowings, they were not concerned with borrowers' ability to repay loans.

In the increased liquidity and the property boom, Wall Street and the US financial industry saw an opportunity to increase their profits. In what has been called 'financial innovation', they invented mortgage-backed securities (MBS) and a range of other new credit instruments related to these securities which enabled investors around the world to invest in the US housing market. It was claimed that this innovation would deepen financial markets as well as reduce and spread risk. However, as we now know, it in fact created huge hidden risks that eventually brought about market failure. Kregel (2008) provides a detailed analysis of the events that underlay this process and the consequences that followed. Section 20 of the Glass-Steagall Act of 1933 restricted commercial banks from affiliating firms that were principally engaged in activities such as under-writing and dealing in securities. During the 1980s the Federal Reserve relaxed this provision, enabling banks to set up affiliates that could engage in such activities. Banks could now use section 20 affiliates to generate fee income rather than being dependent on business lending and net interest margins for their income. This led to the Gramm-Leach-Bliley Act of 1999, which in effect reversed the Glass-Steagall Act and permitted banks to undertake almost any kind of financial activity. The Basel 1 accord under which all banks operated reinforced this trend in the banking industry. Under this accord, while banks were required to hold a capital reserve of 8 per cent against their loan portfolio, there was no capital requirement for what was termed 'reputational' credit lines. Such credit lines covered liquidity backstops that sponsoring banks could provide to off-balance sheet affiliates to maintain their reputation. As a result of this regulatory environment, banks moved much of their lending off their balance sheets to vehicles, gave such vehicles a line of credit to ensure a triple A rating for any securities issued by the latter, and moved their own focus to maximizing fee and commission incomes.

This more relaxed regulatory framework for both commercial and investment banks, the latter of which in any case already faced less strict regulatory rules and oversight, provided the environment for the subsequent financial innovation which brought the US mortgage market – and its increasingly important sub-prime component – into the mainstream of international financial markets. In this structure, banks provided the mortgages. They then used an off-balance sheet special purpose affiliate to pool all these loans and issue mortgage-backed securities against the underlying mortgages. Further innovation was undertaken by combining the mortgage backed security with a credit default swap (CDS), whereby a risk buyer such as a mono-line insurer like AIG would insure the loans in question in case of a default. The mortgage-backed security would then be tranched into collateralized debt obligations (CDO) with different estimated risk profiles based on assessments by the risk rating agencies. A further re-tranching of the CDOs was also undertaken to create what came to be known as CDO-squared securities. A large fraction of the CDOs issued since around 2000 had in fact sub-prime residential mortgages-backed securities as their underlying asset, and by 2006, almost 55 per cent of all such debt obligations were of the re-tranched CDO-squared kind. Based on the statistical models of the rating agencies, the senior tranches of these CDOs were given triple A ratings which thereby made them instruments of the highest investment grade. Finally, a new set of structured investment vehicles (SIV) was created by financial institutions. These SIVs bought the CDOs and financed all of this by issuing their own short- and medium-term investment notes. This commercial paper was then purchased by private and institutional investors, as well as being held in many of the money market mutual funds offered by financial institutions.

The impact of these financial structures and instruments was to change the normal system whereby a lender, such as a bank, assessed the risk by doing due diligence on the borrower and making a credit assessment before giving a loan. Once a loan had been given, the lender carried it to maturity and bore any default risk that may have been involved. Kregel (2008) indicates that the financial innovation described above introduced a new 'originate and distribute' system into the mortgage market. In this banks and other financial institutions involved in the mortgage market sought to maximize the fee and commission income from being bond originators without taking on any of the risks of the mortgage loan. The sale of the mortgage-backed security by the off-balance sheet affiliate transferred the risk of the loan from the mortgage originator to the investors in these securities. Consequently, a bank or other mortgage originator had no interest in undertaking a proper credit evaluation since the interest and principal on the loan would be repaid to the final buyers of the collateralized assets. The final buyers of these assets purchased them on the basis of a statistically based rating provided by the credit rating agencies. They were unaware or unconcerned by the fact that the credit rating agencies themselves faced a conflict of interest in doing these ratings, since they were the recipients of a fee income from those issuing mortgage-based commercial paper. In developing this complex structure the system removed any knowledge of the underlying borrower from the assessment of loan risk. Altogether, therefore, perverse incentives were created amongst financial institutions originating loans, credit rating agencies, the mortgage brokers, and the final borrowers themselves, whereby the focus of activity became one of increasing the quantum of home loans without any concern for the risk this created to the actors themselves or the system as a whole.

Within this new framework of low regulation, unrestricted borrowing and financial innovation, financial markets had become highly leveraged to the value of the underlying asset (i.e. residential houses). The structured investment vehicles operated like an unregulated parallel banking system through which capital ratio requirements could be circumvented and almost unlimited credit could be created so long as there was an appetite for the paper that these organizations issued. While the leverage ratio, (i.e. total debt to total equity,) of a conservative bank is typically 10 to 15, by 2007 this ratio for Wall Street investment banks had increased to almost 30. The credit default swap market was even more unregulated and by some estimates the gross notional amount of debt covered by such contracts had reached over 50 trillion US dollars in 2007. The monoline insurers, such as AIG, of course had nowhere near the required capital to honour the contracts that they had issued in case the economy worsened and thus caused the default rate to increase over what their statistical models had assumed.

The perverse incentives in this system are evident from the fact that in creating this huge mountain of leverage and risk Wall Street enjoyed enormous short-run payoffs. In 2006 investment banks made record revenues and Wall Street executives earned record compensation levels, taking home cash bonuses of almost 24 billion US dollars. In the same year Moody's, the credit-rating agency, earned 44 per cent of its revenues from the rating of structured finance products (Coval et al. 2009). Of course while property prices were increasing there was no problem. However, between June 2004 and June 2006, to cool the economy, the Federal Reserve raised interest rates 17 times. This then had a major impact on house prices. Property values began to decline, causing a wholesale fall in the value of the collateralized debt obligations. Initially this affected the credit insurers or risk buyers such as AIG. They could not meet their obligations and began to fail. Subsequently, however, the entire US financial system – particularly those institutions that were highly leveraged and had been deeply involved in the creation of the new debt instruments – began to experience stress and go bankrupt. This was because a significant proportion of the mortgage-backed instruments created continued to be held on the balance sheets of the banks themselves and these had declined precipitously in value. For instance, out of the 30 CDOs underwritten by Merrill Lynch in 2007, 27 saw their triple A ratings down-graded to junk, with the prices of many falling by over 90 per cent. Thus Wall Street investment banks were the first to be affected wholesale. Of the five largest investment banks three went bankrupt in 2008 and the other two were assisted to become commercial banks with support from the Federal government. During 2007 and 2008, the sub-prime related credit crunch and ensuing financial crisis in the US banking system spread throughout the developed world and played a central role in bringing about the 2007–2009 world recession.

Bibliography

Abramovitz, M. (1956), 'Resource and output trends in the United States since 1870', *American Economic Review Papers and Proceedings*, **46** (2): 285–313.

Acemoglu, D., S. Johnson and J. Robinson (2002), 'Reversal of fortune: geography and institutions in the making of the modern world income distribution', *Quarterly Journal of Economics*, **117** (4): 1231–94.

Akerlof, G. and R. Shiller (2009), *Animal Spirits: How Human Psychology Drives the Economy and Why It Matters for Global Capitalism*, Princeton, NJ: Princeton University Press.

Akerlof, G. and J. Yellen (1990), 'The fair wage-effort hypothesis and unemployment', *Quarterly Journal of Economics*, **105** (2): 255–83.

Alchian, A.A. (1950), 'Uncertainty, evolution and economic theory', *Journal of Political Economy*, **58**: 211–21.

Alesina, A. (1997), 'The political economy of high and low growth', in B. Pleskovic and J.E. Stiglitz (eds), *Annual World Bank Conference on Development Economics 1997*, Washington, DC: World Bank, pp. 217–48.

Alfaro, L. and A. Chari (2009), 'India transformed? Insights from the firm level 1988–2005', Harvard Business School, working paper no. 10-030.

Allen, G.C. (1981), *The Japanese Economy*, London: Weidenfeld and Nicolson.

Allen, R.C. (2007), 'India the great divergence', in T.J. Hatton, K. O'Rourke and A.M. Taylor (eds), *The New Comparative Economic History*, Cambridge, MA: MIT Press, pp. 9–32.

Alvarez, L.W., W. Alvarez, F. Asaro and H.V. Michel (1980), 'Extra-terrestrial cause for the cretaceous-tertiary extinction', *Science*, **208** (4448): 1095–108.

Amsden, A. (1989), *Asia's Next Giant: South Korea and Late Industrialization*, New York: Oxford University Press.

Amsden, A. (2004), *The Rise of the Rest: Challenges to the West from Late Industrializing Economies*, Oxford: Oxford University Press.

Anderson, E. and H. Waddington (2007), 'Aid and the MDG poverty target: how much is required and how should it be allocated?', *Oxford Development Studies*, **35** (1): 1–32.

Aoki, M. (2007), 'Endogenizing institutions and institutional changes', *Journal of Institutional Economics*, **3** (1): 1–31.

Arbache, J. and J. Page (2008), 'Hunting for leopards: long run country income dynamics in Africa', World Bank policy research working paper no. 4715, Washington, DC.

Arbache, J., D. Go and J. Page (2008), 'Is Africa's economy at a turning point?', World Bank policy research working paper no. 4519, Washington, DC.

Arrow, K.J. (1969), 'The organization of economic activity: issues pertinent to the choice of market versus non-market allocation', in *The Analysis and Evaluation of Public Expenditures: The PBB-System*, Washington, DC: Government Printing Office.

Arrow, K.J. (1974), *The Limits of Organization*, New York: W.W. Norton.

Arrow, K.J. (1986), 'Rationality of self and others in an economic system', in R.M. Hogarth and M.W. Reder (eds), *Rational Choice: The Contrast between Economics and Psychology*, Chicago, IL: University of Chicago Press, pp. 201–15.

Arrow, K.J. (1994), 'Methodological individualism and social knowledge', *American Economic Review*, **84** (2): 1–9.

Arrow, K.J. and G. Debreu (1954), 'The existence of an equilibrium for a competitive economy', *Econometrica*, **XXII**: 265–90.

Ashraf, N., C. Camerer and G. Lowenstein (2005), 'Adam Smith, behavioural economist', *Journal of Economic Perspectives*, **19** (3): 131–45.

Bagchi, A. (1982), *The Political Economy of Underdevelopment*, Cambridge: Cambridge University Press.

Bairoch, P. (1967), *Diagnostic de l'evolution economique du tiers monde 1900–1966*, Paris: Gauthiers-Villars.

Bairoch, P. and M. Levy-Leboyer (1981), *Disparities in Economic Development since the Industrial Revolution*, London: Macmillan.

Bardhan, P. (1984), *The Political Economy of Development in India*, Oxford: Basil Blackwell.

Bardhan, P. (1989), 'The new institutional economics and development theory: a brief critical assessment', *World Development*, **17** (9): 1389–95.

Bardhan, P. (1999), 'Understanding underdevelopment: challenges for institutional economics from the point of view of poor countries', mimeo, Berkeley, CA: University of California.

Bardhan, P. (2000), 'The nature of institutional impediments to economic development', in M. Olson and S. Kahkonen (eds), *A Not-So-Dismal Science: A Broader View of Economics and Societies*, Oxford: Oxford University Press, pp. 245–67.

Bardhan, P. (2001), 'Distributive conflicts, collective action, and institutional economics, in G.M. Meier and J.E. Stiglitz (eds), *Frontiers of Development Economics*, Oxford: Oxford University Press, pp. 269–90.

Barro, R. (1989), 'Economic growth in a cross-section of countries', National Bureau of Economic Research paper no. 3120, Cambridge, MA.

Barro, R. (1996), 'Determinants of economic growth: a cross-country empirical study', National Bureau of Economic Research paper no. 5698, Cambridge, MA.

Barro, R. (1996a), 'Democracy and growth', *Journal of Economic Growth*, **1** (1): 1–27.

Barzel, Y. (2002), *A Theory of the State*, Cambridge: Cambridge University Press.

Bates, R.H. (1989), *Beyond the Miracle of the Market: The Political Economy of Agrarian Development in Rural Kenya*, Cambridge: Cambridge University Press.

Bates. R.H. (1995), 'Social dilemmas and rational individuals: an assessment of the New Institutionalism', in J. Harris, J. Hunter and C.M. Lewis (eds), *The New Institutional Economics and Third World Development*, London: Routledge.

Bloom, D. and J. Sachs (1998), 'Geography, demography and economic growth in Africa', *Brookings Papers on Economic Activity*, **1998** (2): 207–73.

Brinkerhoff, D. and J. Brinkerhoff (2002), 'Governance reforms and failed states: challenges and implications', *International Review of Administrative Sciences*, **68** (4): 511–31.

Brown, J.M. (1985), *Modern India: The Origins of an Asian Democracy*, Oxford: Oxford University Press.

Brunnermeier, M. (2009), 'Deciphering the liquidity and credit crunch 2007–2008', *Journal of Economic Perspectives*, **23** (1): 77–100.

Burnside, C. and D. Dollar (1997), 'Aid, policies and growth', World Bank policy research working paper no. 1777, Washington, DC.

Butterfield, N.J. (2007), 'Macroevolution and microecology through deep time', *Palaeontology*, **51** (1): 41–55.

Caldwell, B. (1993), 'Economic methodology: rationale, foundations, prospects', in U. Maki, B. Gustafsson and C. Knudsen (eds), *Rationality, Institutions and Economic Methodology*, London: Routledge, pp. 45–60.

Carothers, T. (1999), *Aiding Democracy Abroad*, Washington, DC: Carnegie Endowment for International Peace.

Caselli, F. (2005), 'Accounting for cross-country income differences', in P. Aghion and S. Durlauf (eds), *Handbook of Economic Growth*, Amsterdam: Elsevier-North Holland, ch. 9.

Chakravarti, A. (2006), *Aid, Institutions and Development: New Approaches to Growth, Governance and Poverty*, Cheltenham, UK and Northampton, MA, USA: Edward Elgar.

Chang, H.J. (2002), *Kicking Away the Ladder: Development Strategy in Historical Perspective*, London: Anthem Press.

Chang, H.J. (2004), *Globalisation, Economic Development and the Role of the State*, London: Zed Books.

Chang, H.J. (2011), 'Institutions and economic development: theory, policy and history', *Journal of Institutional Economics*, **7** (4): 1–26.

Chaudhri, K.N. (1978), *The Trading World of Asia and the English East India Company*, Cambridge: Cambridge University Press.

Clower, R. (1994), 'Economics as an inductive science', *Southern Economic Journal*, **60** (4): 804–14.

Clower, R. (1995), 'Axiomatics in economics', *Southern Economic Journal*, **62** (2): 307–19.

Coase, R. (1937), 'The nature of the firm', *Economica*, **4**: 386–405.

Coase, R. (1960), 'The problem of social cost', *Journal of Law and Economics*, **3**: 1–44.

Coase, R. (1984), 'The New Institutional economics', *Journal of Institutional and Theoretical Economics*, **140** (1): 229–31.

Coase, R. (1992), 'The Institutional structure of production', *American Economic Review*, **82** (4): 713–19.

Colander, D., P. Howitt, A. Kirman, A. Leijonhufvud and P. Mehrling (2008), 'Beyond DSGE models: towards an empirically based macroeconomics', Middlebury College economics discussion paper no. 08-08, Middlebury, VT.

Coleman, J. (1986), 'Psychological structure and social structure in economic models', in R.M. Hogarth and M.W. Reder (eds), *Rational Choice. The Contrast between Economics and Psychology*, Chicago, IL: University of Chicago Press, pp. 181–5.

Coleman, J. (1990), *Foundations of Social Theory*, Cambridge, MA: Harvard University Press.

Coleman, J. (2000), 'Social capital in the creation of human capital', in P. Dasgupta and I. Serageldin (eds), *Social Capital: A Multifaceted Perspective*, Washington, DC: World Bank, pp. 13–39.

Collier, P., A. Hoeffler and C. Pattillo, (2004), 'Africa's exodus: capital flight and the brain drain as portfolio decisions', *Journal of African Economies*, **13** (Suppl.2): 15–54.

Collins, S. and B. Bosworth (1996), 'Economic growth in East Asia: accumulation versus assimilation', *Brookings Papers on Economic Activity*, **1996** (2): 135–91.

Commons, J.R. (1934), *Institutional Economics*, New York: Macmillan.

Cosmides, L. and J. Tooby (1994), 'Evolutionary psychology and the invisible hand', *American Economic Review*, **84** (2): 327–32.

Coval, J., J. Jurek and E. Stafford (2009), 'The economics of structured finance', *Journal of Economic Perspectives*, **23** (1): 3–25.

Croson, R. (1995), 'Expectations in voluntary contribution mechanisms', Department of Operations and Information Management, The Wharton School, University of Pennsylvania working paper no. 95-03-02.

Crotty, J. (2009), 'Structural causes of the global financial crisis: a critical assessment of the "new financial architecture"', *Cambridge Journal of Economics*, **33**: 563–80.

Darwin, C. ([1859]1996), *The Origin of Species*, Oxford: Oxford University Press.

Dawkins, R. (2006), *The Selfish Gene*, Oxford: Oxford University Press.

Debreu, G. (1959), *Theory of Value*, New York: Wiley.

Denzau, A. and D. North (1994), 'Shared mental models: ideologies and institutions', *Kyklos*, **1994** (1): 3–31.

Dollar, D. and A. Kray (2000), 'Growth is good for the poor', World Bank policy research working paper no. 2587, Washington, DC.

Easterly, W. (2000), 'The effect of IMF and World Bank programs on poverty', World Bank policy research working paper no. 2517, Washington, DC.

Easterly, W. (2001), 'The middle class consensus and economic development', World Bank policy research working paper, Washington, DC.

Easterly, W. and R. Levine (2003), 'Tropics, germs and crops: how endowments influence economic development', *Journal of Monetary Economics*, **50** (1): 3–39.

Eaton, J. and S. Kortum (2001), 'Trade in capital goods', *European Economic Review*, **91** (4): 795–813.

Economist (2007), 'Special report on central banks', 20 October.

Economist (2008), 'Special report on international banking', 17 May.

Economist (2010), 'Special report on financial risk', 11 February.

Eldredge, N. (1985), *Unfinished Synthesis: Biological Hierarchies and Modern Evolutionary Thought*, Oxford: Oxford University Press.

Eldredge, N. and S.J. Gould (1972), 'Punctuated equilibria: an alternative to phyletic gradualism', in J. Schopf (ed.), *Models in Paleobiology*, San Francisco, CA: Freeman, Cooper and Company, pp. 82–115.

Engels, F. (1962), *Feuerbach and the End of Classical German Philosophy*, Moscow: Foreign Languages Press.

Engermann, S.I. and K.L. Sokoloff (1997), 'Factor endowments, institutions and differential paths of growth among New World economies: a view from economic historians of the United States', in S. Haber (ed.), *How Latin America Fell Behind: Essays on the Economic Histories of Brazil and Mexico 1800–1914*, Stanford, CA: Stanford University Press, pp. 260–304.

Erwin, D.H. (1993), *The Great Paleozoic Crisis: Life and Death in the Permian*, New York: Columbia University Press.

Evans-Pritchard, E.E. (1941), *The Nuer*, Oxford: Clarendon Press.

Fama, E. (1970), 'Efficient capital markets: a review of theory and empirical work', *Journal of Finance*, **25** (2): 383–417.

Fama, E., L. Fisher, M. Jensen and R. Roll (1969), 'The adjustment of stock prices to new information', *International Economic Review*, **10**: 1–21.

Fehr, E., E. Kirchler and A. Weichbold (1994), 'When social forces remove the impact of competition: an experimental investigation', mimeo, Department of Economics, University of Vienna.

Fortes, M. and E.E. Evans-Pritchard ([1940]1970), *African Political Systems*, Oxford: Oxford University Press.

Frank, A.G. (1998), *ReOrient: Global Economy in the Asian Age*, Berkeley, CA: University of California Press.

Friedman, M. (1953), *Essays in Positive Economics*, Chicago, IL: University of Chicago Press.

Friedman, M. (1957), *Theory of the Consumption Function*, Princeton, NJ: Princeton University Press.

Fukuyama, F. (1995), *Trust: The Social Virtues and the Creation of Prosperity*, London: Penguin Books.

Furubotn, E. and R. Richter (2005), *Institutions and Economic Theory*, Ann Arbor, MI: University of Michigan Press.

Glaeser, E., R. La Porta, F. Lopez-de-Silanes and A. Shleifer (2004), 'Do institutions cause growth?', *Journal of Economic Growth*, **9**: 271–303.

Gordon, A. (2003), *A Modern History of Japan*, Oxford: Oxford University Press.

Gould, S.J. (1978), *Ever Since Darwin: Reflections in Natural History*, London: Burnett Books.

Gould, S.J. (1989), *Wonderful Life: The Burgess Shale and the Nature of History*, New York: W.W. Norton & Co.

Government of the Republic of South Sudan (2005), *Comprehensive Peace Agreement*, Juba.

Government of the Republic of South Sudan (2005a), *Interim Constitution of Southern Sudan*, Juba.

Government of the Republic of South Sudan (2006), *Council of Ministers' Handbook*, Juba.

Government of the Republic of South Sudan (2006a), *200-Day Action Plan*, Juba: Office of the President.

Granovetter, M. (1985), 'Economic action and the social structure: the problem of embeddedness', *American Journal of Sociology*, **91** (3): 481–510.

Greenwald, B. and J. Stiglitz (1986), 'Externalities in economics with imperfect information and incomplete markets', *Quarterly Journal of Economics*, **101** (2): 229–64.

Greif, A. (1998), 'Cultural beliefs and the organization of society: a historical and theoretical reflection on collectivist and individualist societies', in M.C. Brinton and V. Nee (eds), *The New Institutionalism in Sociology*, New York: Russell Sage Foundation, pp. 77–104.

Greif, A. (2006), *Institutions and the Path to the Modern Economy*, New York: Cambridge University Press.

Grether, D.M. and C.R. Plott (1979), 'Economic theory of choice and the preference reversal phenomenon', *American Economic Review*, **69**: 623–68.
Grossman, S. and J. Stiglitz (1980), 'On the impossibility of informationally
efficient markets', *American Economic Review*, **70** (3): 393–408.
Hall, R. and C. Jones (1999), 'Why do some countries produce so much more
output per worker than others?', *Quarterly Journal of Economics*, **114** (1):
83–116.
Hamilton, W.D. (1964), 'The genetical evolution of social behavior I and II',
Journal of Theoretical Biology, **7**: 1–16 and 17–52.
Hamilton, W.D. (1996), *Narrow Roads of Gene Land Vol.1: The Evolution of
Social Behaviour*, Oxford: Oxford University Press.
Hausman, D. (1989), 'Economic methodology in a nutshell', *Journal of
Economic Perspectives* **3** (2): 115–27.
Hayami, Y. and V. Ruttan (1985), *Agricultural Development: An International
Perspective*, Baltimore, MD: Johns Hopkins University Press.
Hayek, F. (1937), 'Economics and knowledge', *Economica*, **4** (Feb): 33–54.
Hayek, F. (1945), 'The uses of knowledge in society', *American Economic
Review*, **35** (Sept): 519–30.
Hayek, F. (1960), *The Constitution of Liberty*, London: Routledge and Kegan
Paul.
Hayek, F. (1973), *Law, Legislation and Liberty*, Chicago, IL: University of
Chicago Press.
Hodgson, G. (2006), 'What are institutions?', *Journal of Economic Issues*, **40**
(1): 1–25.
Hodgson, G. and E. Screpanti (1991), 'Introduction', in G. Hodgson and E.
Screpanti (eds), *Rethinking Economics: Markets, Technology and Evolution*,
Cheltenham, UK and Northampton, MA, USA: Edward Elgar, pp. 1–18.
Hoff, K. (2000), 'Beyond Rosenstein-Rodan: the modern theory of coordina-
tion problems in development', in B. Pleskovic and N. Stern (eds), *Annual
World Bank Conference on Development Economics 2000*, Washington,
DC: World Bank, pp. 145–76.
Hoff, K. and J.E. Stiglitz (2001), 'Modern economic theory and development',
in G.M. Meier and J.E. Stiglitz (eds), *Frontiers of Development Economics*,
Oxford: Oxford University Press, pp. 389–463.
Holm, J. (1988), 'Botswana: a paternalistic democracy', in L. Diamond (ed.),
Democracy in Developing Countries: Africa, Boulder, CO: Lynne Rienner,
pp. 179–216.
Hoover, K. (2001), 'Is macroeconomics for real?', in U. Maki (ed.), *The
Economics World View*, Cambridge: Cambridge University Press.
Hughes, H. (2001), 'Evolution of dual economies in East Asia', in D. Lal and
R. Snape (eds), *Trade, Development and Political Economy: Essays in
Honour of Anne O. Krueger*, New York: Palgrave, pp. 268–84.

Hutchison, T. (1938), *The Significance and Basic Postulates of Economic Theory*, New York: A.M. Kelly.

Inter-Governmental Authority on Development (2004), *Power Sharing Protocol*, Naivasha, Kenya.

Ito, T. (1997), 'What can developing countries learn from East Asia's economic growth?', *Annual World Bank Conference on Development Economics 1997*, Washington, DC: World Bank, pp. 183–216.

Jensen, M. (1968), 'The performance of mutual funds in the period 1945–64', *Journal of Finance*, **23**: 389–416.

Jevons, W.S. ([1871] 1970), *The Theory of Political Economy*, edited by R.D. Collison Black, London: Pelican Books.

Jones, E. (1981), *The European Miracle*, New York: Cambridge University Press.

Kahneman, D. and A. Tversky (1979), 'Prospect theory: an analysis of decision under risk', *Econometrica*, **47** (2): 263–291.

Kahneman, D., J. Knetsch and R. Thaler (1986), 'Fairness as a constraint on profit seeking: entitlements in the market', *American Economic Review*, **76** (4): 728–41.

Kahneman, D., J. Knetsch and R. Thaler (2008), 'The endowment effect: evidence of losses valued more than gains', *Handbook of Experimental Economics Results*, vol. 1, chapter 100, Amsterdam: Elsevier B.V. North Holland.

Kaufmann, D. and A. Kray (2002), 'Growth without governance. World Book discussion paper', Washington, DC.

Kaufmann, D., A. Kray and P. Zoido-Lobaton (1999), 'Governance matters', World Bank policy research working paper no. 2196, Washington, DC.

Keefer, P. (2007), 'Governance and economic growth', in A. Winters and S. Yusuf (eds), *Dancing With Giants*, Washington, DC: World Bank., chapter 7.

Keeley, L. (1996), *War Before Civilization*, New York: Oxford University Press.

Keynes, J.M. (1936), *The General Theory of Employment, Interest, and Money*, London: Macmillan.

Keynes, J.M. (1937), 'The General Theory of Employment', *Quarterly Journal of Economics*, **51**: 209–23.

Khan, M.S. and D. Villanueva (1991), 'Macroeconomic policies and long term growth: a conceptual and empirical framework', African Economic Research Consortium special paper 13, Nairobi.

Killick, T. (1995), *IMF Programmes in Developing Countries*, Overseas Development Institute, London: Routledge.

Killick, T. (1997), 'Principal agents and the failings of conditionality', *Journal of International Development*, **9** (4): 483–96.

Kirby, K. and R. Hernstein (1995), 'Preference reversal due to myopic discounting of delayed rewards', *Psychology Science*, **6** (2): 83–9.

Knack, S. and P. Keefer (1995), 'Institutions and economic performance: cross country tests using alternative institutional measures', *Economics and Politics*, **7** (3): 207–28.

Knudsen, C. (1993), 'Equilibrium, perfect rationality and the problem of self-reference in economics', in U. Maki, B. Gustafsson and C. Knudsen (eds), *Rationality, Institutions & Economic Methodology*, London: Routledge, pp. 133–70.

Kohli, A. (2006), 'Politics of economic growth in India 1980–2005', *Economic and Political Weekly*, 1 April: 1251–9.

Kohn, M. (2005), *Origins of Western Economic Success: Commerce, Finance and Government in Pre-industrial Europe*, Hanover, NH: Dartmouth College.

Kregel, J. (2008), 'Minsky's cushions of safety: systemic risk and the crisis in the U.S. sub-prime mortgage market', The Levy Institute of Bard College public policy brief no. 93, New York.

Laibson, D. (1997), 'Golden eggs and hyperbolic discounting', *Quarterly Journal of Economics*, **112** (2): 443–78.

Lal, D. and I. Natarajan (2001), 'The virtuous circle: savings, distribution and growth interactions in India', in D. Lal and R. Snape (eds), *Trade, Development and Political Economy: Essays in Honour of Anne O. Krueger*, New York: Palgrave, pp. 213–27.

Lall, S. (1996), 'Paradigms of development: the East Asian debate', *Oxford Development Studies*, **24** (2): 111–32.

Landes, D. (1998), *The Wealth and Poverty of Nations*, New York: Norton.

Langlois, R. (1986), 'The New Institutional Economics: an introductory essay', in R. Langlois (ed.), *Economics as a Process: Essays in the New Institutional Economics*, Cambridge: Cambridge University Press, pp. 1–25.

Levi, M. (1988), *Of Rule and Revenue*, Berkeley, CA: University of California Press.

Levine, R. and D. Renelt (1992), 'A sensitivity analysis of cross-country growth regressions', *American Economic Review*, **82** (4): 942–63.

Levy, B. (2004), 'Governance and economic development in Africa: meeting the challenges of capacity building', in B. Levy and S. Kpundeh (eds), *Building State Capacity in Africa*, Washington, DC: World Bank.

Liebenstein, H. (1989), 'Organizational economics and institutions as missing elements in economic development analysis', *World Development*, **17** (9): 1361–73.

Lienhardt, G. (1958) 'The Western Dinka', in J. Middleton and D. Tait (eds), *Tribes Without Rulers*, London: Routledge & Paul, pp. 102–32.

Lipset, S.M. (1960), *Political Man: The Social Basis of Modern Politics*, New York: Doubleday.

Little, I.M.D., M. Scott and T. Scitovsky (1970), *Industry and Trade in Some Developing Countries*, London: Oxford University Press.

Lockwood, W.W. (1968), *The Economic Development of Japan: Growth and Structural Change*, Princeton, NJ: Princeton University Press.

Lockyer, C. (1711), *The Account of Trade in India*, London: S. Crouch.

Lucas, R.E. (1986), 'Adaptive behaviour and economic theory', in R.M. Hogarth and M.W. Reder (eds), *Rational Choice: The Contrast between Economics and Psychology*, Chicago, IL: University of Chicago Press, pp. 217–42.

Maddison, A. (1971), *Class Structure and Economic Growth: India and Pakistan Since the Mughals*, London: Allen and Unwin.

Maddison, A. (1998), *Chinese Economic Performance in the Long Run*, Paris: OECD.

Maddison, A. (2001), *The Asian Economy in the Twentieth Century*, Cheltenham, UK and Northampton, MA, USA: Edward Elgar.

Maddison, A. (2006), *The World Economy: A Millennial Perspective*, Paris: OECD.

Marshall, A. ([1920]1956), *Principles of Economics*, 8th edn, London: Macmillan.

Marx, K. ([1859]1958), *Preface to a Contribution to the Critique of Political Economy*, Moscow: Foreign Languages Publishing House.

Marx, K. (1981), *Grundrisse: Foundation of the Critique of Political Economy*, London: Penguin Books.

Marx, K. and F. Engels (1958), *Selected Works*, Moscow: Foreign Languages Press.

Mauro, P. (1995), 'Corruption and growth', *Quarterly Journal of Economics*, **110** (3): 681–712.

Maynard Smith, J. (1982), *Evolution and the Theory of Games*, Cambridge: Cambridge University Press.

Maynard Smith, J. (1995), *The Theory of Evolution*, Cambridge: Cambridge University Press.

Menger, C. ([1883]1963), *The Problems of Economics and Sociology*, translated by F.J. Nock, Urbana, IL: University of Illinois Press.

Mill, J.S. ([1848]1923), *Principles of Political Economy*, London: Longmans, Green & Co.

Mill, J.S. ([1843]1949), *A System of Logic*, London: Macmillan.

Mill, J.S. ([1836]1967), 'On the definition of political economy and the method of investigation proper to it', *Collected Works of John Stuart Mill*, Vol. 4, Toronto, ON: University of Toronto Press.

Minsky, H. (1977) 'A theory of systemic fragility', in E.I. Altman and A.W.

Sametz (eds), *Financial Crises: Institutions and Markets in a Fragile Environment*, New York: John Wiley and Sons.

Modigliani, F. and M. Miller (1958), 'The cost of capital, corporation finance and the theory of investment', *American Economic Review*, **48** (3): 261–97.

Moe, T.M. (1990), 'Political institutions: the neglected side of the story', *Journal of Law, Economics and Organization*, special issue (7): 213–53.

Moe, T.M. (1991), 'Politics and the theory of organization', *Journal of Law, Economics and Organization*, special issue (7): 106–29.

Moll, J. and J. Grafman (2006), 'Human fronto-mesolimbic networks guide decisions about charitable donations', *Proceedings of the National Academy of Sciences*, **13** (42): 15623–8.

Molutsi, P. and J. Holm (1990), 'Developing democracy when civil society is weak: the case of Botswana, *African Affairs*, **89** (356): 323–40.

Montes, L. (2008), 'Newton's real influence on Adam Smith and its context', *Cambridge Journal of Economics*, **32**: 555–76.

Montesquieu, C. (1748), *De l'esprit des lois*, Paris: Editions du Seuil.

Montinola, G., Y. Qian and B. Weingast (1996), 'Federalism Chinese style: the political basis for economic success', *World Politics*, **48** (1): 50–81.

Moore, B. Jr. (1967), *Social Origins of Dictatorship and Democracy*, London: Penguin Books.

Mosley, P., T. Subasat and J. Weeks (1995), 'Assessing adjustment in Africa', *World Development*, **23** (9): 1459–74.

Nabli, M. and J. Nugent (1989), 'The New Institutional Economics and its applicability to development', *World Development*, **17** (9): 1333–47.

Nath, S.K. (1969), *A Reappraisal of Welfare Economics*, London: Routledge & Kegan Paul.

National Sample Survey Eighth Round (1954–55), *1958*, Delhi: Indian Statistical Institute.

Nayar, B.R. (1980), *India's Mixed Economy: The Role of Ideology and Interest in its Development*, Bombay: Popular Prakashan.

Ndulu, B. and A. O'Connell (1999), 'Governance and growth in sub-Saharan Africa', *Journal of Economic Perspectives*, **13** (3): 41–66.

Newton, I. ([1687]1999), *Mathematical Principles of Natural Philosophy*, edited by I.Cohen and A. Whitman, Berkeley CA: University of California Press.

Newton, I. ([1704]1979), *Opticks: or A Treatise of the Reflections, Refractions, Inflections and Colours of Light*, London: William Innys.

North, D. (1981), *Structure and Change in Economic History*, New York: Norton.

North, D. (1989), 'Institutions and Economic Growth', *World Development*, **17** (9): 1319–22.

North, D. (1990), *Institutions, Institutional Change and Economic Performance*, Cambridge: Cambridge University Press.

North, D. (1992), 'The New Institutional Economics and development', mimeo, Washington University, St. Louis, MO.

North, D. and B.R. Weingast (1989), 'Constitutions and commitment: the evolution of institutions governing public choice in 17th century England', *Journal of Economic History*, **49** (4): 803–32.

North, D., J.J. Wallis and B.R. Weingast (2009), *Violence and Social Orders: A Conceptual Framework for Interpreting Recorded Human History*, New York: Cambridge University Press.

Olson, M. (1965), *The Logic of Collective Action: Public Goods and the Theory of Groups*, Cambridge: Harvard University Press.

Olson, M. (2000), 'Dictatorship, Democracy and Development', in M. Olson and S. Kahkonen (eds), *A Not-So-Dismal Science: A Broader View of Economics and Societies*, Oxford: Oxford University Press, pp. 119–37.

Otterbein, K. (1989), *The Evolution of War: A Cross Cultural Study*, New Haven CT: HRAF Press.

Persson, T. and G. Tabellini (2000), *Political Economics: Explaining Economic Policy*, Cambridge, MA: MIT Press.

Persson, T. and G. Tabellini (2007), 'The growth effect of democracy: is it heterogeneous and how can it be estimated?', Centre for Economic Policy Research working paper no. 6339, London.

Pesendorf, W. (2006), 'Behavioural economics comes of age', *Journal of Economic Literature*, **44**: 712–21.

Pirenne, H. (1953), *Economic and Social History of Medieval Europe*, translated by I.E. Clegg, London: Routledge and Kegan Paul.

Plott, C.R. (1986), 'Rational choice in experimental markets', in R.M. Hogarth and M.W. Reder (eds), *Rational Choice: The Contrast between Economics and Psychology*, Chicago, IL: University of Chicago Press, pp. 117–43.

Plott, C.R. and V. Smith (2008), *Handbook of Experimental Economics Results*, vol. 1, Amsterdam: Elsevier.

Polanyi, K. (1944), *The Great Transformation*, Boston MA: Beacon Press.

Polanyi, K., C. Arensberg and H. Pearson (1957), *Trade and Market in the Early Empires*, New York: Free Press.

Pomeranz, K. (2000), *The Great Divergence: China, Europe and the Making of the Modern World*, Princeton, NJ: Princeton University Press.

Popper, K. (1959), *The Logic of Scientific Discovery*, London: Hutchinson.

Putnam, R.D. (1992), *Making Democracy Work: Civic Traditions in Modern Italy*, Princeton, NJ: Princeton University Press.

Rabin, M. (1998), 'Psychology and economics', *Journal of Economic Literature*, **36** (1): 11–46.

Radcliffe-Brown, A.R. and D. Forde (1970), *African Systems of Kinship and Marriage*, Oxford: Oxford University Press.

Raychaudhri, T. and I. Habib (1982), *The Cambridge Economic History of India*, Cambridge: Cambridge University Press.

Robbins, I. (1935), *An Essay on the Nature and Significance of Economic Science*, London: Macmillan.

Robinson, J. (1999), 'When is a state predatory?', Center for Economic Studies, University of Munich working paper no. 178, Germany.

Robinson, J. and Q. Neil Parsons (2006), 'State formation and governance in Botswana', *Journal of African Economies*, **15** (1): 100–40.

Rodrik, D. (1996), 'Understanding economic policy reform', *Journal of Economic Literature*, **34** (1): 9–41.

Rodrik, D. (1999), 'Institutions for high quality growth: what they are and how to acquire them', unpublished paper, Harvard University, Cambridge, MA.

Rodrik, D. and R. Wacziarg (2005), 'Do democratic transitions produce bad economic outcomes?', *American Economic Review*, **95** (2): 50–55.

Rodrik, D., A. Subramaniam and F. Trebbi (2002), 'Institutions rule: the primacy of institutions over geography and integration in economic development', Harvard University, Center for International Development working paper, Cambridge, MA.

Rosenberg, N. (1986), *How the West Grew Rich*, New York: Norton.

Roubini, N. (2008), 'How will financial institutions make money now that the securitization food chain is broken?', accessed 19 May at www.rgemonitor.com/blog/roubini.

Rozman, G. (1973), *Urban Networks in Ch'ing China and Tokugawa Japan*, Princeton, NJ: Princeton University Press.

Rudolph, S.H. and L.I. Rudolph (2001), 'Redoing the constitutional design: from an interventionist to a regulatory state', in A. Kohli (ed.). *The Success of India's Democracy*, Cambridge: Cambridge University Press, pp. 127–62.

Rudolph, S.H. and L.I. Rudolph (2002), 'New dimensions of Indian democracy', *Journal of Democracy*, **13** (1): 52–66.

Rutherford, S (1644), *Lex Rex*, London: John Field.

Sachs, J. (2003), 'Institutions don't rule: direct effects of geography on per capita income', National Bureau of Economic Research working paper no. 9490, Cambridge, MA.

Sachs, J. and A. Warner (1995), 'Economic reform and the process of global integration', *Brookings Papers on Economic Activity*, **1** (1): 1–118.

Schadler, S., F. Rowadowski, S. Tiwari and D. Robinson (1993), 'Economic adjustment in low income countries: experience of the ESAF', IMF occasional paper no. 106, Washington, DC.

Schapera, I. (1940), 'The political organization of the Ngwato of Bechuanaland Protectorate', in M. Fortes and E. Evans-Pritchard (eds), *African Political Systems*, Oxford: Oxford University Press, pp. 56–82.

Schapera, I. (1955), *Handbook of Tswana Law and Custom*, Oxford: Oxford University Press.

Searle, J.R. (2005), 'What is an Institution?', *Journal of Institutional Economics*, **1** (1): 1–22.

Sen, A. (1993), 'The concept of development', in H. Chenery and T.N. Srinivasan (eds), *Handbook of Development Economics*, Amsterdam: Elsevier, pp. 9–26.

Shafir, E. and A. Tversky (1992), 'Thinking through uncertainty: nonconsequential reasoning and choices', *Cognitive Psychology*, **24** (4): 449–74.

Shafir, E., A. Tversky and P. Diamond (1997), 'Money illusion', *Quarterly Journal of Economics*, **112** (2): 341–74.

Shen, T.Y. (1984), 'The estimation of X-efficiency in eighteen countries', *Review of Economic Statistics*, **66** (1): 98–104.

Shiller, R. (1981), 'Do stock prices move too much to be justified by subsequent changes in dividends?', *American Economic Review*, **71**: 421–36.

Shiller, R. (2000), *Irrational Exuberance*, Princeton, NJ: Princeton University Press.

Simon, H. (1957), *Models of Man*, New York: Wiley.

Simon, H. (1965), 'Mathematical constructions in social science', in D. Braybrooke (ed.), *Philosophical Problems of the Social Sciences*, New York: Macmillan, pp. 83–98.

Simon, H. (1979), 'From substantive to procedural rationality', in F. Hahn and M. Hollis (eds), *Philosophy and Economic Theory*, New York: Oxford University Press pp. 65–86.

Simon, H. (1982), 'The role of expectations in an adaptive or behaviourist model', in H.A. Simon (ed.), *Models of Bounded Rationality: Behavioural Economics and Business Organization*, vol. 2. Cambridge, MA: MIT Press.

Simon, H. (1986), 'Rationality in psychology and economics', in R.M. Hogarth and M.W. Reder (eds), *The Behavioural Foundations of Economic Theory*, *Journal of Business* (supplement): S209–S224.

Smith, A. (1759), *Theory of Moral Sentiments*, London: Ward, Lock & Co.

Smith, A. ([1776]1904), *An Inquiry into the Nature and Causes of the Wealth of Nations*, edited by E. Canaan, London: Modern Library Edition.

Smith, V. (1989), 'Theory, experiment and economics', *Journal of Economic Literature*, **3** (1): 151–69.

Smith, V. (1991), *Papers in Experimental Economics*, Cambridge: Cambridge University Press.

Sober, E. (1984), *The Nature of Selection: Evolutionary Theory in Philosophical Focus*, Cambridge, MA: MIT Press.

Sober, E. and R. Lewontin (1982), 'Artifact, cause and genic selection', *Philosophy of Science*, **49** (2): 157–80.

Solow, R. (2001), 'Applying growth theory across countries', *World Bank Economic Review*, **15** (2): 283–88.

Spear, P. (1978), *A History of India*, London: Penguin Books.

Sperry, R. (1964), *Problems Outstanding in the Evolution of Brain Function*, New York: American Museum of Natural History.

Sperry, R. (1966), 'A modified concept of consciousness', *Psychological Review*, **76** (6): 532–36.

Stein, H. (1995), 'Policy alternatives to structural adjustment in Africa,' in H. Stein (ed.), *Asian Industrialisation and Africa*, London: St. Martin's Press.

Stiglitz, J.E. (1974), 'Incentives and risk sharing in sharecropping', *Review of Economic Studies*, **41**: 219–55.

Stiglitz, J.E. (1989), 'Markets, market failures and development', *American Economic Review*, **79** (2): 197–203.

Stiglitz, J.E. (2001), 'From miracle to crisis to recovery: lessons from four decades of East Asian experience', in J.E. Stiglitz and S. Yusuf (eds), *Rethinking the East Asian Miracle*, Washington, DC: World Bank.

Stiglitz, J. E. (2010), 'The non-existent hand', *London Review of Books*, **32** (8): 17–18.

Summers, L. (1986), 'Does the stock market rationally reflect fundamental values?', *Journal of Finance*, **41** (3): 591–601.

Taleb, N. (2007), *Fooled by Randomness: The Hidden Role of Chance in Life and in the Markets*, London: Penguin Books.

Taylor, M. (1982), *Community, Anarchy and Liberty*, Cambridge: Cambridge University Press.

Thaler, R. (1980), 'Towards a positive theory of consumer choice', *Journal of Economics, Behaviour and Organization*, **1** (1): 39–60.

Thurnwald, R. (1932), *Economics in Primitive Communities*, Oxford: Oxford University Press.

Tobin, J. (1969), 'A general equilibrium approach to monetary theory', *Journal of Money, Credit and Banking*, **1** (1): 15–29.

Toye, J. (1995), 'The New Institutional Economics and its implications for development theory', in J. Harriss, J. Hunter and C. Lewis (eds), *The New Institutional Economics and Third World Development*, London: Routledge.

Tversky, A. (1969), 'Intransitivity of preferences', *Psychology Review*, **76**: 31–48.

Tversky, A. and D. Kahneman (1986), 'Rational choice and the framing of decisions', *Journal of Business*, **59** (4): S251–S278.

Tversky, A. and R. Thaler (1990), 'Anomalies: preference reversals', *Journal of Economic Perspectives*, **4** (2): 201–11.

Tversky, A., P. Slovic and D. Kahneman (1990) 'The causes of preference reversal', *American Economic Review*, **80**: 204–18.

United Nations (2004), *Report of the Joint Assessment Mission*, Khartoum, Sudan.

USAID (2004), 'Poverty reduction papers. How do they treat the private sector?', USAID issues paper no.4, Washington, DC.

Van Eeghen, P-H. (1997), 'The capitalist case against the corporation', *Review of Social Studies*, **55**: 85–113.

Van Eeghen, P-H. (2008), 'Money and banking tutorial letter no. 103', Unpublished paper, University of South Africa, Pretoria.

Vanberg, V. (1993), 'Rational choice, rule following and institutions: an evolutionary perspective', in U. Maki, B. Gustafsson and C. Knudsen (eds), *Rationality, Institutions & Economic Methodology*, London: Routledge, pp. 171–202.

Veblen, T. ([1899]1949), *The Theory of the Leisure Class*, second impression, London: George Allen and Unwin.

Viner, J. (1927), 'Adam Smith and laissez faire', *Journal of Political Economy*, **35** (2): 198–232.

Wade, R. (2004), *Governing the Market*, Princeton, NJ: Princeton University Press.

Wallis, J.J. and D. North (1986), 'Measuring the transaction sector in the American economy 1870–1970', in S. Engermann and R. Gallman (eds), *Long Term Factors in American Economic Growth*, Chicago, IL: Chicago University Press.

Walras, L. ([1877]1954), *Elements of Pure Economics*, Cambridge, MA: Harvard University Press.

Weber, M. (1927), *General Economic History*, translated by F.H. Knight, London: George Allen & Unwin.

Weber, M. (1965), *The Protestant Ethic and the Spirit of Capitalism*, Translated by T. Parsons, London: Unwin University Books.

Weber, M. (1968), *The Theory of Social and Economic Organization*, translated by A.M. Henderson and T. Parsons, New York: Free Press.

Weber, M. (1975), *Roscher and Knies: The Logical Problems of Historical Economics*, London: Collier Macmillan.

Weingast, B.R. (1995), 'The economic role of political institutions: market preserving federalism and economic development', *Journal of Law, Economics and Organization*, **11** (2): 1–31.

Williamson, O.E. (1975), *Markets and Hierarchies: Analysis and Anti-Trust Implications*, New York: Free Press.

Williamson, O.E. (1985), *The Economic Institutions of Capitalism*, New York: Free Press.

Williamson, O.E. (2000), 'The New Institutional Economics: taking stock, looking ahead', *Journal of Economic Literature*, **38** (3): 594–612.

Williamson, O.E. and W.G. Ouchi (1981), 'The markets and hierarchies and visible hand perspectives. The markets and hierarchies program of research: origin, implications, prospects', in A.H. Van de Ven and W.F. Joyce (eds), *Perspectives on Organizational Design and Behaviour*, New York: John Wiley, pp. 347–70.

Wilson, D.S. (1983), 'The group selection controversy: history and current status', *Annual Review of Ecology and Systematics*, **14**: 159–88.

Wilson, D.S. and E. Sober (1994), 'Reintroducing group selection to the human behavioural sciences', *Behavioural and Brain Sciences*, **17** (4): 585–654.

Wilson, E.O. (2000), *Sociobiology: The New Synthesis*, Cambridge, MA: Harvard University Press.

Wilson, T. (1976), 'Sympathy and self-interest', in T. Wilson and A. Skinner (eds), *The Markets and the State: Essays in Honour of Adam Smith*, Oxford: Clarendon Press, pp. 73–99.

World Bank (1983), *World Development Report*, Washington, DC: World Bank.

World Bank (1993), *The East Asian Miracle, Economic Growth and Public Policy*, Washington, DC: World Bank.

World Bank (1994), *Adjustment in Africa, Reforms, Results and the Road Ahead*, Washington, DC: World Bank.

World Bank (1999), *Comprehensive Development Framework*, Washington, DC: World Bank.

World Bank (2000), *Poverty Reduction Strategy Source Book*, Washington, DC: World Bank.

World Bank (2001), *World Development Report 2000/2001*,Washington, DC: World Bank.

World Bank (2001a), *Rethinking the East Asian Miracle*, Washington, DC: World Bank.

World Bank (2008), *African Development Indicators 2008/09*, Washington, DC: World Bank.

World Bank (2008a), World Development Indicators data accessed at the World Bank website. www.worldbank.org

Young, A. (1995), 'The tyranny of numbers: confronting the statistical realities of the East Asian growth experience', *Quarterly Journal of Economics*, **110**: 641–80.

Index

accountability 67, 150, 151, 157, 185
Acemoglu, D. 81, 85, 88, 141, 143
adaptation 20–21, 37, 49, 128, 171, 188,
    190–91, 197
Africa 54, 57–8, 61, 62–9, 70–73, 76,
    78, 194
African Development Indicators 55, 66,
    67, 68, 72
agricultural policy 63–4
agriculture 100, 101, 103, 127, 128–9,
    132–3, 135, 139, 143–4, 146
Akerlof, G. 25, 178–9, 191
Alchian, A.A. 46, 172
Allen, G.C. 127–8
Allen, R.C. 105–7
altruism 21–2, 24-5, 33, 170
Amsden, A. 59, 61, 62, 175
animal spirits 34, 178–9
anthropology 38–9, 122, 171, 198, 203
anti-corruption 62, 69, 70, 71, 140, 141,
    149, 166, 167, 204
Arbache, J. 55, 63, 65–6
Arrow, K.J. 15–16, 17, 19, 20, 28, 31,
    33–4, 42, 172–3, 181–2, 200
Asia (excluding Japan) 54–5, 78, 85, 97,
    98, 99–100, 120, 126

Bairoch, P. 99–100
banking sector 128, 185–6, 190, 192,
    210, 211–13
Bardhan, P. 29, 30, 49, 50, 105, 124,
    127, 131, 136, 139, 199
Barro, R. 8, 74, 81, 83, 89, 90
Bates, R.H. 40–41, 50–51, 63, 173
behavioural economics 22–6, 27, 170,
    179, 181–2, 198–202
belief perseverance 23
beliefs
    discontinuous institutional change
        135, 139, 145, 169, 206
    institutional change 198, 199, 201,
        203–4

new institutionalism 41, 44
beneficence 11, 12
Bloom, D. 86, 88
Bosworth, B. 74, 75–6, 78
Botswana 125, 141–3, 144, 148, 202,
    206
bounded rationality 19–20, 45, 171, 172,
    180, 182, 184, 188, 190–91
brain physiology 20–21
Britain 61, 102, 105, 132
    see also England
Brown, J.M. 131, 133
Burnside, C. 57

capital 13–14, 56, 58, 64, 79, 93
    see also capitalist class; capitalist
        developmental state; human
        capital; physical capital; social
        capital
capitalist class 108, 120, 127–8, 129,
    130, 132, 136, 139, 146, 195
capitalist developmental state 60, 61, 64,
    112, 130, 140, 146, 148, 174, 175,
    204, 205
Caselli, F. 79
cattle ranching 141–2, 143, 144
causation 4, 6, 71, 145, 198
central banks 186, 210, 213
centralized political power 100, 142
Chakravarti, A. 57, 70–73, 200
Chang, H.J. 19, 61, 121, 175
China 12, 89–92, 93–5, 97–8, 99–102,
    107, 109, 120, 174, 195, 196
Christianity 107, 108, 109, 205
classical economics 11–14, 15, 25, 27–8,
    29, 35–6, 44–5
classical liberal economics
    deductive methodology 6
    institutions 11–13, 14, 15, 25, 27–8,
        29, 35, 44–5, 184, 187–8, 190
    person responsibility 184
    rights 12, 38

Clower, R. 7
Coase, R. 40, 41–2, 47, 49–50, 51, 171
codes of conduct 41, 45, 175
cognitive capabilities 19–20, 170–71,
    189–90
cognitive psychology 17, 19–22, 170,
    198
Colander, D. 32, 182
Coleman, J. 25–6, 198, 206, 207
collateralized debt obligations (CDOs)
    189, 190, 211–12, 213
collective action
    development strategies and
        performance 64, 175
    institutional change 4, 46–7, 48, 49,
        52, 53, 124, 125, 197, 201,
        202–3
    old institutionalism 37–8, 40
collective bargaining 111–12, 113–14,
    115, 118, 119, 120, 121
    see also relative bargaining power
Collier, P. 64–5
Collins, S. 74, 75–6, 78
colonial exploitation 99, 101–2, 105,
    107, 132, 133–4, 153
commercial banks 192, 213
common law 38, 114, 116, 117
common pool problem 166–7, 169
Commons, J.R. 37–8, 180
communism 93, 94, 96, 125, 148, 195,
    207
competition 12, 27–8, 46, 181
complex systems 32, 182, 183, 184, 188,
    189–90, 201
Comprehensive Development
    Framework (CDF) (World Bank)
    69–73
Comprehensive Peace Agreement (CPA)
    (Southern Sudan) 151, 155–6,
    158, 160, 161–2, 163
conditionalities for development aid 57,
    63, 65
confiscatory powers 102, 103, 104, 105,
    109, 110, 112, 113, 115, 116, 132,
    194
conflict of interest 36, 37, 39, 53, 170,
    180–81, 198
conflict resolution 37, 39, 40, 48, 120,
    152, 164
conspicuous consumption and leisure 36

constitutions
    China 95
    classical liberal economics 13
    development strategies and
        performance 71
    India 134–5, 136
    institution definition 2, 3, 4
    Japan 129, 130
    new institutionalism 41
    Southern Sudan 151, 157–9, 160,
        161–2
    Western Europe 109, 113–15, 116,
        119
constrained maximization 25–6, 27
consumption 14–15, 16, 18, 174
contractual rights
    development strategies and
        performance 62
    economic growth 80, 81, 82, 83, 84,
        89, 95, 119–20, 196
    India 105, 137
    institutional change, effects on 124
    new institutionalism 41, 42, 43, 173
    Southern Sudan 161, 168
    Western Europe 108, 109–11, 174
cooperation 32–3, 37, 39, 40, 198
coordination 40, 45, 47–8, 59, 62, 162,
    175–6, 190, 192–3, 198
coordination problems 19, 49, 61, 175,
    180, 188, 193–4
corporations 184–6, 188, 191
corruption
    development strategies and
        performance 67, 68, 69, 71
    economic growth 80, 81, 82, 83, 84,
        93, 119
    India 139, 140
    Southern Sudan 165–7, 167
    see also anti-corruption
Cosmides, L. 20–21
costs and benefits, institutional change
    46–7, 49–50
Country Policy and Institutional
    Assessment (CPIA) (World Bank)
    66–7, 68
Coval, J. 187, 189, 190, 210, 213
credit 105, 109–10
crony capitalism 60
culture 17–18, 41, 44, 198, 201, 203–4,
    205

customs
  economic historical evidence on
    institutional change 108, 109,
    113–14
  institution definition 2, 4, 17
  institutional change 198, 199, 204
  marginalism 15
  new institutionalism 41, 44, 46, 52
  old institutionalism 37–8, 39, 48

Darwinism/neo-Darwinism 20–21, 37,
    207–9
Dawkins, R. 21, 32–3
Debreu, G. 15–16, 17, 19
decentralized knowledge 187–8
decentralized political power
  China 100
  Southern Sudan 152, 153, 154,
    157–9
  Western Europe 107–8, 109, 111–12,
    114–15, 118–19, 203
  see also federalism; feudalism
decision-making structures, Southern
    Sudan 163–5
deductive methodology 5, 6, 7
democracy
  classical liberal economics 13
  development strategies and
    performance 66–7, 68, 69, 70,
    71
  discontinuous institutional change
    145, 148, 149, 204
  Botswana 141, 142–3
  India 134–5, 138–40
  Japan 129–30
  Southern Sudan 150, 151, 155–7,
    158, 159, 160, 161, 162–3,
    164, 166, 169
  economic growth 81, 82, 84, 87, 88,
    89–95, 195
  international assistance 150–51,
    156–7
  United States 144
Democracy and Governance (DG)
    Programme 150–51, 156–7, 158,
    160, 161, 162–3, 164, 166
despots 101, 102, 103, 104, 106, 107,
    109, 120, 132, 174
developed countries 31, 54, 76, 78, 79,
    124, 175–6, 180–92

developing countries
  discontinuous institutional change
    124–5
  economic historical evidence on
    institutional change 99
  government intervention 56, 58–62,
    175, 176, 193–6, 202, 203–4
  institutional change 123–4
  investment rates 58, 59
  market failure 18–19, 174, 175, 176,
    193–4, 202
  neoclassical economics approaches to
    economic development 1
  per capita GDP growth 54–5, 76–7
  predation 30, 31, 64, 148, 194,
    201–2, 203
  total factor productivity contribution
    to output growth 76, 77–8
  X-inefficiency 79
development aid *see* international
    assistance/development aid;
    structural adjustment programmes
development strategies and performance
  African economic performance 62–9
  current approaches to development
    69–73
  development strategies 56–8
  East Asian model 58–62, 195, 196
  per capita GDP growth of developing
    versus developed countries
    54–5
dictatorships 30, 64, 87, 89, 91, 100,
    119, 155–6, 194
diminishing utility 22–3, 27
Dinka tribe 142, 152, 165
discontinuous biological change 207–8
discontinuous institutional change
  Botswana 125, 141–3, 144, 148, 202,
    206
  characteristics 124–5, 144–6, 147–9,
    197–8, 202, 204–9
  India 125, 131–40, 145, 146, 148
  institutional transitions 124–5
  Japan 126–31, 202
  non-Western societies 122
  see also Southern Sudan: case study
    in discontinuous institutional
    change
Dollar, D. 8, 57
domestic investment 95, 165

downward causation 4, 145, 198, 199
Dutch institutional evolution 118–19,
    120, 174

East Asia 55, 56, 58–62, 65–6, 74, 76,
    175, 189, 196, 202
East Asian financial crisis 1997–1998
    60, 189
Easterly, W. 57, 81, 85, 88, 200, 205
economic backwardness 100, 101–3,
    105–7, 174
economic deregulation 100, 192, 211,
    212–13
economic development 1–2, 7–8
economic governance quality 66–7, 68,
    70–71, 77
economic growth 7–8, 42, 77, 119–21,
    194–6, 201
    see also per capita GDP growth
economic historical evidence on
        institutional change
    Asia (excluding Japan) 97, 98,
        99–100, 120
    China 97, 98, 99–102, 107, 109, 120,
        174
    Dutch institutional evolution 118–19,
        120, 174
    English institutional evolution 105,
        106, 109, 112, 114–17, 120,
        174
    Islam and the Ottoman Empire 97,
        98, 102–3, 107, 108, 109, 111,
        174
    Mughal India 97, 98, 99–100, 104–7,
        109, 132, 174
    Western Europe 51–2, 97–100,
        101–2, 105, 106, 107–14, 120,
        121, 123, 174, 197, 202–3
economic history 5–6
    see also economic historical evidence
        on institutional change
economic reform programmes 57, 63,
    92–4, 136–8
education
    development strategies and
        performance 69, 71
    discontinuous institutional change
        128, 130, 133, 134, 135–6,
        138, 146, 148
    economic growth 75–6, 82, 84, 87,
        88

institutional change 205–6
efficiency 42, 43, 44, 45, 79, 82, 93,
    175, 176, 198
efficient markets hypothesis 1, 16–17,
    19, 28, 176–80, 184, 188–9, 192
embeddedness 3–4, 38–9, 41, 48, 180,
    200
empiricism 6–8
endogenous view of institutional change
    classical economics 35, 36, 44–5
    economic historical evidence on
        institutional change in Western
        Europe 120, 123, 202–3
    institution definition 3
    institutional change 53
    neoclassical economics 35–6, 44–5
    new institutionalism 46–8
endowment effect 23, 27
enforcement
    classical liberal economics 12, 13,
        29
    institutional change 200
    new institutionalism 42, 43, 45, 198
    old institutionalism 38, 39, 40, 145
    property rights 4, 13, 29, 30, 43, 204
Engels, F. 13–14, 15
Engermann, S.I. 143–4
England 49, 105, 106, 109, 112, 114–17,
    120, 174, 195
entrepreneurs 56, 128, 133, 135, 175
equality 152
equilibrium prices 25, 26
Evans-Pritchard, E.E. 44, 142, 149, 152,
    166
evolutionary biology 21–2, 32–3, 207
evolutionary psychology 20–21, 170–71
evolutionary stable strategy (ESS) 32–3
evolutionary view of institutions 35–6,
    45–8, 120, 123, 199–202
exchange rate 59, 65, 70, 95
executive, Southern Sudan 155, 157,
    158–9, 160–61, 162–6
exogenous view of institutional change
    3, 36, 53, 124, 203–4, 205, 209
expected utility model 22–3, 24, 27
experimental markets 25–6, 27, 170
exploitation 100, 101, 103, 104, 107
    see also colonial exploitation;
        confiscatory powers;
        opportunism; predation

export-oriented industrialization 56, 59–60
externalities 1, 18, 40–41, 45, 50, 174–5

factors 79
fairness 12, 25, 27–8, 179, 200
Fama, E. 16–17, 176, 177
federalism
  discontinuous institutional change in India 134, 140
  discontinuous institutional change in Southern Sudan 155, 156, 157–9, 161–2, 163, 168, 169
  market preserving federalism in China 93, 95, 195
feudalism 52, 103, 106, 107–8, 112, 126–31, 132, 135, 174, 195, 207
financial crises 1, 60, 167, 178, 183–4, 189, 190, 192, 210–13
financial deregulation 192, 211, 212–13
financial markets 1, 16–17, 176–8, 179, 180, 183–4, 188–90, 191, 210, 211–13
financial products 187, 188–90, 191, 211–13
financial sector 128, 185–7, 188–91, 210–13
firms 41, 173, 175
  see also corporations; industrialization; private sector; state-owned enterprises
fiscal policies 70, 94, 95
foreign investment 66, 70, 92, 93, 94, 95, 165
formal institutions
  classical economics 11–12, 13, 14, 15
  economic historical evidence on institutional change 110–12
  versus informal rules 44–5
  institution definition 2
  institutional change 198–9, 200, 201, 202
  markets in an institutional framework in developed countries 180–81, 182–3, 184, 191–2
  neoclassical model 4, 17
  new institutionalism 41–4, 45, 46, 53, 173, 175–6
former Soviet Union countries 125, 148–9, 201–2, 206–7

Fortes, M. 142, 152, 166
framing effects 23, 27
free markets 1, 13, 18, 19, 61, 187–8, 192, 196
free rider problem 46–7, 51, 52
Friedman, M. 6–7, 16, 33
Furubotn, E. 1, 41, 42, 206

game theory 32–3, 50, 181–2
generalizations 5, 6
genetic theory 21–2, 170, 198
geographical factors, economic growth 84, 85, 86, 88
Glaeser, E. 86–7, 88, 205–6
governance 4, 41, 173
governance quality
  Botswana 141
  development strategies and performance 62, 66–7, 68–9, 70–71, 72–3
  discontinuous institutional change 140, 204
  economic development 1–2
  economic growth 80, 81, 82, 83, 84, 85, 86, 89, 92, 93, 119
  Southern Sudan 150–51, 156–7, 160, 161, 162–3, 164, 165
government consumption 80, 82, 83, 86, 90
government debt 71–2
government deficit 86
government expenditure 63, 69, 70, 71–2, 82, 117
government failure 62, 176, 195, 196
government finance 116, 118
  see also government debt; government deficit; government expenditure; taxes
government intervention
  developing countries 56, 58–62, 175, 176, 193–6, 202, 203–4
  discontinuous institutional change 127–8, 135–6
  East Asia development model 58–62, 175
  economic performance 56, 58–62, 175, 201
  neoclassical model critique 18, 19
Government of Southern Sudan (GOSS) 155, 159, 160, 161, 164, 165, 166–7, 169

governments
   Africa 63–4
   classical liberal economics 12, 13
   Government of Southern Sudan
      (GOSS) 155, 159, 160, 161,
      164, 165, 166–7, 169
   historical determinism 14
   India 134–5, 138–9, 140
   neoclassical economics 4, 43
   new institutionalism 43, 51, 52, 53
   old institutionalism 38, 39
   predation 29–30
Greif, A. 5, 6, 110–12
growth accounting studies 74, 75–80

habits 2, 15, 17, 36, 37–8, 39, 48
Hall, R. 77–8, 83, 88
harmony 11, 12, 14, 28, 37, 39, 44–5
Hausman, D. 6, 7
Hayami, Y. 46, 49
Hayek, F. 2, 35, 44–5, 46, 184, 187–8,
   190, 197
health care 69, 71
health/mortality 83, 84, 85, 86, 87, 89,
   90, 103
heterogeneous agents 32, 33
hierarchies
   corporations 185, 186–7, 188, 191
   institutions 3, 4, 38, 46
   political authority 117, 135, 142, 152,
      154, 160, 164
High Performing Asian Economies
   (HPAEs) 58–9
historical determinism 13–14, 15, 199,
   201
Hodgson, G. 2–3, 4, 19, 45, 145, 169,
   198
Hoff, K. 30, 123–4
Holm, J. 142–3
honesty 38, 121, 200, 206
Hoover, K. 32, 182
human agency 11, 13, 40, 141, 144, 145,
   148, 149, 173–4, 197–8, 209
human behaviour 3–4, 17, 19–26, 33–4,
   36–8, 39, 45, 170–71
   see also altruism; fairness;
      opportunism; predation;
      rationality; reciprocal altruism;
      self-interest
human capital 74, 75–6, 77–8, 80, 82,
   83, 86, 87, 88, 90

human nature 11, 15–16, 19, 171,
   199–200, 205
human rights/civil liberties 69, 70, 71,
   82, 84, 88, 156, 157, 158, 159,
   161

ideas/ideologies
   discontinuous institutional change 48,
      144, 145, 146, 148, 156,
      202–3, 205, 206
   new institutionalism 41, 44, 53, 196
IMF 2, 9, 57, 69, 137, 150
immediate gratification 24, 25, 27
imperfect information
   institutional change, effects on 124
   market failure 18, 19, 174, 175, 193
   markets in developed countries 180,
      181, 182, 183, 184, 187–90,
      191
   markets in developing countries
      193–4
   neoclassical model critique 20, 28,
      172, 173
   new institutionalism 40–41, 45, 172,
      173
import substitution industrialization 56,
   61
incentives 3–4, 41, 43, 44, 124, 173–4,
   183, 191–2, 199, 202
   see also perverse incentives
increasing returns 18, 19, 47, 50
independence
   Botswana 141–2, 143
   discontinuous institutional change
      125, 145, 148
   India 133, 134, 135–40, 146
   rent-seeking 145
   Southern Sudan 149, 153, 157, 168–9
India
   discontinuous institutional change
      125, 131–40, 145, 146, 148,
      206
   economic and political history 92–3
   economic growth 89–93, 97–8,
      99–100, 196
   economic historical evidence on
      institutional 97, 98, 99–100,
      104–7, 109, 132, 174
   per capita GDP growth 131–2, 136–7
individual utility function 22–3, 24

individual utility maximization 14–15,
 16–17, 19–20, 21–2, 24–7, 28,
 170
inductive methodology 5–6, 7
industrial policies 59–61, 62, 135–6
industrialization
 China 100
 developing countries 175, 176, 202
 development strategies 56
 India 133, 135–6, 137–8, 146
 Japan 128, 129–30
 Western Europe 61, 108–9
inertial forces, historical determinism
 13–14, 15
informal rules
 classical economics 11, 12, 15
 economic historical evidence on
  institutional change 110, 111
 versus formal institutions 44–5
 institution definition 2–3
 institutional change 198–200, 201,
  202, 206
 markets in an institutional framework
  in developed countries 182–3,
  191–2
 markets in an institutional framework
  in developing countries 196
 neoclassical model critique 4, 17–18,
  28
 new institutionalism 41, 44, 45, 46,
  53, 173, 175, 198
 old institutionalism 36, 37–8, 39,
  48
 see also customs; reputation; social
  capital; social norms; tradition
information costs 42, 173
information theory 123–4, 209
institutional blueprints 204
institutional change
 developing *versus* developed
  countries 122–3
 evolutionary view 45–6, 123,
  199–202
 model 198–202
 neoclassical economics 45–7, 49,
  199, 200, 201
 new institutionalism 46–8, 49–53,
  123–4, 198
 old institutionalism 36–7, 38, 40, 49
 ontology of institutions 4

institutional deficits 148, 149–50, 153–5,
 186, 201–2, 206
 see also confiscatory powers;
  corruption; despots;
  opportunism; predation
institutions
 classical economics 11–14, 15, 25,
  27–8, 29, 35–6
 classical liberal economics 11–13, 14,
  15, 25, 27–8, 29, 35, 44–5,
  184, 187–8, 190
 definition and concept 2–5
 development strategies and
  performance 62, 66–7, 68–9,
  70–73
 economic development approaches
  1–2
 economic growth 77, 80–89, 119–21,
  201
 marginalism 14–15, 16, 35–6
 markets in developed countries
  175–6, 180–92
 neoclassical economics 1, 2, 3–4,
  15–16, 17–18, 28, 44–5, 48
 neoclassical model critique 1, 15–16,
  17–18, 28, 171
 visible hand *versus* invisible hand
  44–5
 see also formal institutions;
  government intervention;
  informal rules
instrumentalist methodology 6–7
interactive processes 36–7, 198–9, 200,
 202, 205
international assistance/development aid
 56, 67, 72, 73, 149, 150–51, 154,
 165, 204
 see also development strategies and
  performance; structural
  adjustment programmes
international financial institutions 57–8,
 62–3, 67, 69
 see also IMF; World Bank
international trade 61, 66, 102, 105, 108,
 109–11, 119
investment
 developing countries 58, 59, 65–6, 69
 economic growth 93, 94, 95
 neoclassical growth model 16, 56, 74,
  80, 82, 90

see also domestic investment; foreign
    investment; investment banks;
    private investment
investment banks 192, 213
irrationality 34, 178, 179
Islam 97, 98, 99–100, 102–7, 108, 109,
    111
Ito, T. 65

Japan 61, 125, 126–31, 175, 202, 206
Jevons, W.S. 14, 15
joint liability 110–11
Jones, C. 77–8, 83, 88
Jones, E. 98–9, 101, 103, 104, 109,
    112
judgement biases 23, 27
judiciary
    classical liberal economics 12
    development strategies and
        performance 69, 70, 71
    discontinuous institutional change
        140, 158, 159, 161
    economic historical evidence on
        institutional change 110, 111,
        116, 117
old institutionalism 38

Kahneman, D. 22–3, 25
Kaufmann, D. 84, 85, 88, 141
Keefer, P. 80–81, 82–3, 92, 163
Keeley, L. 122, 171
Keynes, J.M. 34, 172, 173, 178–9, 191
Knack, S. 80–81, 82–3
Kohn, M. 30, 51–2, 107, 109–10,
    113–14
Kray, A. 8, 84, 88, 141
Kregel, J. 210, 211, 212

labour 74, 75–6, 79, 92
labour productivity 74, 75–8, 83, 84
land tenure 50, 103, 104, 107, 116,
    128–9, 130–31, 132, 135, 136,
    143–4
Landes, D. 98–9, 101, 102
landlords 128–9, 132, 133, 135
Latin America 47, 54, 55, 58, 70–73, 76,
    84, 85, 143–4
laws/rule of law
    Botswana 141
    classical liberal economics 12

development strategies and
        performance 67, 69, 71
discontinuous institutional change
        205
economic growth 80, 81, 82, 83, 84,
        89, 93
financial sector 192, 211
historical determinism 14
India 104, 134–5, 140
institution definition 2, 3
Japan 128, 130
markets 194–5, 196, 201, 204
neoclassical model critique 4, 17
new institutionalism 40–41, 42, 45,
        52, 175–6
old institutionalism 38, 39–40
Southern Sudan 154–5, 156, 158,
        159–61, 165, 168
Western Europe 108, 109, 110, 112,
        113, 115, 118–19
leisure classes 29, 36
Levine, R. 74, 81, 85, 88
Levy-Leboyer, M. 99–100
Liebenstein, H. 79–80
local knowledge 204
Lockwood, W.W. 126, 127, 129, 130
loss aversion 22–3, 27
Lucas, R.E. 7, 33

macroeconomic liberalization 57, 92–3,
        137–8, 195
macroeconomic management 66–7, 68,
        75
macroeconomic policies 75, 92–3, 94,
        95, 165
macroeconomic stability/instability 59,
        65–7, 68, 70
macroeconomics 32, 33–4
Maddison, A. 8, 54–5, 85, 97–8, 99–100,
        101, 105, 107, 108, 126, 131, 132
Magna Carta 109, 114–15, 116
managerial power 185, 186–7
marginalism 14–15, 16, 17, 35–6
market failure
    developing countries 18–19, 174,
        175, 176, 193–4, 202
    development strategies and
        performance 58–9, 60, 61
    neoclassical model critique 18–19,
        174–6, 184
    new institutionalism 40–41, 45, 51

market-oriented development strategies
China 93–4, 195, 196
discontinuous institutional change
145, 148
East Asia development model 58–62,
175, 196
economic performance 56–7, 58, 60,
61, 62–3, 84, 196
India 93, 136–8, 139, 146, 148
Southern Sudan 151
market prices 2, 15, 16–17, 18, 45,
176–7, 188–90, 191
market size 92
markets
classical liberal economics 44–5
developed countries 19, 174–6,
180–84
discontinuous institutional change in
Japan 128
institutional change 201
institutional framework in developed
countries 175–6, 180–92
marginalism 15
neoclassical model 2, 15–16, 25, 27,
44–5, 48
neoclassical model critique 1, 17–18,
19, 25–6, 28–9, 30–31, 171,
174–6
new institutionalism 41, 42, 45,
173–6, 180
old institutionalism 38, 39–40,
173–4, 180–81
Marshall, A. 2, 14, 15, 16
Marx, K. 11, 13–14, 15, 38, 204
Marxism 11, 13–14, 15, 35, 38, 41, 43,
51–2, 99, 194, 204
Maynard Smith, J. 21, 32
Menger, C. 2, 35–6, 44, 46
mental models 44, 121, 173
mercantile economies 100, 102, 105,
107, 108–13, 118, 120, 121
merchant classes 101, 102, 105, 108,
109–12, 118, 119, 120, 127, 129
middle classes
India 133–4, 135–6, 138, 139, 140,
146, 148, 206
institutional change 200, 202, 205
Japan 131, 206
Southern Sudan 168
Middle East 55, 76

military
Africa 63
China 101
India 104
Japan 127, 128, 129–30
social order 51, 123
Southern Sudan 153–4, 155–6, 157,
160–61, 163–4, 168
Western Europe 107, 108, 109, 110,
112, 118, 128
Mill, J.S. 6, 11, 13, 15, 29
Minsky, H. 173, 178, 191
modernization 125, 127–8
Montinola, G. 93–5, 163, 195
moral hazard 185–6, 191
mortgage-backed securities (MBSs) 187,
189, 190, 211–12, 213
mortgage sector 187, 189, 190, 192,
210–13
motivation 14–15, 19, 21, 24–5, 31, 36,
46, 52–3, 84, 171
see also altruism; beliefs; customs;
fairness; habits; ideas/
ideologies; incentives;
opportunism; predation;
reciprocal altruism; self-
interest
Mughal India 97, 98, 99–100, 104–7,
109, 132, 174
multiple equilibria 20, 47–8, 50

natural history 20–21, 207–8, 209
natural liberty 11, 12, 13, 14
natural selection 20–21, 37, 207
Ndulu, B. 63–4, 66, 76–7
neoclassical economics
critique 17–19, 53, 170–76, 177–8,
181–2, 184, 188–90, 192
rationality, opportunism and
predation 26–31, 170–71,
199, 200
representative agent 17, 31–3,
170-71
economic development 1, 2
efficient markets hypothesis 1,
16–17, 28, 176–80, 184,
188–9, 192
human behaviour 3–4, 17, 19–26,
33–4, 170–71, 181
institutional change 45–7, 49, 199,
200, 201

institutions 1, 2, 3–4, 15–16, 17–18,
    28, 44–5, 48, 171
  rational choice theory described
    16–17
  research methodology 6–7
neoclassical growth model
  cross-country regression studies
    80–89
  described 56, 74, 75
  development strategies 56–7, 58, 60,
    61, 62–3, 70
  growth accounting studies 74, 75–80
Netherlands 118–19, 120, 174
new institutionalism
  described 40–44
  institutional change 46–8, 49–53,
    123–4, 145–6, 198
  markets 41, 42, 45, 173–6, 180,
    182–3, 196
  neoclassical model critique 172–4
  political economy 48–53
  predation 41, 43, 53, 173, 194, 195
non-cooperative games 181
non-technological factors 75, 76, 77
non-Western societies 123, 124–5,
    144–5, 148–9, 197, 199, 209
North, D. 2, 5, 19, 41, 42–3, 44, 46, 47,
    48, 49, 51, 113, 115, 116–17,
    122–3, 125, 180, 182, 194, 195,
    198
Nuer tribe 44, 142, 152, 165

O'Connell, A. 63–4, 66, 76–7
oil 54, 56, 65, 67, 68, 69, 165, 166–7,
    168, 169
old institutionalism 36–40, 48, 49, 51–2,
    53, 66, 145, 173–4, 180–81
Olson, M. 5, 30, 46, 47
openness 82, 83, 84, 85, 86, 92, 93
opportunism
  institutional change 199, 201
  markets in developed countries 180,
    181, 183, 184, 190, 191
  markets in developing countries 193,
    195
  neoclassical model critique 28–9, 30,
    31, 33, 170, 171, 184
  new institutionalism 41, 45, 53, 173
  old institutionalism 39
  principal-agent problem 185–6

opportunism, absence of 192, 199
Ottoman Empire 97, 98, 102–3, 107,
    108, 109, 111, 174
ownership 37, 63, 93, 131, 133, 143,
    165, 185, 210
  see also contractual rights; land
    tenure; landlords; property
    rights

Page, J. 63, 65–6
Pareto superior equilibrium 50–51, 124
path dependence 46, 47–8, 209
per capita GDP growth
  Asia (excluding Japan) 54–5, 85,
    97–8, 99–100, 101–2, 126
  Botswana 141
  developed countries 54
  developing countries 54–5
  East Asia 55, 56, 58, 65–6, 74, 76
  India 131–2, 136–7
  Japan 126
  Sub-Saharan Africa 55, 65–9
  Western Europe 54, 97–8, 99–100,
    101–2, 126
per capita income 79, 80, 82, 84, 85, 86,
    88, 90, 91, 97–8, 144, 193
person responsibility/irresponsibility
    184–6
Persson, T. 81, 89, 91, 194
perverse incentives 184–7, 190, 191,
    212, 213
physical capital 74, 75–6, 77–8
physical infrastructure development 64,
    69, 71
Plott, C.R. 21–2, 23, 25, 27
Poland 49
Polanyi, K. 38–40, 180–81
political economy 48–53
political governance
  development strategies and
    performance 66–7, 68–9, 70,
    71
  discontinuous institutional change
    134–5, 138–40, 141
  economic growth 77, 81, 82, 84, 87,
    88–95
  economic historical evidence on
    institutional change 112–13
  see also despots; dictatorships;
    governments; political

institutions; political leadership
quality; political power
political history 63–4
political institutions 133, 134–5, 138–9,
146, 194–6
see also democracy; laws/rule of law;
separation of powers
political leadership quality 62, 63–4,
151, 155–6, 159, 164–5, 166, 197
political power
China 100, 101, 174
development strategies and
performance 63–4
India 104, 105, 107, 132, 174
institutional change 199–200
Japan 127, 128, 129–30
markets in developing countries
194–5, 196
Ottoman Empire 102, 103, 174
Western Europe 112, 113, 114, 115,
116–17, 118, 120
see also centralized political power;
confiscatory powers;
decentralized political power;
political governance
political reforms 93–5
political stability 82, 83, 87
politics 14, 39
polity indicators 66, 67, 68, 69
Pomeranz, K. 99
positivism 6–7
poverty 99, 100, 104, 106, 107, 141,
143, 144, 203
poverty reduction 1–2, 8, 57, 63, 69–73,
167
Poverty Reduction Strategy 2, 63, 69–73
Power Sharing Protocol (Southern
Sudan) 155, 156, 157–9
predation
developing countries 30, 31, 64, 148,
194, 201–2, 203
economic historical evidence on
institutional change 101, 104,
113, 120, 145, 174
institutional change 197, 199, 200,
201
institutional deficits 148, 149, 201–2,
207
markets in an institutional framework
in developed countries 180,
181, 183, 184

Marxism 43, 51–2, 194
neoclassical model critique 29–31,
33, 170, 171
new institutionalism 41, 43, 53, 173,
194, 195
old institutionalism 36, 39, 51–2, 180
predation, control of 179, 192, 199, 200
predictability 3, 6–7, 172–3, 192
preference reversals 23, 24
price information 17, 176–7, 179, 183,
188, 191
primitive societies 122–3, 152, 171, 199,
200, 201
see also feudalism; tribal societies
principal-agent problem 185–6
private investment 58, 65–6, 69, 70, 95,
136–7, 150, 165
private sector 63–6, 69, 70, 95, 128,
136–8, 161, 165, 167
pro-poor government expenditure 63, 70,
71–2
probabilities 21, 172, 173, 191
production 13–15, 18, 40–41, 74, 75–8,
79, 83, 174–5
productivity 74, 75, 76, 77, 84
profit maximization 16, 185–6, 190, 211
property rights
Botswana 141–2, 143, 144, 206
development strategies and
performance 62, 69, 205
economic growth 80, 81, 82, 85, 89,
95, 119–20, 195, 196
India 105, 132, 133, 134, 135, 137,
139, 206
Latin America *versus* US 143–4
legal enforcement 4, 13, 29, 30, 43,
204
markets 195, 196, 204
new institutionalism 40–41, 42, 43,
46, 50, 51, 173
Ottoman Empire 102, 103
Southern Sudan 158, 161, 168
Western Europe 108, 109, 112, 113,
114, 115, 174
public goods 1, 18, 24–5, 40–41, 45, 174
public sector 56, 60, 66–7, 71, 136

quantity theory of money 33–4

Rabin, M. 23, 24–5, 27

rational expectations 172–3, 176–80
rationality
    classical liberal economics 13
    evolutionary stable strategy (ESS)
        32–3
    marginalism 15
    neoclassical model 179, 199, 200,
        201
    neoclassical model critique 17,
        19–21, 22, 27, 170–71
    new institutionalism 40, 41
    rational choice theory 16–17
    social change 205
reciprocal altruism 21, 24–5, 170
reconstitutive downward causation 4,
    145, 198
reference levels, neoclassical model
    critique 22–3
regulations
    classical liberal economics 13
    development strategies and
        performance 69
    discontinuous institutional change in
        Southern Sudan 165
    economic performance 56
    markets 18, 19, 201
    new institutionalism 41, 45, 175–6
    old institutionalism 39
    private sector in Africa 63–4
relations of production 13–14
relative bargaining power 46, 49, 50, 51,
    52, 53, 121, 124
relative preference changes 46, 47
relative price changes 46, 47, 49, 50
religion 4, 39, 41, 199, 205
    see also Christianity; Islam
rent-seeking
    classical liberal economics 197
    institutional change 123, 124, 145
    institutional decay 148, 149
    Latin America 144
    new institutionalism 41, 53, 174, 194,
        195
representative agent 17, 31–3, 170–71
representative assemblies 113–14, 118,
    120, 134, 138, 139, 141, 142–3,
    161–2, 163
reputation 38, 110, 211
research methodology 5–8
Richter, R. 1, 41, 42, 206

rights 12, 38, 52, 112–13, 117
    see also contractual rights; human
        rights/civil liberties; property
        rights
risk
    economic growth 80–81, 82–3, 85,
        86–7, 119
    entrepreneurship 175
    neoclassical model critique 22–3,
        172, 188–90
    perverse incentives 185–6, 187, 212,
        213
risk assessment 188–90, 191, 192, 212
Robinson, J. 64, 81, 85, 88, 141
Rodrik, D. 60, 61–2, 84, 88, 89, 90, 91,
    176, 204
Rudolph, L.I. 139–40
Rudolph, S.H. 139–40
rule of law see laws/rule of law
ruling elites
    Africa 63–4, 194
    Botswana 141–3, 144, 148, 206
    China 100–101, 120
    development strategies and
        performance 62
    discontinuous institutional change
        145, 146, 148, 149, 197
    historical determinism 14
    India 104, 107, 132, 135, 138–9, 148,
        206.
    institutional change 51, 52, 53, 123,
        125, 199–200, 202–3
    Japan 127, 128, 129–30, 206
    old institutionalism 36
    Ottoman Empire 102, 103
    predation 29–30, 31, 194, 195
    Southern Sudan 150
    Western Europe 107, 109, 114, 120
Russia 207
Ruttan, V. 46, 49

Sachs, J. 57, 81, 83, 86, 88
savings 58, 59–60, 65–6, 69
scientific innovation 99, 102
Searle, J.R. 3
security 11, 12, 13
self-commitment and control 24
self-enforcement 113, 114, 115, 117,
    120, 123, 145, 146, 168, 194–5,
    198, 200, 206

self-interest
   classical liberal economics 11, 25,
      27–8, 44
   evolutionary stable strategy (ESS)
      32–3
   marginalism 15, 35
   neoclassical model 16, 19, 44, 46, 47,
      181, 199, 200, 201
   neoclassical model critique 17, 20,
      21–2, 24–5, 26–31, 32–3, 53,
      170
self-regulation
   markets 1, 27–8, 29, 39, 44–5,
      180–81, 182, 184, 190, 192,
      209
   natural history 208
senior managers' remuneration 185–6,
   187, 213
separation of powers
   classical liberal economics 12
   development strategies and
      performance 71
   discontinuous institutional change
      135, 139, 151, 156, 157, 158,
      159, 168
   economic growth 84, 86, 87, 89,
      194–5
   economic historical evidence on
      institutional change 113, 117
Shen, T.Y. 79
Shiller, R. 177–9, 191
Simon, H. 19–20, 41, 171
Singapore 59–60
Smith, A. 11–12, 14, 15, 25, 27–8, 31,
   44, 197, 200
Smith, V. 26, 27
social backwardness 101, 102, 103
social capital 52, 196, 198, 199, 200,
   201, 203, 206, 207
social change 14, 125, 140, 199, 204–6
social institutions 40–41, 45
social norms 41, 110, 198, 206
social order 37, 39, 44, 51, 122–3, 176,
   198
social relations 3, 17–18, 39, 45
Sokoloff, K.L. 143–4
Solow, R. 74, 75
Southern Sudan: case study in
   discontinuous institutional change
   Comprehensive Peace Agreement

(CPA) 151, 155–6, 158, 160,
   161–2, 163
   constitution 151, 155, 157–9, 160,
      161–2
   Democracy and Governance
      Programme 150–51, 156–7,
      158, 160, 161, 162–3, 164, 166
   executive 155, 157, 158–9, 160–61,
      162–7
   federalism 155, 156, 157–9, 161–2,
      169
   institutional development 2005–2009
      167–9
   institutions during the civil war
      149–50, 153–5
   legal framework 161
   legislature 155, 158, 159–61
   traditional society 149, 152–3
standard of living 8, 106
   see also per capita GDP growth; per
      capita income; poverty; wages;
      wealth
state *see* governments
state-owned enterprises 60, 92, 93, 94,
   128, 135, 137
Stein, H. 59–60, 61
Stiglitz, J.E. 1, 19, 30, 60, 123–4, 174–5
stock prices 16–17, 177–8, 179
structural adjustment programmes 57–8,
   63, 65, 69
sub-prime mortgage crisis 1, 178, 183–4,
   187, 189, 190, 192, 210–13
Sub-Saharan Africa 55, 64–9, 76–7, 90,
   148, 149, 201–2, 206
Sudan People's Liberation Movement
   (SPLM) 151, 154–6, 157, 158,
   159, 160, 162, 163, 164, 165, 166,
   168
Summers, L. 179
survival 21, 106, 171, 199

Tabellini, G. 81, 89, 91, 194
tariff barriers 56, 59, 61
taxes
   Africa 63
   China 94, 95, 100, 101
   classical liberal economics 13
   development strategies and
      performance 59–60
   India 104, 136

Japan 128
new institutionalism 43
Southern Sudan 155, 159, 162, 165
Western Europe 108, 109, 110, 112,
    113–14, 115, 116, 117, 118
technological backwardness 101, 102–3,
    107
technological innovation 75, 78, 100,
    102, 120, 202–3
Thaler, R. 13, 23, 25
theorization 6–7
time consistency/inconsistency 23, 24,
    27
Tooby, J. 20–21
total factor productivity 75, 76, 77–8
trade liberalization 57, 61, 70, 84, 86
trade protectionism 56, 59, 61, 112
tradition 2, 4, 135, 139, 149, 152–3,
    166–7, 169, 205
transaction costs
    Africa 63
    institutional change, effects on 124
    markets in an institutional framework
        in developed countries 180,
        181, 182, 183
    markets in developing countries 193
    new institutionalism 41–3, 44, 45, 47,
        49–50
transactions 37
transparency 69, 70, 71, 156, 157, 166,
    189, 192
tribal societies 142–3, 149, 150, 152,
    154, 158, 160, 164, 169, 206
    see also Dinka tribe; Nuer tribe;
        Tswana tribe
trust 28, 45, 175, 179, 182, 183, 198,
    200, 206
Tswana tribe 141–3, 144
Tversky, A. 22–3, 24

uncertainty
    markets in an institutional framework
        in developed countries 181,
        182, 183, 188, 189, 191
    neoclassical model critique 18, 20,
        28, 172, 173, 178
    new institutionalism 41, 42
United Nations 149, 150, 156, 158, 163
United States 1, 54, 61, 76, 77–8, 85,
    143, 144, 177, 178, 182, 183–4,

186–7, 189, 190, 191, 192,
    210–13
upward causation 4, 199
urbanization 64, 85
USAID's (United States Agency for
    International Development's) DG
    Programme 150–51, 156–7, 158,
    160, 161, 162–3, 164, 166

validity, research methodology 5, 6, 7
Van Eeghen, P.-H. 184–5, 186
Veblen, T. 29, 36–7, 38, 145, 180
violence 51–2, 122–3, 198, 202–3

Wade, R. 59, 61, 175
wages 105–6
Wallis, J.J. 42–3, 51, 122–3, 182
Walras, L. 14–15, 17, 27, 188
wars/civil wars
    China 101, 102
    discontinuous institutional change
        127, 148–9
    India 104, 106
    institutional change, effects on 52,
        122, 123, 198
    Japan 127
    Southern Sudan 149–50, 153–5, 168
    Western Europe 108, 109, 114, 115,
        117, 118, 119
wealth
    Africa 63, 142, 144, 152
    classical liberal economics 11, 13, 29
    India 104, 132
    Japan 127
    Marxism 35, 43
    neoclassical model 16, 19, 21, 22,
        170
    new institutionalism 40, 49
    Western Europe 99–100, 107, 108,
        113, 115, 116, 117, 119, 120
Weber, M. 13, 204–5
Weingast, B.R. 51, 93, 113, 115, 116–17,
    122–3, 163, 194, 195
Western Europe 51–2, 54, 97–100,
    101–2, 105, 106, 107–14, 120,
    121, 123, 126, 174, 197, 202–3
Western societies 128, 130, 135, 139,
    151, 155–6, 165, 202, 205
Williamson, O.E. 3–4, 28–9, 30, 31, 35,
    41, 185, 188

World Bank 2, 56–7, 58–60, 62–3, 65, 66–73, 92, 95, 150, 156, 163, 166

world financial crisis and recession 2007–2010 1, 7, 178, 180, 186, 190, 191, 213

X-inefficiency 79–80

zero transaction costs 42, 47, 49–50